GRAMSCI AND FOUCAULT: A REASSESSMENT

Gramsci and Foucault: A Reassessment

Edited by

DAVID KREPS
University of Salford, UK

ASHGATE

Published by
Ashgate Publishing Limited
Wey Court East
Union Road
Farnham
Surrey, GU9 7PT
England

Ashgate Publishing Company
110 Cherry Street
Suite 3-1
Burlington, VT 05401-3818
USA

www.ashgate.com

British Library Cataloguing in Publication Data
A catalogue record for this book is available from the British Library

The Library of Congress has cataloged the printed edition as follows:
Gramsci and Foucault : a reassessment / [edited] by David Kreps.
pages cm
Includes bibliographical references and index.
ISBN 978-1-4094-6086-2 (hardback) – ISBN 978-1-4094-6087-9 (ebook) – ISBN 978-1-4724-0465-7 (epub) 1. Gramsci, Antonio, 1891–1937. 2. Foucault, Michel, 1926–1984. 3. Social sciences–Philosophy. 4. Political science–Philosophy. 5. Political sociology. I. Kreps, David, 1963–
H61.15.G73 2015
306.2–dc23

2014030034

ISBN 9781409460862 (hbk)
ISBN 9781409460879 (ebk – PDF)
ISBN 9781472404657 (ebk – ePUB)

MIX
Paper from responsible sources
FSC® C013985

Printed in the United Kingdom by Henry Ling Limited, at the Dorset Press, Dorchester, DT1 1HD

Contents

List of Tables

Notes on Contributors

Onur Bakiner is Assistant Professor of Political Science at Seattle University. His research and teaching interests include transitional justice, human rights and judicial politics, particularly in Latin America and the Middle East. His articles have been published in the *International Journal of Transitional Justice*, *Nationalities Papers*, and *Memory Studies*.

Heather Brunskell-Evans is Senior Research Fellow at the Centre for Medical Humanities, University of Leicester. Her current research interests include a focus on the body, in particular the body as it is represented within a variety of medical, social and political contexts. This interest fuses a combination of intellectual themes running throughout her academic and political life with regard to ethics, feminism, the medicalized body and international relations. Her publications include: Brunskell-Evans, H. and Moore, M. (2012) *Reimagining Research for Reclaiming the Academy in Iraq: Identities and Participation in Post-Conflict Enquiry* (SENSE Publishers). She has also been guest editor for *Medicine, Conflict and Survival 1* and the special issue: *CARA Iraq Research Fellowship Programme*.

Brecht de Smet obtained his PhD in Political Science at Ghent University, Belgium, where he also received a Master's degree in History and in Arabic. Since 2013 De Smet has been working as a post-doctoral assistant in the department of Conflict and Development Studies at Ghent University. De Smet's empirical research focuses on political and syndical activism in contemporary Egypt, whereas his theoretical work engages with critical theories of mass agency, revolution and societal change. He has published in international peer-reviewed journals on Gramsci, the Egyptian revolution, and working class subjectivities, and is preparing two academic books that deal with the same topics.

Alex Demirovic is Visiting Professor of Critical Social Theory at the Goethe University Frankfurt am Main for. His main subjects of research include state theory, theory of democracy, critical political epistemology, and critical theory. His publications include: *Der nonkonformistische Intellektuelle. Die Entwicklung der Kritischen Theorie zur Frankfurter Schule* (Suhrkamp Taschenbuch Wissenschaft, Frankfurt am Main, 1999); *Nicos Poulantzas. Aktualität und Probleme materialistischer Staatstheorie* (Münster, 2007); *Demokratie in der Wirtschaft. Positionen? Probleme?* (Perspektiven, Münster, 2007); (in collaboration with Stephan Adolphs und Serhat Karakayal): *Das Staatsverständnis von Nicos*

Poulantzas. Der Staat als gesellschaftliches Verhältnis, (Baden-Baden, 2010); (in collaboration with Christina Kaindl und Alfred Krovoza): *Das Subjekt? zwischen Krise und Emanzipation* (Münster, 2010); (in collaboration with Julia Dück, Florian Becker und Pauline Bader): *VielfachKrise. Im finanzmarktdominierten Kapitalismus* (Hamburg, 2011); (in collaboration with Heike Walk): *Demokratie und Governance. Kritische Perspektiven auf neue Formen politischer Herrschaft* (Münster, 2011); (in collaboration with Christina Kaindl): *Gegen den Neoliberalismus andenken. Linke Wissenspolitik und sozialistische Perspektiven* (Hamburg, 2012).

Jean-Paul Gagnon is a university postdoctoral research fellow at the Australian Catholic University. His research is on critical, social and political philosophy – focusing especially on democratic theory. His two books are *Evolutionary Basic Democracy* (Palgrave Macmillan, 2013) and *Democratic Theorists in Conversation: Turns in Contemporary Thought* (Palgrave Macmillan, 2014). He co-edits the journal *Democratic Theory* (Berghahn) and the Palgrave Macmillan book series on *The Theories, Concepts and Practices of Democracy* (both with Dr Mark Chou).

Efe Can Gürcan is a PhD student in Sociology at Simon Fraser University. He holds a SSHRC-Joseph-Armand Bombardier CGS Doctoral Scholarship – Category A. His research interests lie in the areas of Marxism, political sociology, Latin America (Cuba, Venezuela, Argentina), development and food studies, and Turkish politics and society. His works have been or will be published in journals such as *Rural Sociology*, *Dialectical Anthropology*, *Latin American Perspectives*, *Review of Radical Political Economics*, *Capital & Class*, and *Socialism and Democracy*.

Sonita Sarker is Professor of Women's, Gender, and Sexuality Studies, and English at Macalester College (St. Paul, Minnesota, USA). Among her publications are *Trans-Status Subjects: Gender in the Globalization of South and South-east Asia* (Duke University Press, 2002), and *Sustainable Feminisms* (JAI Press, 2007); numerous articles on post/coloniality and post/modernity. She has presented on Antonio Gramsci at the Re-thinking Marxisms conference and the International Gramsci Conference; she has also taught on subalternity and feminisms as located in the histories of feminisms, capitalisms, and democracies. She is currently writing on Gramsci and Grazia Deledda in relation to the idea of the subaltern situated within twentieth-century nation-state structures. Two book-length manuscripts – one on women as 'natives making modernity' in early twentieth-century history and another on interdisciplinarity and late-capitalist democracies – are in progress.

Marcus Schulzke is Research Director for the Project on Violent Conflict at the University at Albany. He received his PhD in Political Science from the University at Albany in 2013 with a dissertation on how soldiers make ethical decisions during counterinsurgency operations. His primary research interests are contemporary political theory, applied ethics, political violence, comparative politics, and new technologies. He has published articles and book chapters on a wide range of issues including legal theory, international law, political theory, applied ethics, just war theory, security studies, and media studies.

Ngai-Ling Sum is Reader in Cultural Political Economy in the Department of Politics, Philosophy and Religion, and Co-Director (with Bob Jessop) of the Research Centre at Lancaster University. She has interests in international political economy, Gramsci and Foucault, globalization and competitiveness, corporate social responsibility and BRIC economies. She was awarded (with Bob Jessop) the Gunnar Myrdal Prize by the European Association of Evolutionary Political Economics for their co-authored book, *Beyond the Regulation Approach* (Edward Elgar Publishing, 2006). Her latest book is *Towards a Cultural Political Economy* (Edward Elgar Publishing, 2013) with Bob Jessop. She also publishes in journals such as *Critical Policy Studies*, *Development Dialogue*, *New Political Economy*, *Critical Asian Studies*, *Competition and Change*, *Capital & Class*, *Urban Studies*, *Journal of Language and Politics*, and *Economy and Society* as well as edited collections.

Jelle Versieren obtained his Master's degree in History at Ghent University and is working on a doctoral dissertation in Early Modern History at the University of Antwerp, at the Centre for Urban History on guild craftsmen and wage workers in the economic transition of capitalism in the Low Countries. This dissertation focuses on the formation and development of modern labour concepts, the disappearance of precapitalist corporative institutions, the making of the early factory system and the historical processes between technology and social relations of production. He has also published on the history of economic thought, value theory, Marxist philosophy and theoretical humanities, and the history of the Belgian labour movement.

Foreword

An Archaeology of the Future, to be Excavated by the Post-Modern Prince?

Stephen Gill

I am happy to have been invited by David Kreps to write the foreword to this rich and thoughtful book. It focuses upon two principal thinkers of the twentieth century, and it searches for diverse ways in which to harness their insights to help move towards an understanding of the conditions of our time and the potentials for our future. The contributions are ambitious and wide-ranging involving questions of epistemology, political economy, power, education and critical pedagogy, democracy and history in processes of complexity and change. Other chapters address new innovations in regional and global politics, political transitions and religion, and child psychology in the process euphemistically called 'post-conflict reconstruction' (in Iraq after the US invasion of 2003). Most of these reflective chapters point towards very interesting ways to develop radical new research agendas premised upon epistemological and political challenges to prevailing orthodoxies and rationalizations of dominant power.

As a constructive contribution to these new avenues of enquiry, drawing on the two thinkers and relating them to international questions, my foreword will try to reflect on some potential aspects of the global conjuncture. I will suggest that we should imagine a post hegemonic 'archaeology of the future' to be excavated by the products of the collective actions associated with the new and emergent forces that form the figure of what I call 'the post-modern Prince' (Gill 2008).

By post-modern I simply refer to a set of political, material and ecological conditions (not postmodernism as a mode of literary or philosophical thought) that are generating new forms of political agency (many of which are based on collective action and solidarity amongst peoples, although some of them are deeply reactionary). At issue is the degree to which new forms and patterns of emancipatory political agency can emerge under these conditions.

In so doing, we might invoke Gramsci's favourite political maxim 'pessimism of the intelligence, optimism of the will'. This maxim underlines the need to clarify, with intellectual pessimism and in all its violence, some of the key conditions of existence in the emerging world order of the twenty-first century, including its key structures, discursive formations, and elements of its 'common sense'.

This is required in order to look beyond the constitution of dominant power and to assess, with an optimism of the will, the potentials for insurgent and emancipatory power to engage not only in what I have called 'transformative resistance' but also the creation of new imaginaries and forms of political agency, involving innovations in power/knowledge and considerations involving a long shadow of our global future. Thus new forces in global politics are associated with complex epistemologies and practices that recognize the social, biopolitical and biospheric limitations of dominant forms of development, and they are searching for new frameworks of governance and regulation to produce a more just and sustainable world order. At issue, therefore, is how far postmodern conditions may be changed and allow new modes of politics that transcend the claims to hegemony and the disciplinary practices of modernist reductionisms, neo-liberalism, imperialism and eco-myopia.

This approach is consistent, I think, with the concerns of both Foucault and of Gramsci when they attempted to theorize the relationships between disciplinary power, hierarchy, processes of rule and the constitution of subjects in the making of history.

A starting point, then, is a sober assessment of key aspects of world order, and clearly this cannot be effectively dealt with in a short foreword. So here I will simply briefly address some cultural and political aspects of actually-existing capitalism as the primary shaping force in world order. I will underline how this is linked to a global restructuring of power associated with an extraordinary concentration of wealth and power in the hands of a very small proportion of the world's population – a global plutocracy and an associated governing class that principally rules on behalf of capital. This situation is overseen by the geopolitical preponderance of the United States which uses panoptic power to keep friends and enemies alike under a condition of constant and omniscient surveillance, guarding the citadels of corporate power. This aspect of power was, of course initially theorized by Foucault, drawing upon the eighteenth-century utilitarian philosopher Jeremy Bentham's designs for the all-purpose institution that would be productive and transformative of its subjects.

It can be asserted however that the modernist dystopia of panoptic power – whether it is in the form of the National Security Administration coordinating its global surveillance activities with the United Kingdom's GCHQ – can be neither omnipotent nor omniscient, nor indeed can it effectively place under surveillance and thereby render docile and pliant the vast numbers of multiple moments and movements of resistance that are localized throughout contemporary globalization (Gill 1995b, 2008). However, whilst it is true that power is distributed, multiple and localized and that it circulates within a set of relations, power is also structural in a broader macro sense: there is a global order that is structured hierarchically that is simultaneously class-based, racialized, and gendered within and across jurisdictions. It operates to systematically empower corporate capital and the associated privileged social strata and specifically the multi-millionaires and billionaires, as well as the affluent more generally, who are the principal beneficiaries of disciplinary neo-liberal 'market civilization' (Gill 1995a). Giant corporations, such as Apple routinely exploit inter-jurisdictional competition between states to attract capital, allowing the firms to locate their profits and losses in the most advantageous locations, especially tax havens, such as Ireland, the Cayman Islands or the City of London, allowing them to lower their taxes. The offshore world therefore structurally reinforces the relational hierarchies associated with contemporary globalization.

Nevertheless, this does not mean that the power of capital, and specifically its disciplinary power, is uncontested; indeed one of the reasons why such power is not hegemonic is because of its distributional consequences, which raise fundamental issues of inequality and social justice. Indeed one of the most crucial issues of our time is the deepening of inequality and its link to crises of capital accumulation; in fact such issues were underlined just before the global crash of 2007–08 by that leading organ of capitalism, the *Financial Times* which asked how, without reading Marx's *Capital*, could one possibly explain why the world's richest 2 per cent of people now owned more than 50 per cent of the world's global assets. By contrast perhaps 90 per cent of the world proletariat are subjected to the rigours of wage labour and are 'unprotected' or precarious workers, people who are non-unionized and deemed to be disposable by the employers. They are often landless workers and peasants who are marginalized from integration into world capitalism but still subjected to many of its forces and pressures, insofar as they are dispossessed of their basic means of livelihood and forced to migrate to the urban centres of the Third World, usually to live in slums and shantytowns, searching for work in the entirely unregulated labour markets.

This is the dark side of market civilization and the global panopticon. Indeed, Marx noted that the dominant model of civilization of the nineteenth century took a specific historical form (bourgeois society) as the counterpart to the dominance of the capitalist mode of accumulation and imperialist expansion. As in the nineteenth century, we can hypothesize therefore that the current neo-liberal form of market civilization is historically specific: it combines the old with the radically new. For example, one novel element is how the boundaries and borderlands of the commodity form spread to heretofore unimagined aspects of human existence to encompass the commodification of social reproduction, the body, and of life forms more generally, e.g. in recent developments associated with new reproductive technologies and commercial surrogacy: the biopolitics of Foucault merge with the commodity form of Marx. The broader pattern is the expropriation of the commons by the forces of commodification, creating new enclosures not simply on land but of life-forms more generally.

So when we consider the nature and future trajectory of market civilization and the forms of power and rule that go with it, we should remember that these are contested, transient and governed by violence as well as by forms of mutability that are not all progressive nor inevitable. Indeed, following Vico and Gramsci, these are the products of human collective action, for good or for otherwise. Vico observed in 1725 in *The New Science* that society is created by the human mind, i.e. by human beings rather than being the product of a divine, cosmic consciousness. For Vico, any explanation of society required the identification of changes in thought – and the conditions that configured action. It is possible to argue that it was therefore Vico who first propounded the essentials of Marx's maxim that human beings make their own history but not necessarily under conditions of their own choosing. Indeed, in this very volume there is an important case study of the Dalit women in Nepal who are making history and forging new knowledge and the creation of rights, not simply through a localized strategy but one that makes links globally so that their political identities and political possibilities might be transformed.

These conditions are uneven and unequal in their consequences. For some, the market civilization of world capitalism involves very specific and beneficial types of acceleration in flows of images, information, commodities and currencies in ways that seem to speed up and render immediate their sense of time and connectivity. On the other hand for most others there is a crisis in global health care, and the spread of infectious diseases and various other maladies once thought to have been conquered in the name of progress, so that even the super-affluent plutocrats are not immune from the negative effects of neo-liberal globalization, and the repercussions of how the commodity form has penetrated into and weakened the provision of health services that were once seen in a number of countries as non-exclusive and governed by public collective organizations in the biopolitical management of populations à la Foucault.

But what of the other political forms that characterize market civilization? These have principally involved passive revolution (see Chapter 7 of this volume for elaboration). For Gramsci, a passive revolution was a non-hegemonic form of intellectual, moral and political change that relied on dominance and the imposition of rule from above, in the absence of consent to the leadership of a ruling class. The condition of passive revolution applies to many of the transformations that have been occurring in the Third World, the former Soviet Union and parts of the communist world since the late 1980s, involving the reintroduction of market-governed disciplinary neo-liberal capitalism. Whilst the world is not fully post-communist – China is still ruled by the Communist Party and committed to principles of socialism, at least formally – the general shift to capitalism is perhaps the key geopolitical development since 1917. Chinese development is linked to global capitalism by the political economy equivalent of an umbilical cord.

With respect to the apex of world order structures, some of my earlier work identified in rather precise terms a 'G7 nexus' that embodies the prevailing relations of force. It includes not only governments but also networks of transnational corporations and other social forces active and influential in political and civil society across borders, a nexus that has been gradually expanding to incorporate some of the ruling forces of other states (e.g. the G8+5 initiative launched in 2007, to add not only Russia but also five influential Third World states including China and India to some – but not all – of the summit discussions at the 'top table'; this is now extended to the G20).

At the apex of this nexus – that is leading the forces of disciplinary neo-liberalism – is a historical bloc of social, economic, cultural and political forces, one that is transnational in its structures and scope. The material and political base rests on the power of giant oligopolistic firms and market forces that operate politically both 'outside' and 'inside' the state and that form part of the 'local' and 'global' political structures. Its social nucleus is the relatively small percentage of affluent people who are the primary beneficiaries of neo-liberal political economy: I call this the 'social reproduction of affluence' and it is politically central to the constitution of market civilization and the forces which tend to support its continuance. It is important to remember however that this historical bloc incorporates much smaller and mid-sized businesses, such as contractors or suppliers, import export businesses, stockbrokers, accountants, consultancies, lobbyists, educational entrepreneurs, architects, and designers. Many of these people provide legitimation for the shift to more marketized systems of value, as do the sports and other stars of entertainment and the celebrity culture.

Again one of the characteristics of market civilization is the way in which risk is increasingly privatized for the majority of the population, and governed by market forces (e.g. their savings/pensions are invested through institutional investors and other intermediaries in the stock and money markets). This is part of the increasing subordination of virtually all state forms to capital following some socialization and nationalization of the means of production especially in the post-World War II era. Socialization and nationalization has occurred during what Hobsbawm called the 'short 20th century'. The existence of the USSR between 1917 and 1991 provided a social and political alternative to capitalist forms of rule, and thus we entered a new era of much more global capitalism with its collapse. Now we see a restructuring of the state's obligations for social reproduction, rolling back welfare, redistribution and public provisions connected to the family, education and healthcare, leading to privatization of risk, and a shift towards greater social atomization. The pattern worldwide is one of intensified exploitation of human beings and nature allied to tendencies towards extreme inequality of income, wealth and life chances. The intensification of exploitation, longer working hours, more intensity of work, and even falling real wages is the converse of rising stock prices and the growing fortunes of the plutocracy.

As noted earlier, one of the salient features of our times is acceleration in the ongoing process of 'primitive accumulation', involving expropriation or dispossession of producers of their means to subsistence – in ways that have parallels with early capitalist forms of dispossession, enclosure and colonization. As peasants are forced off their smallholdings of land, or from land that is common or collectively owned, they become 'free labourers' who have no choice but to sell their labour-power to the private owners of such assets in order to survive. Many move to the rapidly growing cities of the Third World in search of income, in a new great transformation or shift from predominantly rural forms of livelihood to life in urban shantytowns. In this way the fates of communities and their livelihood are increasingly governed by private ownership and by capital, e.g. privatization of public assets and common resources and lands, as well as growing private, particularly corporate control over food supplies.

Even here attempts by corporate capital to gain domination over the 'security' of world food supplies show some of the ecological contradictions of capital accumulation, contradictions which are aided and abetted by compliant governments and lack of global regulation to protect the commons.

Two recent pieces of evidence can be cited here. One is the collapse in fish stocks on the high seas, which from the vantage point of political economy can be considered as perhaps the largest 'offshore' location for capital accumulation, and as such it is a vast and unregulated zone for corporate activity. Global fish stocks have been recently estimated to be 87 per cent overfished or on the verge of collapse, partly as a result of massive fuel subsidies given to industrial fishing fleets and nations such as Spain, France, the UK, the USA and Japan. Another example of how capital accumulation coincides with ecocide is how commercial chemical insecticides have contaminated the environment of the planet so pervasively that global food production is now significantly at risk and will remain so in the future. In ways that recall the problems detailed in Rachel Carson's 1962 book *Silent Spring*, which showed how blanket use of DDT was destroying the environment (thereby triggering the growth of the environmental movement) today the problem is the massive use of other pesticides, and in particular long-lasting neurotoxins (e.g. neonicotinoids). These are sprayed on crops and, in consequence absorbed by seeds so that they spread to all parts of plants as well penetrating the soil and groundwater. Evidence is accumulating that these neurotoxins are increasingly poisoning creatures essential to the cycle of global food production, from bees to earthworms. The side effect of these chemicals is to harm or kill bees and other pollinators and organisms that create healthy soils, with chronic impact on global biodiversity, ecological sustainability and food security. Very little is known about the long-term effects of these chemicals or their effects on reptiles and mammals.

All of this is deeply contested. However to sustain the domination of giant corporations and the financial power of Wall Street, the City of London and other financial centres which lie at the heart of the investment strategies and profit orientations of neoliberal capitalism requires the coercive power of the state apparatuses to prevail. It has gone with the restructuring of state apparatuses and police powers as a response to the global state of emergency effectively declared by the US Bush Administration after 911, when the World Trade Centre was destroyed and the Pentagon attacked. This has meant the strengthening of the already vast internal and external aspects of national security apparatuses and mechanisms of military and political surveillance, as revealed, for example, by the Snowden revelations concerning the NSA and GCHQ. There is also growing intolerance and criminalization of displays of dissent by neoliberal leaderships, most obviously reflected in the paramilitary policing strategies and mass arrests that have occurred at recent WTO and IMF meetings or at G8 and G20 summits and the criminalization of protests against austerity measures in Europe, for example in Spain. World leaders from the G20 countries have used huge public financial resources in responding to the global financial collapse of 2008, whilst enormous numbers of people have been pushed towards the brink of starvation; badly needed resources to bolster public health initiatives and to deal with primary healthcare issues were being and are still being cut (Gill 2015: 188–91).

However the present crisis is very deep and it involves much more than a crisis of capitalist accumulation or a necessary self-correction aided by macroeconomic intervention and bailouts. Many of the issues and problems noted above are connected to the basic logic of the dominant pattern of accumulation in the global political economy (what I call disciplinary neo-liberalism) and the unequal and unjust development it fosters. This pattern is ecologically unsustainable – it is premised upon energy-intensive, consumerist and ecologically myopic patterns of economic activity – a market civilization which by definition is exclusive and can be only available to a minority of the population of the planet, but which is nevertheless serving to consume the vast bulk of global resources. And as we have noted, there is widespread resistance to this particular form of capitalist ecocide, and that resistance encompasses not only those communities that are being dispossessed of their livelihoods but also scientists and activists concerned with the longer-term threats to the integrity of biosphere associated with contemporary patterns of production and consumption.

One can hypothesize that all this signals what Gramsci called an 'organic crisis' of world order and global capitalism (Gill 2012a). We may have reached an impasse such that: 'The crisis consists precisely in the fact that the old is dying and the new cannot be born; in this interregnum a great variety of morbid symptoms appear' (Gramsci 1971: 276). These morbid symptoms are some of the social conditions that will constitute – although not necessarily determine – the archaeology of the foreseeable future.

As we ponder the future, our 'pessimism of the intelligence' might characterize the current moment in world order as reflecting an impasse shaped by the degenerative forces of disciplinary neoliberalism, with no clear or generalized progressive solution(s) yet in sight; indeed where authoritarianism and greater coercive power may prevail in the context of intensifying global competition for resources and food and the ongoing politics of austerity.

On the other hand an 'optimism of the will' might highlight not only developments discussed in this volume, such as ALBA (see Chapter 8) but also the myriad and capillary forms of contestation to re-think lifestyles and sustainability and to challenge the hyper-consumerism, mass advertising, ecological myopia and waste associated with the affluent development patterns of market civilization. Deadlock over climate change and food and health security is linked to political struggles over growing corporate domination and private control over world agriculture, food production and distribution, life sciences, medicine, and pharmaceutical industries.

Indeed many scientists are increasingly convinced that the global economic system is careening out of control, driven by an economic paradigm that is a threat to ecological sustainability as global capitalism is associated with the intensification of global warming, threats to biodiversity and soil degradation, posing fundamental dangers to our collective futures. Increasingly scientists are identifying with and joining activists, participating in various forms of resistance associated with environmental direct action, protests, blockades and opposition to market civilization. The political status quo is increasingly understood as having an ostrich mentality; its political leaders and state managers are seen as enslaved by short term or immediate interests and beholden to various forms of political expediency, coercion and repression.

Indeed, a study that was partly sponsored by NASA's Goddard Space Flight Centre has 'highlighted the prospect that global industrial civilization could collapse in coming decades due to unsustainable resource exploitation and increasingly unequal wealth distribution', factors which combined to precipitate the collapse of several complex and sophisticated civilizations in the past such as the Roman and Mesopotamian Empires. The NASA model was developed by a team of natural and social scientists and mathematicians and it proposed that the two key solutions required to pave the way to a more stable civilization are to reduce inequality and ensure a fairer distribution of resources, and to significantly reduce the consumption of non-renewable resources and population growth.

Thus the stakes are very high and they concern new imaginaries and mechanisms for the future of global governance. Indeed, if we could combine the insights of Gramsci and Foucault to imagine new forms of political agency (see Chapter 5) one might add that the Dalit women (Chapter 6) and the Latin American movements (noted in Chapter 8) are examples of new forces engaging in basic questions of equality, justice, livelihood, racism, and the relations between men and women, thinking both locally and globally to generate alternative forms of power/knowledge and to challenge and displace neo-liberal common sense.

It may be possible therefore to discern an emerging, innovative form of global theory and praxis, intimating new potentials for a transformative politics. I have termed these potentials, following Machiavelli and Gramsci, the 'post-modern Prince' – the emergence of a set of emancipatory and insurgent movements understood as political, social and pedagogical processes, in many ways consistent with the work of Paulo Freire (Gill 2008, 2012b). The 'post-modern Prince' should therefore be understood in the plural and the local but having in common the development of imagined and real alternatives to disciplinary neo-liberalism and market civilization, in ways that go beyond their reductionist and nihilistic epistemologies to collectively produce a complex, historically grounded, integrated and holistic long term perspective on the conditions of existence and the transformation of possibilities for future generations. The post-modern Prince encompasses largely subaltern but progressive political forces still in formation and needs to be understood as a democratic process in formation that does not necessarily provide a unified response to all problems. It is thus not a traditional political party with restrictive membership requirements, but it is nonetheless premised on not only a relatively shared recognition of common problems and principles. It embraces diversity, difference, recognition and redistribution.

It encompasses both North and South. It does not simply focus on industrial workers as its 'vanguard'; its leadership encompasses peasants, other workers, feminists, ecologists, anarchists, indigenous peoples and a wide range of forces, including churches and experts with scientific and technological expertise. Its leaders are millions of organic intellectuals interlinked locally and globally through powerful modes of communication and radical media outlets that deconstruct narratives and tropes of dominant power and lay bare and place unethical and illegitimate practices under scrutiny; a form of 'democratic surveillance' (Gill 1995b).

Such innovations in praxis on the part of countless organic intellectuals involve not only critique but also new ways of thinking and imagining beyond the dominant ideologies of our times. They combine both traditional and indigenous knowledge premised upon a long-run time scale as well as the systematic learning and research on the integrity and sustainability of complex systems that is at the cutting edge of new scientific thinking about the relationship between prevailing development patterns and the integrity of the biosphere (see Chapter 10). Perhaps therefore, the (progeny) of the post-modern Prince will excavate not only the archaeology of modernist and post-modern knowledge but more importantly, recreate the very social and ecological 'archaeology of the future'?

References

Gill, S. 1995a. Globalisation, market civilisation & disciplinary neoliberalism. *Millennium* 24(3): 399–423.

—. 1995b. The global panopticon? The neo-liberal state, economic life and democratic surveillance. *Alternatives* 20(1): 1–49.

—. 2008. *Power and Resistance in the New World Order.* London and New York: Macmillan-Palgrave. Second fully-revised, updated and enlarged edition.

—. 2012a (editor and contributor). *Global Crises and the Crisis of Global Leadership.* Cambridge and New York: Cambridge University Press.

—. 2012b. Towards a radical concept of praxis: Imperial 'common sense' versus the post-modern Prince. *Millennium: Journal of International Studies* 40(3): 502–21.

—. 2015 (editor and contributor). *Critical Perspectives on the Crisis of Global Governance: Reimagining the Future.* Basingstoke and New York: Palgrave Macmillan

Polanyi, K. 1944. *The Great Transformation: The Political and Economic Origins of Our Time.* Boston: Beacon Press.

Preface

This volume first came about through a paper I presented at the Media, Communication and Cultural Studies Association (MeCCSA) conference in January 2011. The paper focused on Social Networking and Transnational Capitalism, and appeared at the end of that year in *tripleC – Cognition, Communication, Co-operation* (Kreps 2011). Acknowledging that social networking sites, like Facebook, have become a key component of users' experience of the internet, this paper argued strongly that whilst much has been made in academic literature of the social dynamics of such websites, the influence of the structures and operations of these sites – and the business models behind them – on users is rarely accounted for. The argument stressed that behind the social behaviours supported by such sites, there has been and continues to be a fundamental shift towards viewing online communities as commodities, and social networking sites as an extension of mainstream capitalist ideologies fostered by existing patterns of commercialization and consumption. (Indeed there were already indications that some of the corporations behind such commercialization were adept at avoiding paying tax (Shaxson 2011).) Using the works of Gramsci, Gill, and Hardt and Negri to provide a critical grounding, the paper explored the hugely popular social networking site Facebook and suggested that although such a site may feel to its users to be free, social, and personal, in fact such sites are just business as usual.

In the paper, I noted:

> Gramsci's work is today situated within the literature of cultural criticism alongside other writers such as Loius Althusser, and Michel Foucault, both of whom have their criticisms of Gramsci's approach, and present their own alternatives. This is not the place for a wider discussion of these issues, save to present the caveat, in using the notion of cultural hegemony, that there are foundational assumptions about the nature of capitalist societies, divisions in society related to the concept of class, and a particular understanding of the nature and expression of power inherent in Gramsci's work that are not shared by other cultural theorists in the field. Foucault in particular refused to see power as something exercised by a dominant over a subservient class, insisting that power is derived from discourses – accepted ways of thinking, writing, and speaking – and practices that amount to power. (Kreps 2011: 692)

During the question and answer session following my presentation, it was the dissonances and potential synergies between Gramsci and Foucault that formed the core of what became a lively and stimulating discussion. Further work on this theme, in the ensuing weeks, revealed that, apart from the few journal papers and book chapters reviewed in my introduction to this volume, there seems to be a gap in the literature concerning these dissonances and synergies between arguably two of the most important radical/critical thinkers of the twentieth century. This volume, then, is my attempt to stimulate further discussion to fill this gap. Clearly I am not the first, and I hope, not the last! Indeed, a workshop at the University of Lancaster, co-organized by the 'Foucault and Critical Realism' Research Cluster entitled, 'Marx, Gramsci and Foucault', in July 2009, could be regarded as having blazed the trail, including as it did among its five papers a plenary by Alex Demirovic, and a paper by the workshop's co-host, Ngai-Ling Sum, both contributors to this volume.

David Kreps
October 2014

References

Kreps, D. 2011. Social networking and transnational capitalism. *tripleC – Cognition, Communication, Co-operation* 9(2): 689–701.

Shaxson, N. 2011. *Treasure Islands*. London: Bodley Head.

Chapter 1
Introduction

David Kreps

In this introduction, by way of presenting a review of the scant pre-existing literature I have been able to find which considers the work of Gramsci and Foucault together, I attempt firstly to set out a conceptual framework by which the reader may see what is common among the papers in this volume – which makes it valid to call these papers a meaningful collection, and thereby to call each paper a chapter; and secondly, in exploring the tensions between Gramsci and Foucault, I attempt a discussion of what are the kinds of differences among the chapters that make it interesting to collect them together. Lastly, I offer a brief explanation of each chapter, and how it contributes to that picture.

The Three Camps

The few already published journal articles, book sections and chapters on Foucault or Gramsci that consider the two writers together, or mention the other writer in passing, are to be found across a range of disciplines, including feminist philosophy and human geography, along with the more obvious radical political theory and cultural studies. Joan Cocks (1989), a feminist philosopher, puts forward the primary argument of much of this volume, that taken together (although quite how remains the core of the discussion) Foucault's and Gramsci's sociological insights present something of more value than either of them taken in isolation. As she says:

> There are [between Gramsci and Foucault] certain striking thematic repetitions, certain similar analytical obsessions – certain ways, too, in which their arguments and insights are reciprocally illuminating. What is flawed in each argument alone, moreover, is improved by the selective combination of the arguments together. For in some cases there is too great a faith in subjective agency, in others too great an emphasis on objective determination. Some defend an overly centrist strategy of resistance, others an overly localist one. In certain arguments we find a naïve esteem for a final harmony in social relations, and in others, a hypertrophied sensitivity to the possibilities of repression in any collective way of life. (Cocks 1989: 26)

In other words, Foucault's attention to the micro-levels of power over individual bodies and Gramsci's attention to the macro-level of institutions, classes and societies offer a broader and deeper picture when considered together.

Jane Kenway (1990) makes the same assertion, suggesting a 'poststructuralist reading of Gramsci' (Kenway 1990: 172) makes a good adjunct to Foucault's work, and that the two writers' oeuvres should be considered complementary, although she makes no attempt to combine them. Indeed – combining the two seems to be something no-one has attempted, pointing out, when it is considered, the fundamental dissonances between their approaches that would prevent such a synthesis. Inconsistencies within the *Prison Notebooks*, and the gradual development and shifts of Foucault's thought over the course of his career, moreover, render both these 'oeuvres' quite diffuse in places, on such critical issues as Gramsci's definition of hegemony – which is never definitive – and the freedom of the individual to escape disciplination, which in the early Foucault appears negligible, but later appears possible but only through individual – and sometimes counterintuitive – effort. Combining such diffuse oeuvres seems, from certain perspectives, quite impossible. Finally, as human geographers, Ekers and Loftus (2008), put it, 'what was often a fiercely anti-Marxist stance on Foucault's part' (2008: 698), and the fact that the poststructuralist turn of the 1960s quite simply post-dates Gramsci's death and is therefore absent in his work, present, for many authors, fundamental oppositions between the two.

Thus, Marxist Norman Geras (1990) points out, forcefully, that there is simply no possibility of combining the work of the two thinkers, because the way Foucault uses the concept, in particular, of hegemony, is expressive of a totally different standpoint to that of Gramsci. Richard Day's *Gramsci is Dead* (2005) meanwhile, attacks the whole notion of hegemony, from a Foucauldian perspective. Arguably, however, as Olssen (2006) points out, Geras's objections seem to stem from a standpoint that simply does not accept the fundamental premises of poststructuralism, preferring the objective certainties of classical Marxism. Day (2005), in a similar vein, seems overly determined to deconstruct everything to the level of the individual (as indeed Foucault arguably did) without the possibility of any collectivity. Barnett (2005) views attempts to use the two thinkers together – at least in the considerations of human geographers – as 'theoretically clumsy, and politically confused' (Ekers and Loftus 2008: 699). Is it, as Barnett would have it, that 'Marxist and Foucauldian approaches imply different models of the nature of explanatory concepts; different models of causality and determination; different models of social relations and agency; and different normative understandings of political power' (Barnett, 2005: 8). Or is it merely that the two thinkers focused upon differing aspects of a wider picture that do not exclude each other? Does Foucault's concentration upon the micro-politics in society that add up to and constitute the central figure of the State undermine and discount, or complement and mirror Gramsci's concentration on the hegemonic reach of that centre out into the minutiae of social relations? Or is it, as Scott Lash (2007) argues, that 'power over', in contemporary society, has simply become post-hegemonic, and that the more Foucauldian conception of 'power from within' is now the only game in town.

Attempts at combination aside, there are, nonetheless, many examples of authors using the two together to address a range of concerns: in human geography (Larner 2000; 2003; Peet 2001; Sparke 2006; Watts 2003; Ekers and Loftus 2008), in feminism (Mercer 1980; Cocks 1989; Kenway 1990; Harstock 1990), and in critical thinking (Driver 1985; Smart 1985 and 1999; Barrett 1991; Burchell et al. 1991; Marsden 1999; Torfing 1999; Morera 2000; Ives 2004; Stoddart 2005; Olssen 2006; Jessop 2007), along, no doubt, with other areas this author has no knowledge of.

Marxist scholar Paul Ives (2004) sees many points of contact between the two – particularly between the notion of 'grammars' and of 'discourse'. As he points out,

> in a way that is closer to Foucault's analysis of power, Gramsci's notion of spontaneous grammar shows how political influence works at the micro level and how even those who seem to have little power, working-class children for example, exert their dominance over peasant or immigrant children by making fun of the way they speak. Even the benign form of correcting someone's grammar or asking for clarification is not free of power relations or politics. (Ives 2004: 143)

Granting Gramsci, in this way, insight into where Foucault would later take the consideration of the micro-level of power relations, chimes with a range of literature in which, as Ekers and Loftus argue, citing Chantal Mouffe (1979), 'Gramsci approached many of the theoretical concerns that were to become central to Foucault's oeuvre' (Ekers and Loftus 2008: 699).

Yet, if Gramsci's thought in some ways tentatively prefigured where Foucault would later flesh out detailed analysis, as Radhakrishnan (1990) suggests, Gramsci's thought elsewhere seems to complete, in advance, some of the gaps left in Foucault's later analysis. Radhakrishnan argues that Foucault's attention to the micro-level of politics stems from his critique of his own position as a European intellectual, and that without direct experience of the 'subjugated knowledges' he interrogates he cannot conceive the macro-political necessity of leadership. Gramsci's earlier concentration on the relationship between the individual and the group, therefore, provides the very theoretical foundation upon which such leadership can be created in a way that evades the pitfalls Foucault describes.

Combinations, then, at least of specific elements of each thinker's ideas, do appear in the literature. The noted neo-Gramscian Stephen Gill (2003) has drawn substantially on Foucauldian notions of panopticism to develop his new concepts of disciplinary neo-liberalism. Hardt and Negri's (2000) *Empire* is conceived as more of a Foucauldian discursive formation than an old European imperialist power, yet it exerts thoroughly Gramscian hegemonic dominance, for all that that dominance may be in a more theoretical form of rulership than Gramsci may have envisaged. Indeed, 'the rule of Empire operates on all registers of the social order extending down to the depths of the social world' (Hardt and Negri 2000: xv).

Most strikingly of all, perhaps, the work of Laclau and Mouffe (1982; 1985; 1987), and that of Jacob Torfing (1999) present for us a very enlightening combination of the two great thinkers. Accepting the decentring of the subject in poststructuralism and the notion that 'Discourse theory abandons the notion of a true or perfect definition together with a conception of social identities as rooted in pregiven essences' (Torfing 1999: 3), Laclau and Mouffe undertake an updating of Gramsci's thought into the poststructuralist mode. 'The essentialist remnant in Gramsci, which made him insist on the privileged position of the fundamental classes in hegemonic struggles, is removed' by this update, 'thereby allowing Laclau and Mouffe to reformulate the concept of hegemony' (Torfing 1999: 13). This reconceptualizing of hegemony as a discursive phenomenon, allows Laclau and Mouffe to redefine it:

> Hegemony is no longer to be conceived of in terms of the unification of political forces around a set of paradigmatic interests that are constituted elsewhere. Rather, hegemony involves the articulation of social identities in the context of social antagonism. As in the work of Derrida, the articulation of identity is taken to be conditioned by the deconstruction of the very notion of structure, which reveals the discursive, and thus the contingent, character of all social identities. (Torfing 1999: 14)

From this review of the literature that considers Foucault and Gramsci together, then, three camps emerge: (i) the Marxists for whom Foucault's conception of power ignores historical realities – such as 'the fundamental classes'; (ii) the poststructuralists for whom Foucault's nominalism, or 'sociological singularism' as Olssen (2006) puts it, precludes any totalizing theoretic such as Gramsci's – and for whom the 'fundamental classes' do not exist; and (iii) those for whom these differences constitute the site of complementarity between the two writers. In this third camp, there seems little evidence of any genuine attempt to combine the theories of the two, without in some shape or form granting one or the other the upper hand – Radhakrishnan to Gramsi; Laclau, Mouffe and Torfing to Foucault – in some fundamental respect.

It seems, then, from the literature, that there are fundamental differences between the two thinkers that have prevented, beyond the few papers cited above, much discussion between them: they exist in separate worlds – incompatible ones, if Geras (1990) or Day (2005) are to be believed – and many scholars seem either to belong to one or the other. From a classical Marxist perspective, Foucault's use of such terms as hegemony sets up inescapable inconsistencies; from a poststructuralist perspective, the totalizing – and scientistic – approach of Marxist historical materialism completely fails to appreciate the far more nuanced, pervasive understanding of power as situated in discursive contexts. The consequence has been a form of parallel and exclusive paradigm conflict between divergent camps within radical thought that has undoubtedly been detrimental to the broader aims of both sides of the divide: social change.

But it is also clear that there are ample areas in which the two writers complement one another, and, as Olssen in particular points out, they 'present a more powerful perspective on social structure taken together than each does on his own' (Olssen 2006: 116). I would like, then, at this point, to put forward a notion of my own concerning the possibility of combining the works of the two thinkers that has thus far – if my searches of the literature have been sufficiently exhaustive – failed at least to appear in print. It strikes me that, beyond the linguistic and poststructuralist turns which knock down the essentialism to which Gramsci, in the 1930s, remained true, there is a further 'turn' that similarly post-dates Foucault's lifetime, and which has brought the worlds of poststructuralism and scientific materialism into a new and strikingly innovative confluence: the 'complexity turn' (Urry 2005). I have devoted the final chapter of this volume to a more thorough treatment of this idea, and refer the reader there for more detail. For now, let me briefly introduce it.

As Kaufmann asserts, the fundamental problem with scientific materialist thought (in its reductionist mode), is that to represent a *complex* system (as opposed to one that is merely complicated) one must, of necessity, reproduce the system in its entirety. The representation, usually something like an algorithm – the 'shortest description' which can capture the essential elements of a system – can only capture the entirety of a complex system, because a complex system is already its own shortest description, (Kaufmann 1995: 22). Thus – if human society can be considered as a complex system, as indeed many sociologists are now beginning to do – Foucault's exclusive attention to the micro-level is indeed justified. Yet with the help of Kaufmann's theories, and those of others working in the field of complexity, it may be possible to evince what he describes as 'generic lawlike behaviours' in these systems that may be not dissimilar to those attempted by Gramsci. I refer the reader to my concluding chapter, in this volume, for a fuller explication of this potential combination.

Introduction to Each Chapter in this Collection

It should be said that none of the chapters in this collection could be considered to fall into the first or second of the above 'three camps'. Yet in the third camp – those for whom the differences constitute the site of complementarity between the two writers – any attempt to combine the theories of the two seems inevitably to in some shape or form grant one or the other the upper hand. This collection proves little different, although the chapters have been ordered thematically rather than in terms of their preference for a Gramscian Foucauldianism, or a Foucauldian Gramscianism.

The collection begins with Alex Demirović, who examines the relation between discourse and reality, as exposed through the differing but related positions of

Foucault and Gramsci on truth. While for both writers, 'truths are understood as historically relative practices which nevertheless determine the subsequent social and intellectual processes', Foucault, Demirović asserts, concentrates upon the ethics of truth, and how subjectivities and identities derive their underpinnings from the multiple layers of discourses where truths are created and deployed in networks of power relations. Gramsci, meanwhile, concentrates upon the politics of a truth that is provisional and transient, and how it is marshalled by the institutions of power and deployed for the dominance of the subaltern; for Gramsci the overriding importance is to speak the truth in politics, for all that it may be a provisional one. Demirović looks ultimately to the potential synergy of the two writers' oeuvres from which 'a politics and ethics of truth emerges, through which truth itself – its very status and power – can be changed'.

Next Ngai-Ling Sum considers what Gramsci termed the regularities of the determined market and their relation to the state in its integral sense, alongside what Foucault called liberal and neo-liberal economic rationality and their relation to governmentality and statecraft. Gramscianizing Foucault, and working towards the potential contribution of Gramsci and Foucault to the development of the emerging agenda of cultural political economy, Sum presents six 'discursively selective' moments in the production of hegemonies – a heuristic schema to help in locating social relations within meaning-making. He then illustrates this schema by applying it to discourses on 'competitiveness', seeking ultimately to both governmentalize Gramsci and Gramscianize Foucault.

Then Marcus Schulzke seeks a Gramscian interpretation of Foucault's theory of power that helps it avoid making resistance either impossible or pointless. Through Gramsci's theory of hegemony he offers in this chapter a clearer explanation of the agent, tactics, and goals of resistance – in particular through the political party. As he points out,

> Those who attempt to derive theories of resistance from Foucault offer strong explanations of how power can be mobilized by ordinary people, but they offer insufficient accounts of how individuals can ever hope to rise above the multiple sources of power acting on them to the extent that they can carry out acts of resistance.

In this chapter, using the ideas of Gramsci, Schulzke helps to map a route by which this cul-de-sac might fruitfully be escaped – specifically through the social tool of education.

Then Jean-Paul Gagnon focuses on education and democracy, suggesting that Gramscian and Foucauldian theory support a democracy focused on citizen-experts who actively resist power. Citizens, he asserts, require expert knowledge, and this knowledge 'should be about diluting power'. They must also understand their 'role as selves in dialectic to the role of citizen'. This expertise, it is hoped, 'will allow for an emancipated politics for the self, association and demos. Awareness of the need to be an expert will, in other words, rescue democracy'.

Taking the Gramscian term, 'subaltern', in her chapter, Sonita Sarker shows how the famous theorist Gayatri Spivak remodelled it as a 'position without identity' (Spivak 2005: 476), and how it remains relevant to this day, in the plight of the Dalit in India and indigenous women in Texas, USA. Sarker places the dialectic of subalternity in the context of a discussion of time and history – specifically the history of our thinking around time – linking Gramscian 'subalternity' with Foucauldian 'subjugated knowledges', to show that subalternity exists in an unstructured stream of time outside of hegemonic history.

Then Jelle Verserien and Brecht de Smet focus on religion and modernity, and the transitions and modernizations associated with them, and how the work of both Gramsci and Foucault addresses these issues. How is the 'modern' defined by each author? How do their differing 'historicisms' render similar stories and transformations? Echoing Sarker's thoughts on time and history, this chapter speaks of 'history as an ensemble of multiple temporalities' and asserts that Gramsci and Foucault share 'a mutual core element: the historical and conceptual status of modernity as historicity'.

Then Efe Can Gürcan and Onur Bakıner describe counter-hegemonic practice in action in Latin America, arguing that 'post-neoliberal regional integration has emerged as a political, economic, and cultural alternative to neoliberal hegemony' in the South American continent, particularly through such regional organizations as ALBA, the Bolivarian Alliance for the Peoples of Our America. Not just education, but the significance of Revolutionary leadership is argued for in this chapter, incorporating Paulo Freire's pedagogy of the oppressed, and the real and substantial education efforts of ALBA.

Heather Brunskell-Evans situates her discussion in the context of a small case study of paediatric care – using imported Western psychological discourses – in post-invasion Iraq, focussing on the different slants both Gramsci and Foucault gave to the concept of humanism. She reminds us of Gramsci's suspicion that sociology cannot 'objectively' study the conditions of a historically constructed 'human nature' since 'the will and initiative of human beings, in transforming the social conditions of their existence, cannot be left out of the account'. Similarly, she points to Foucault's archaeological understanding of the creation of 'man' in the late eighteenth century, through the 'sciences' and disciplines of 'reason', with ministering to the psyche – or secular soul – undertaken not by the priest but by the doctor, and increasingly focussed around the newly constituted social arrangement of the 'private' nuclear family. Thus understanding the well-being of the child and of the family as constitutively social, Brunskell-Evans can turn, with this picture of the 'child with psychological needs' as a device of normalizing power, to consideration of how paediatric care in post-invasion Iraq is undertaken – paradoxically allied to the ultimately Westernizing agenda of the invaders.

Finally I conclude with my own chapter about the possibility of viewing a potential combination of the ideas of Gramsci and Foucault through the lens of the complexity turn in sociological thought.

Summary

In sum, we can conclude that a third way – considering the work of both Foucault and Gramsci, without attempting to combine them – is far more fruitful than merely dismissing the one in favour of the other. Moreover, although Foucault does look exclusively at the micro-level, it is impossible to get a 'shorter description' than the full detail (Kaufman 1995). Yet despite Foucault's reticence – and even hostility – towards the issue, we need to, and can discern 'generic lawlike behaviours' in the structures and institutions of collectivities. Gramsci gives us a suggestion of what kinds of laws to look for, and indeed combining things in this way might even improve Gramsci's thought, using Foucault and the poststructuralist turn to escape the essentialism for which he is rightly criticized.

This collection explores the nature, politics and ethics of truth; markets and governmentality in the context of discourses of competitiveness; theories of resistance; citizen-experts who actively resist power; the notions of subalternity and subjugated knowledges; 'history as an ensemble of multiple temporalities'; counter-hegemonic practice in action in Latin America; and the hegemony of Western psychological discourses in post-invasion Iraq. Finally, through an introduction to the sociology of complexity, it suggests that the ideas of Foucault and Gramsci deserve to be considered together, to the benefit of each, and of us all.

References

Barnett, C. 2005. The consolidations of 'neoliberalism'. *Geoforum* 36(1): 7–12.

Barrett, M. 1991. *The Politics of Truth: From Marx to Foucault.* Cambridge: Polity.

Burchell, G., Gordon, C. and Miller, P. (eds) 1991. *The Foucault Effect: Studies in Governmental Rationality*, translated by C. Gordon. Hemel Hempstead: Harvester Wheatsheaf.

Cocks, J. 1989. *The Oppositional Imagination: Feminism, Critique and Political Theory.* London: Routledge.

Day, R. 2005. *Gramsci is Dead: Anarchist Currents in the Newest Social Movements.* London: Pluto Press.

Driver, F. 1985. Power, space, and the body: A critical assessment of Foucault's 'Discipline and Punish'. *Environment and Planning D: Society and Space* 3: 425–46.

Ekers, M. and Loftus, A. (2008) The power of water: Developing dialogues between Foucault and Gramsci. *Environment and Planning D: Society and Space* 26: 698–718.

Geras, N. 1990. *Discourses of Extremity: Radical Ethics and Post-Marxist Extravagances.* London and New York: Verso.

Gill, S. 2003 *Power and Resistance in the New World Order.* Basingstoke: Palgrave.

Gramsci, A. 2007. *Selections from the 'Prison Notebooks'*, edited and translated by Q. Hoare and G.N. Smith. London: Lawrence and Wishart.

Hardt, M. and Negri, A. 2000. *Empire*. London: Harvard University Press.
Harstock, N. 1990. Foucault on power: A theory for women? In *Feminism/ Postmodernism*, edited by L. Nicholson. New York: Routledge.
Ives, P. 2004. *Language and Hegemony in Gramsci*. London: Pluto Press.
Jessop, B. 2007. From micro-powers to governmentality: Foucault's work on statehood, state formation, statecraft and state power. *Political Geography* 26(1): 34–40.
Kaufmann, S. 1995. *At Home in the Universe*. Oxford: Oxford University Press.
Kenway, J. 1990. Education and the Right's discursive politics: Private vs. state schooling. In *Foucault and Education: Discipline and Knowledge*, edited by S.J. Ball. London: Routledge, 167–206.
Laclau, E. and Mouffe, C. 1982. Recasting Marxism: Hegemony and new political movements. *Socialist Review* 12: 91–113.
—. 1985. *Hegemony and Socialist Strategy*. London: Verso.
—. 1987. Post-Marxism without apologies. *New Left Review* 166: 79–106.
Larner, W. 2000. Neoliberalism: Policy, ideology, governmentality. *Studies in Political Economy* 63(Fall): 5–25.
—. 2003. Neoliberalism? *Environment and Planning D: Society and Space* 21: 509–12.
Lash, S. 2007. Power after hegemony: Cultural studies in mutation? *Theory, Culture, and Society* 24(3): 55–78.
Marsden, R. 1999. *The Nature of Capital: Foucault after Marx*. London: Routledge.
Morera, E. 2000. Gramsci's critical modernity. *Rethinking Marxism* 12(1): 16–46.
Mouffe, C. 1979. Hegemony and ideology in Gramsci. In *Gramsci and Marxist Theory*, edited by C. Mouffe. New York: Routledge, 168–204.
Olssen, M. 2006. *Michel Foucault: Materialism and Education*. London: Paradigm Publishers.
Peet, R. 2001. Ideology, discourse and the geography of hegemony: From socialist to neoliberal development in South Africa. *Antipode* 34: 54–84.
Radhakrishnan, R. 1990. Toward an effective intellectual: Foucault or Gramsci? In *Intellectuals: Aesthetics, Politics, Academics*, edited by B. Robbins. University of Minnesota Press, 57–99.
Smart, B. 1985 *Foucault* London: Tavistock Press
—. 1999. The Politics of Truth. In *Foucault: A Critical Reader*, edited by D.C. Hoy. Oxford: Blackwell.
Sparke, M. 2006. Political geographies of globalization: (2) Governance. *Progress in Human Geography* 30: 357–72.
Stoddart, M. 2005. The Gramsci–Foucault nexus and environment sociology. *Alternative Routes* 21: 26–40.
Torfing, J. 1999. *New Theories of Discourse: Laclau, Mouffe and Zizek*. Oxford: Blackwell.
Urry, J. 2005. The complexity turn. *Theory, Culture and Society* 22(5): 1–14.
Watts, M. 2003. Development and governmentality. *Singapore Journal of Tropical Geography* 24(1): 6–34.

Chapter 2
The Politics of Truth: For a Different Way of Life

Alex Demirović

Truth – A Praxis?

There exists a problem which, despite occupying the minds of a number of authors we count to western Marxism, remained rather limited in its impact and reception. It is a problem concerning the relationship between truth and politics. Being so strongly tied to the more widely discussed concept of reason it seems to have faded somewhat into the background. Critical Theory – and by that I mean the theory of Marx and those who took up his work and the problems he dealt with – claims to be scientific and true. What does such a claim imply? A number of true statements which can be coherently assembled into a systematic theory? Does praxis automatically follow on from truth? Is there are particular persuasiveness or capacity to act connected to a scientifically true theory? Are there individuals or social groups who are willing to engage and commit themselves – both for and following – the theory, for the only reason of it being true? Why do we expect that the truth of a theory attracts people and that this truth should or might become binding for them, maybe insomuch as it might motivate them to certain practice?

Though power can be bound to cynicism and an instrumental relation to truth, truth also represents something emancipatory: clarity and rational and universally comprehensible arguments. The relation between truth and power on the one side, and truth and emancipation on the other raises a batch of questions: does reference to truth hinder those fighting for emancipation, and does this same reference to truth contribute to moderate and limit the fervour necessary to resolutely engage oneself for change? Does truth contribute to emancipation? Is truth a form in which emancipation is performed and fulfilled? Does the will to truth secure the intellectual continuity of emancipatory knowledge? Does veridiction give the strength necessary to fight for social change? I want to discuss these questions referring myself to the thoughts of Antonio Gramsci and Michel Foucault. Though working in widely different historical contexts both of these authors thought about these problems. Given the historical defeat of the workers movement and the Stalinization of the Communist party, Gramsci wondered how a particular understanding of reality, science and truth could become an instrument for anti-emancipatory tendencies in the left. For this reason he argued for a radical anti-objectivist understanding of truth. Foucault studied the comprehensive effects of the power of knowledge and truth from a historical perspective. Having also observed the effects of this power of knowledge and truth in emancipatory movements, he attempted – despite strong criticism – to conceive a radical practice of veridiction tied to life. I will attempt to show that although Foucault never explicitly refers to Gramsci, the thoughts of both authors concur on a number of matters, and that even where they don't quite agree, it is productive to read them as complimentary approaches.

The Power of Truth

Looking back, Foucault remembers how the French protest movement of May 1968 confronted him with the relationship between the subject and truth in Marxism. He felt bitterly disappointed when in 1968, returning from Tunisia and arriving in Paris, he found himself confronted with the 'cold academic debates on Marxism' (Foucault 1980b: 135). He saw a '"hyper-Marxism" in France, that unleashing of theories, anathemas, the splitting up into factions' (Foucault 1980b: 138–9). 'All of this was really the reverse, the polar opposite of what had attracted me to Tunisia' (Foucault 1980b: 139). During his time teaching in Tunisia he had experienced something different: 'Everyone was drawn into Marxism with radical violence and intensity and staggeringly powerful thrust. For those young people, Marxism did not merely represent a way of analyzing reality; it was also a kind of moral force, an existential act that left one stupefied' (Foucault 1980b: 135). Tunisian students exposed themselves to a great deal of risk, aware that they were susceptible to be sentenced to long prison terms. This led Foucault to the question: what in today's world it is 'that can set off in an individual the desire, the capacity, and the possibility of absolute sacrifice' (Foucault 1980b: 136). His answer to this question is somewhat contradictory and is directly related to the problem of truth. On the one hand, for the young Tunisians Marxism represented the better way of analysing reality, and could therefore unleash the moral energy needed for radical action. On the other hand, referring to theory and truth can also show itself to be damaging. Truth does not appear as a source or motivation for socially transformative practice. 'This is what I saw in Tunisia. The necessity for a struggle was clearly evident there on account of the intolerable nature of certain conditions produced by capitalism, colonialism and neocolonialism' (Foucault 1980b: 136–7). The struggle appeared because of a political world-view, whilst 'The precision of theory, its scientific character, was an entirely secondary question' (Foucault 1980b: 137). Marxism, science, theory and truth are four closely related concepts. Foucault tends to see them as an obstacle to radical emancipation. They are not only secondary to appropriate action, but on a much more fundamental level, truth itself can represent a substantial factor in the hindrance of radical action. To these more prevalent terms, Foucault opposes a number of other more difficult and problematic concepts: world-view, spirituality and myth. Though quite how this opposition functions is both ambivalent and unclear. Foucault therefore seems to suggest that truth is more likely to inhibit or even preclude a critical emancipatory stance.

A basis for this assumption can be found in his discourse analytical studies on the emergence of new discourse formations. Foucault develops a number of relevant ideas on the relationship between discourse and power in his inaugural lecture in 1970. Truth is here mostly understood as a form of repression, insomuch as truth is a mechanism which controls who may speak about what and how. Truth is therefore a practice which censures, regulates, controls and selects what can be said. Speech which wants to be heard has to strive to be considered true. On top of this, it must cross a threshold which – at least in science and academia – is defined by disciplinary rules which control a space of truth: 'one is "in the true" only by obeying the rules of a discursive "policing" which one has to reactivate in each of one's discourses' (Foucault 1970: 61).

Foucault wants to give the discursive event a specific status within reality, discourse should not be obscured by the three authorities of language, consciousness and social reality. Here he is turning against the critique of ideology, which takes linguistic objects as expressions and proof of a reality under the surface. Discourses should not be determined by pre-discursive objects; quite to the contrary, they themselves constitute the objects, the concepts, the ways of arguing and the subject positions. Foucault also clearly distances himself from semiology and deconstruction, even though he shares with them the view that the text in no expression, no representative of an external reality. For Derrida it is the play of signifiers which in the first place generates the meaning which constitute the real (see Derrida 1969). Laclau and Mouffe (1985: 105ff) radicalized this position, supposedly building on Gramsci's theory of hegemony. They criticize Foucault for clinging on to the distinction between discursive and non-discursive practices. They suggest that this brings a non-systematic ontology into play, for he still assumes the existence of such non-discursive elements such as institutions, techniques and economy. According to them, to be systematic, he would need to defend the view that it is the discourses that constitute the practices in the first place and which give them a specific unity. Each object is first constituted as an object of discourse. Laclau and Mouffe don't make this point to deny the existence of objects outside of thought but, seemingly more radically than Foucault, to claim that they can only be constituted under specific discursive conditions. Laclau and Mouffe´s argument is problematic for the following reason: seeing as it is the discourses which give objects significance and meaning as objects for us and in this world in the first place; by accepting the existence of some objects outside of and beyond thought which have no relevance for thought, Laclau and Mouffe are in effect questioning if humans actually interact with, and appropriate, nature at all or on any level. Is there not a form of interaction, a form of appropriation, in which we, nature, and the objects we interact with play an active role? Doesn´t our historically situated and variable outer and inner nature determine this form of appropriation? When discourses are arbitrary in their relation to the reality they constitute, they lead us to a problem that is not solvable on the level of discourse analysis: why do certain specific discourses emerge at particular historic moments and not others? Insomuch as Laclau and Mouffe attempt to explain the historicity of the existence of specific discourses, starting with the French Revolution, they seem to apply a view on the development of the logic of discourses which is not only externalistic, but also tributary of modernization theory (ibid.: 149ff; cf. Demirović 2007). But even if they were more consistent and would accept that historical time and the history of discourses themselves are also constituted discursively, questions would remain. Firstly, what characterizes the sequence and the relation of discourses to each other? Secondly, to what extent are objects outside of discourses – which they accept as existing according to their thinking – perhaps not after all rooted in and part of the dynamic of discursive processes? The following fundamental problem arises: how do specific discourses come into being and emerge, without being solely an expression of some exterior relations, being instead a moment of these very relations and the concrete material human practices as they are performed?

Foucault distances himself from the critique of ideology and deterministic class theory on the one side and semiologically orientated deconstruction on the other. One could understand Foucault in such a way as to state that deconstruction, with the assumption of a free play of signifiers, also denies the specific reality of discourse. It is for this reason that he calls for the sovereignty of the signifier to be lifted (Foucault 1970: 66); the fundamental concepts should no longer be those of structure and sign (ibid.: 68). Foucault insists on the distinction between discourses and things and on the fact that the relation between them is a specific, historic, non-necessary and conflictual one. The world is not an accomplice of our knowledge. There is no pre-stabilized harmony between knowledge and reality. The discourse and its objects represent a historically coherent and specific relationship. Discourse must be understood as violence, 'which we do to things, or in any case a practice which we impose on them' (ibid.: 67). The relationship between the things and discourse is an interdependent one. Things are appropriated under specific social, economic, technical and discursive conditions. Meaning and discursive regularity are forced upon things and the specific materiality of these things evidently cause them to resist. Discourses are therefore to a certain extent always determined by these things. The extent of violence the things are subject to and the conflicts between them is therefore variable, and it is thinkable and possible that this relationship needn't always be a violent one. Here, as with the thinking of Laclau and Mouffe, the question arises as to why this specific discourse and no other emerges? What defines its particular power and what effects does this power deploy? What determines – to use a concept of Gramsci's – the organicity of discourses? How do they become historically relevant and efficacious? Is their violence and contingence also down to the fact that they are themselves as discourses simply randomly set, or is there a historical and social rationality, which means truth and discourses form actors, constitute objects, generate themes and logics of argumentation? Who sets discourses? Why? How can this succeed? Why should these set discourses hold for 'true'? Why does a discourse want to be 'true'? Why does this truth connect itself with power? Why does this truth become binding? In other words, when the words and the things are set in relation to one another through discourse, and that relationship becomes generally binding and obtains a natural and logical character, when it basically obtains the character of objective truth; if it is possible to conceive of this relationship as a contingent one, and one that can possibly be dismantled by critical thinking: how can we take what we think as true, in such a way that this truth can be both binding for us and historical?

Foucault clearly sees truth as a form of violence which turns against the wildness of speech. He advocates for discourse's status as an event, for its freedom and openness, to be restored. By so doing, he questions all institutions which subordinate or regulate discourse, or which contribute to its limitation. What he wants above all however, is to question the will to truth itself and the institutions which support it. He points to a number of institutions, which are of significant importance to its production, circulation, reproduction and limitation. From a Gramscian perspective these institutions can be attributed to civil society. Civil society being here understood as an institution for the organization of spontaneous consent and the ruling of the subaltern. Foucault doesn't just question the will to truth and institutions such as the author-function and scientific disciplines; he questions a number of related elements such as the educational basis and the initiation into specific discursive practices, the publishing industry, learned societies and laboratories (ibid.: 13). Foucault speaks of an apparatus as a specific power relation of institutions, architectonic establishments, regulations, administrative measures and strategies. These apparatuses exist so that discourses and objects can be connected. Argumentative strategies, disciplinary knowledge practices, subject positions, objects and instruments, which render objects visible and the propositions verifiable, are constituted on epistemological foundations. These apparatuses allow these epistemological foundations to be connected (Foucault 1977: 392ff). He leaves no doubt to the fact that it is the bourgeoisie which, in the process of its creation and expansion, created such fields of knowledge. It is these fields of knowledge which perpetuate, immortalize and multiply power relations and further allow the bourgeois class to exist and to exercise their domination and to moralize the working class (ibid.: 402). The bourgeoisie deployed a form of rationality and related institutions which were necessary for the preservation and expansion of its way of life. Academies, professorships and learned societies are established, congresses are organized and journals and book editions established, all as a support for this dominant knowledge. These initiatives strive for medical, hygienic, dietary, pedagogic, psychiatric and social knowledge to be connected with moral, educational practices as well as numerous institutions (marriage, family, social housing, school, savings banks, sanatoriums; Foucault 1974; Donzelot 1979). Much like Gramsci, Foucault is interested in how domination within power relations is formed from below, how power universalizes itself by imbibition, and how it, in this way and carried by a whole range of different power practices, deploys hegemony. Rationality, truth and knowledge are part of complex power strategies in the imposition of specific knowledge orders with which the one is dominated by the other.

Given these insights into the strong links between power, knowledge and truth, Foucault's critique of 'truth' shows itself to be inadequate. What is criticized is that truth operates as a form of power, which limits the freedom of the sayable and regulates discourse. If the subaltern manage, despite their exclusion from the speech, to enter into the discursive order, they are prevented from saying what would need to be said by a number of internal mechanisms. It is not that they are necessarily silenced, but discourse tames their fervour, forces them to say 'it' differently, so that what is said becomes part of a series, assumes an order and regularity and loses its wild and 'event'-based character. The truth toward which discourse coerces, bridles the fervour, renders it incapable of action and shifts its objectives; all by demanding of a discourse crude and obvious facts to furnish itself with arguments, proofs and justifications. A will to truth is spurred on which pushes for better knowledge to be developed or which pushes one to fight for legitimate knowledge. In the fight for truth – for the better arguments, for the more exact empirical analysis, the more complete theory – it is forgotten what is fought for and about. Would it therefore not be more consistent to give up the claim to truth and to advocate a radical anarchy of speech? To do this would be to give up on studying the practices which develop and are deployed with truth; the institutions, the power relations, the strategies and the fights within and about truth.

This is the problem towards which Foucault turns his attention in the seventies, and though truth continues to be seen as a form of power, truth is no longer seen in quite such a negative light. 'Truth is to be understood as a system of ordered procedures for the production, regulation, distribution, circulation and operation of statements' (Foucault 1980a: 133). This production and circulation of truth represents a form of truth order, which is strongly tied to power systems and capitalism. Truth doesn't however function as a purely coercive force which excludes those trying to speak and rein in the speaker. Truth becomes defined as a point of social struggle. Truth is subject to a specific struggle. To be more exact, there is a specific struggle around both truth's status and its economic and political role. Foucault asks himself if such a struggle could lead to the constitution of a new politics and a new truth generating order. Foucault suggests that these politics of truth require a new intellectual practice. Much like Gramsci, he links the question of truth politics with the political question of the intellectual. The question of the intellectual should not be thought of in terms of science and ideology, but in terms of truth and power, for the intellectual acts and fights on the general level of the order of truth, fighting around the rules following which truth and falsehood are distinguished, and following which the true is armed with specific power. Much like Gramsci, Foucault – in a much more suggestive and less explicit way – underlines the fact that it is the relationship between manual and intellectual labour which is here at stake. In other words: giving truth a specific economic and political status implies a specific kind of intellectuality and truth order. This truth order calls for a specific truth politics, which in turn is needed to enforce and support a specific truth regime and to bring forth the intellectuals and intellectual practices which might address the appropriate issues and problems. Both Foucault and Gramsci argue against the assumption that the intellectual is, as such, tied to the principles of equality, freedom and universalism. Foucault attacks the doubly false character of the intellectual's claim to universality: the intellectual as the individual incorporation of the universal, of which the proletariat would be the dark, collective form. Both the intellectual, representing the universal and carrying the values of everyone, and the enlightened jurist and brilliant writer who fights for the rule of law and for freedom, are, through their privileged access to writing and to the public sphere, sacralized figures. In the overreaching theories of writing, as Foucault sees them in the fields of linguistics and semiology (one could also say in Derrida 's 'deconstruction'), Foucault sees an attempt to defend an antiquated truth regime. In contrast, he advocates for the very practical struggles to be taken as starting points: the home, the madhouse, the universities and the families, where concrete tangible and specific knowledge is formed. At stake are specific intellectuals; to be more exact, academics and experts with specific knowledge, which affect political struggles in the name of specific and localized scientific truths. As examples, Foucault gives Darwin, Oppenheim, doctors and social workers, computer scientists and geneticists: 'No longer the rhapsodist of the eternal, but the strategist of life and death' (Foucault 1980a: 129). All of them could potentially, each from their specific place and through an exchange of know-how and experience, be able to contribute to global polarization. Foucault sees as a danger that they might easily, for lack of strategy, be unable to push the struggles around the status of truth. To be clear: he doesn't oppose a specific intellectual to the universal bourgeois intellectual of enlightenment. He doesn't posit a specific intellectual who might, without staking a claim to truth himself, fight at a local level. This new type of intellectual must also fight for universalism and truth. Foucault wants to encourage the whole order of knowledge to be changed and a new network of knowledge and new truth politics to emerge. The power of truth should be freed from: 'The forms of hegemony, social, economic and cultural' (Foucault 1980a: 133) in which they function. This happens when the social division between manual and intellectual labour is reorganized by a new politics of truth which gives the specialist and the expert a new significance. It is however not clear here, whether Foucault wants to question the very principle of the separation between manual and intellectual labour. At this stage he wants to replace specific universal claims and the power effects they produce, with a new type of universality constituted by a horizontally organized network of experts. Foucault calls for a new politics of truth, a new type of intellectual belonging to a different order of knowledge, and which follows goals rooted in life. The politics of truth advocated by Gramsci in contrast, call for an order of knowledge in which the separation of manual and intellectual labour is abolished.

In his last lectures analysing the relationship between veridiction and subject, Foucault is picking up a subject to which he had already alluded in 1980 in conversations with Trombadori: the relationship between truth, passion and commitment. In the sixties it was the structures of discourse which appear as true discourses which had interested him. This approach to knowledge, analysing socio-historic apriority of truth regimes, was far removed from classical philosophy and epistemology. In the eighties we see a new shift and expansion in his field of study:

> Rather than analyzing the forms by which a discourse is recognized as true, this would involve analyzing the form in which, in his act of telling the truth, the individual constitutes himself and is constituted by others as a subject of a discourse of truth, the form in which he presents himself to himself and to others as someone who tells the truth, the form of the subject telling the truth. In contrast with the study of epistemological structures, the analysis of this domain could be called the study of 'alethurgic' forms. (Foucault 1984: 3)

By putting it this way, he is posing a question which necessarily implies a radical critique of the power of truth and with which a long tradition has already sought to deal: 'how to live if I must face up to the fact that "nothing is true"?' (Foucault 1984: 190). Foucault radicalizes the question of the historicity of truth. The question is not how to live and act when truths and the critique of truths, given critical reflection, reveal themselves to be historically relative. He poses a more fundamental question: which type of life, which form of existence would be necessary, if truth were radically questioned and no longer necessary? The question is not asked with any form of resignation; Foucault stays true to the radicalism of his earlier texts, only shifting the problem away from that of epistemology, and towards that of the analysis of a way of life and a stylistic of existence.

In his studies of the Parrhesia, Foucault analyses the disposition of subject, truth and power. Here, truth is not analysed as a form of repression or politics, but it is the status of truth and constellations of ethics of truth which are studied. Foucault is interested in the ways the subject internally binds himself to truth, the ways in which the subject constitutes himself through a relationship to truth, how the subject constitutes himself as a subject of truth and as a subject capable of both truth and true action and how a subject might commit himself to a specific truth regime. How does a subject have the courage of the truth? This encompasses the determination of the intellectual in the social division of labour and his function in the reproduction of the division between manual and intellectual labour. Foucault studies the intellectual's relationship to himself, his stance towards truth, which, depending on the 'political' constellation, might constitute this or that type of intellectual. He seeks a truth ethics in which the element of passion and personal commitment gains its significance. At first, Foucault's words in his conversations with Trobadori could be understood as though Foucault wanted to play truth and myth – insomuch as the myth incites to action – against each other. But here truth and passion are seen in as strongly tied to one another, truth itself being seen as a passion. This leads us to the following questions: how can a truth lead to a stance which both fosters and motivates to action? What does it mean to let oneself be determined and led by truth? Does fearless speech leave us stuck between the alternatives of following a hegemonic public discourse or feeling bound by autonomously acquired knowledge? How can a specific ethics and politics of truth be followed?

Foucault sees two kinds of Parrhesia. There is on the one side the truth-telling oriented towards the Polis, the right to speak publicly, the right for the citizen to talk of things of public interest, to reveal the truth of what has happened and to fulfil a free existence. Foucault however focuses more to the second kind of Parrhesia: an ethical Parrhesia which refers to an examination of the soul. This second kind of Parrhesia can also be of use for the Polis, because it is in the interest of the state that people should take care of themselves and of true discourse.

Foucault first identifies this ethical Parrhesia in the figure Socrates. Socrates distances himself from the politically orientated Parrhesia. This reticence to make use of this political Parrhesia has nothing to do with any possible fear of the consequences of this form of truth-telling. The ethical, non-political, Parrhesia also requires courage. Socrates sees himself entrusted with a mission: to make sure – to take care – that people take care of themselves. To ensure that they examine their soul and accomplish such acts which will help them discover their true opinion and distinguish between true and false. Individuals should not let themselves be guided by the opinion of the majority leaving them to 'to and fro' between different opinions. This leads to false opinions, illogical conclusions which themselves are both physically and psychologically harmful. In contrast, true opinions can hinder the ruin of the soul and lead it back to health (see ibid.: 104f). The true opinion is rooted in a relationship to the self and allows one to commit oneself to truth. Foucault sees something new in Plato 's *Laches*. Ethics of truth are usually bound with the idea that the subject cleanses himself, breaks with the world of the senses and gives up its particular interests. To become a subject of truth, a comprehensive cathartic practice is required: passage from un-pure to pure, from darkness to transparency, from the fleeting to the eternal. In Plato's text another path is present, a path Foucault describes as courage of the truth; a specific kind of resolution and determination, of will, struggle and sacrifice for truth (ibid.: 124f). Socrates' argument for a care of the self sees a significant alternative emerge: either one cares for one's soul, or one cares for one's life (bios). In this alternative, Foucault sees the emergence of two different ways in which the ethical Parrhesia became taken up and passed down in western philosophy. On the one side, taking the soul as a reality distinct from the body, philosophy, concerning itself with the metaphysics of the soul, leads to an ontology of the self. On the other hand, philosophy understands itself as a test of life and mode of knowledge of the self through a way of life. Here a philosophy is constituted which takes as a point of departure an art of the self and an aesthetic of existence, taking the bios as object of aesthetic work and perception. In the history of philosophy this second element, philosophy as an examination, questioning and stylistic of existence finds itself mostly obscured by the metaphysical tradition. Foucault sees the Cynics as having been the ones who picked up these elements: philosophy as an art of the self and way of life through which truth is directly binding and lived. For Foucault, these elements have been largely ignored, rejected and neglected by the officially recognized and sanctioned professional philosophy. This metaphysical philosophy was relayed institutionally in the officially sanctioned sciences and in the consensus of academics, be it in individual teachings, classes, teaching rooms and textbooks. In stark contrast to all this, Foucault sees Cynicism as a universal philosophy which was never passed on by a doctrine, which needed no books and had nothing more than a rudimentary theoretical framework. It corresponded to a simple practice and took place on the streets.

This differentiates Cynicism from the Socratic conception of truth-telling. It is a more radical and carnevalesque development of philosophy, insomuch as it attaches itself to philosophy's most common and central elements, only to show philosophy up for what it is and break with it. It gives the courage of the truth a new form. It is no longer a case of risking one's life by speaking true. It is no longer about the conditions which allow us to identify a statement as being true. The question is, which way of life, which mode of life, allows truth truth-telling to take place and for a better life.

The principles which are affirmed as true are to be simultaneously attested by one's own way of life. But what is a way of life which is internally bound to truth, and can be said to be a true way of life on the merits of it allowing truth to be told? What does this break with philosophy look like? This philosophy which limits itself to truth-telling and an examination of the soul, but otherwise, as in Socrates' case, allows for a normal civic life in the midst of the powerful. In the common antique conception truth is defined by four characteristics: unconcealed, unalloyed and independent, straight, and lastly unchanging and sovereign. Cynicism exaggerates these characteristics and pushes them beyond their own boundaries until they emerge as caricatures of themselves: out of an unconcealed life emerges an obscene and shameless one, an independent life becomes a bare life which needs near to nothing, a straight life becomes one which distinguishes between good and bad and friend and foe, a sovereign life becomes a life of struggle. Foucault's central conclusion here is that Cynicism, unlike traditional philosophy, is not concerned with the soul, with the pure world or with another world. Cynicism asks the question of an 'other', as a different, life. A life that puts the principles of true life into practice is a different life than that which people in general, and philosophers in particular, live. A true life is an 'other' life; any true life must be a radically different one (ibid.: 245ff).

This short summary of Foucault's lectures in 1984 helps us considerably with our problem. Foucault is clearly not sure how to assess the relationship between truth and radical engagement and commitment to a cause. Does reference to truth make radical praxis possible, or does the power of truth serve to confine and curtail emancipatory goals? Foucault's Parrhesia lectures suggest that, after a time in which he focused on a radical critique of the power effects of truth, he then advocates a new specific ethics of truth. These ethics being in turn bound to a specific type of intellectuality. He sketches a new type of intellectual subjectivity who is not concerned with theory or academia and science, or an 'other' and pure world, but who lives close to the people and shares with them a universal way of life. A way of life already lived by some, and which could be lived by all. This way of life asserts itself as truth, constituting a specific subject. Faced with the perspective of a true and 'other' way of life, existing ways of life find themselves rejected. Foucault is therefore not concerned with an existential act of resistance or even the readiness to risk death through engagement and praxis. He is thinking of a new humble, straight and self-determined form of praxis, a new way of living which takes the knowledge of the subaltern seriously. The courage of the truth is the courage to live an 'other' life, the courage of a different subjectivity. The requirement to live adjusted to the rules of the dominant order, to subordinate the self to the politically sovereign, is consciously rejected in the 'other' way of life.

Foucault is once again drawing on, and contributing to, the discussions in the left and social movements in the seventies and eighties. These discussions centred the development of such an alternative way of life – taking in such elements as work, living space, gender roles and knowledge – through specific praxis. These alternative projects however failed to reach and affect the power of capitalist structures. This criticism regarding the inability to affect capitalist structures can also be applied to Foucault's ideas as we find them in the transcription of his last lectures. According to him, over the millennia Cynicism always continued to deploy its effects, all be it at a very limited level. The aim of fashioning humanity was always present. But the other branch of philosophy always remained dominant: the philosophy of metaphysics, of pure knowledge, of the separation of body and soul, of transcendental consciousness and of abstract entities. The intellectual competences – science and academia, theory, the arts – remained cut off from the people and the privilege of the powerful and intellectuals. Though Foucault gives us some hints at a theoretical social explanation, he doesn't elaborate on it. One would have to think about the way in which truth, seen here by Foucault as an 'other' way of life followed by single individuals, can be conceived as to allow for binding, praxis-determining insight, which may indeed become universal and radically transform collective ways of life. At this point, with the plea to think science, world view and way of life together: with the ideas relating to the relationship between knowledge and economy, and particularly when it comes to the question of hegemony, I see a connection with the thought of Gramsci. On a number of important points Gramsci can be read as a critical complement to Foucault.

Gramsci's Philosophy of Praxis

Gramsci's problem, unlike Foucault's, is not that of questioning truth as such. But much like Foucault he is concerned with a new universal way of life, reorganized from the experience and practices of the subaltern. This encompasses a new order of knowledge production and a new order of truth, as well as a historically new function for the intellectual in the social division of labour. Gramsci also thinks extensively about the meaning of knowledge and truth in relation to power. Unlike Foucault, he strives to bind scientific knowledge and world view at an internal level; this with the aim of changing our way of life and allowing the subaltern to take over and control the social production apparatus.

Gramsci conceives of Marxist theory as the basis for a wholly new philosophy of praxis, characterized by a radical historicized and immanentist world view. Thus he radically turns against the common belief that there exists a real objective world 'out there' and defends the idea that this is nothing more than a commonly held 'belief'. He sees the belief in the objective existence of reality to be the: 'most widespread and entrenched ideology ' (Gramsci 1975, *Notebook* 4:41); Gramsci sees the origin of this belief as being rooted in religion, for all religions expound the view that the universe and mankind were created by god. (Gramsci 1975, *Notebook* 11: 17). If there were such an 'extra-historical and non-human objectivity' he asks who might be the judge such an objective reality (ibid.). Mankind doesn't have the benefit of such a standpoint and can't imagine the earth and cosmos as though they weren't there themselves. The sciences can't prove the objective existence of the real as this 'world view' is not a matter for science but one for philosophy (Gramsci 1975, *Notebook* 4: 41). This is why Gramsci – following an immanentist conception – suggests that 'objective' should always mean 'humanly objective' and correspond to the concept of the 'historically subjective'. For him, objectivity is the objectivity of universal subjectivity (Gramsci 1975, *Notebook* 11: 17). This idea poses a problem which was also the object of Laclau's critique of Foucault. The problem being in what way this world view, though seen as radically subjective, might still be connected to real historical processes. It seems to me that Gramsci answers this question in a very original way, complimenting Foucault's theory productively.

That people cling on to this vulgar materialist belief in the objectivity of the world serves to pacify them and leads them to believe they don't really and truly participate in the world. This passivity is for Gramsci the result of domination. For him, everyone is a philosopher insomuch as they enter into a specific relation to reality along shared concepts, terms and feelings. There are however many philosophies and truths. The choice between them is not a 'purely intellectual fact' the real world view is not 'the alleged logic as an intellectual fact', but 'that which is apparent from the actual activity of each inherent in his actions' (Gramsci 1975, *Notebook* 11: 12). It is in this very relation between theory and practice that domination can emerge. For though everyone is a philosopher, the conditions for the fashioning of their world view from their work and practice are themselves subject to domination. Many people live under conditions which reduce them to mere executors of menial work. They are denied the concepts which would be necessary to form a world view based on their practice and to universalize them collectively. They are intellectually unsynchronized and are determined by bizarre combinations of thoughts and feelings. This is down to the fact that they don't possess the conceptual instruments to understand their thinking, feelings and practice and to fashion them into a coherent whole. Often the active subaltern has no clear theoretical consciousness of his action: 'However, a recognition that the world is as it transformed them. His theoretical consciousness can even be historically contrary to his work' (ibid.). The subaltern think and act incoherently and live in different worlds. They can have more than just one shared consciousness; this disunity and contradiction can mean no decision, no choice, no action emerges. That the subaltern live with different world views is conceived by Gramsci immanent-theoretically as a contradiction of socio-historic nature. They can, as a collectively active social group, possess and share an embryonic world view. Their intellectual subjugation however means they remain unable to deploy this world view and they adopt a view which 'is not theirs'. They express this world view in words and think they follow it. 'So that is why philosophy cannot be separated from politics, and it can be shown that the choice and the criticism of a world view in turn is a political fact' (Gramsci 1975, *Notebook* 11: 12).

Gramsci considers the critique of this alien world view and the elaboration of a coherent world view as one of the central tasks for the philosophy of praxis and its intellectuals. A double critique is here at work. First, the rational activities we carry out on a day to day basis must be renewed to allow a new and coherent world view to emerge and a new way of life to be developed. For a new way of life to emerge, this new world view must distinguish itself from that of the ruling class. When a mass of people are brought to think the real present situation coherently this constitutes a philosophical fact more original than any truth brought forth by a philosopher from the context of some intellectual group (ibid.). According to Gramsci, the philosophy of praxis is the heir to classic German philosophy, developing it further: that the 'heir' continues its predecessor's activity, but does so 'in practice' since it has deduced from mere contemplation

> an active will capable of transforming the world and, in this practical activity, there is also contained the 'knowledge' that it is only rather in practical activity that there lies 'real knowledge' and not 'scholasticism'. From this it can also be deduced that the nature of the philosophy of praxis is in particular that of being a mass conception, a mass culture, that of a mass which operates in a unitary fashion, i.e. one that has norms of conduct that are not only universal in idea but 'generalized' in social reality. And the activity of the 'individual' philosopher cannot therefore be conceived except in terms of this social unity, i.e. also as political activity, in terms of political leadership (Gramsci 1999: 536f).

The renewal of the subaltern's thought, the development of a critical consciousness, the abandonment of widespread and common ways of thinking which hold together the historic bloc, the formation of a new historic bloc; all this takes place first in small, embryonic contexts. These elements foster a true universalism. In contrast, the systems drafted by distant professional philosophers and academics, though they use universal arguments and concepts, do not and cannot constitute a true universalism.

Second, the philosophy of praxis criticizes the philosophy of intellectuals; intellectuals understood by Gramsci here as servants of the bourgeois superstructure. Gramsci identifies the bourgeois superstructure with civil society and the political class. They produce the knowledge and the competence of the dominant class, they organize the culture, the way of life and a relation to objectivity as well as the separation between manual and intellectual labour. They help pacify the subaltern, ensuring they remain unable to fully grasp their situation, unable to appropriate the intellectual conceptual tools to develop and own an autonomous world view. Gramsci develops what we might – following Foucault – call a Politics of Truth of the subaltern, aiming for the constitution of a new order of truth. This politics of truth therefore doesn't only affect the truth of a theory; it aims at a way of life in which the world view, the division between manual and intellectual labour and the complete organization of society is reorganized, starting with a reorganization of the socially produced work. This politics of truth includes a transformative praxis in the hegemonic apparatus of civil society as well as a transformation of this very apparatus; this to allow for a new way of life and new way of thinking to emerge.

> The proposition contained in the preface to *A Contribution to the Critique of Political Economy* to the effect that men acquire consciousness of structural conflicts on the level of ideologies should be considered as an affirmation of epistemological and not simply psychological and moral value. From this, it follows that the theoretical-practical principle of hegemony has also epistemological significance, and it is here that Ilyich [Lenin]'s greatest theoretical contribution to the philosophy of praxis should be sought. In these terms one could say that Ilyich advanced philosophy as philosophy in so far as he advanced political doctrine and practice. The realization of a hegemonic apparatus, in so far as it creates a new ideological terrain, determines a reform of consciousness and of methods of knowledge: it is a fact of knowledge, a philosophical fact (Gramsci 2000: 192).

As people in the superstructure attain an organic consciousness of the conflicts within a society, Gramsci sees a necessary conflict around both these superstructures themselves and the historic blocs they and the economy form. To attain consciousness, to think, to feel and act freely is always a specific historic modality. The organization of culture by a dominant group – Foucault speaks of an apparatus, Gramsci of civil society – determines what is sayable in a society. It defines the consciousness, the ways of thinking, cultural practices, the instruments of knowledge, the concepts and ways things are felt in a society. In the case of a dominant bourgeoisie, these cultural organizations take shape in a variety of cultural apparatuses. These include colleges and universities, academic disciplines, learned societies, publishers, libraries, journals and newspapers. Here such apparatuses are isolated from the great mass of the people and the system of production. In contrast, in an immanentist-philosophical conception culture becomes a praxis shared by all and loses its attribute as an organization of the superstructure. It is consciously integrated in the immanence of social everyday life; the type of intellectual changes, connects with manual labour and everyone becomes – no longer just theoretically but in practice – an intellectual. This is why for Gramsci the philosophy of praxis is:

> not the instrument of government of the dominant groups in order to gain the consent of and exercise hegemony over the subaltern classes; it is the expression of these subaltern classes who want to educate themselves in the art of government and who have an interest in knowing all truths, even the unpleasant ones, and in avoiding the (impossible) deceptions of the upper class and – even more – their own. (Gramsci 1999: 549)

For Gramsci, truth is a relationship between concepts, with these concepts being tied to specific activities of intellectuals in the context of specific superstructures. This is organized in such a way either to generate conceptual confusion and to pacify and 'dumb down' the subaltern, or to generate coherence and, in the end, to lift the separation between superstructure and the productive system. As such, truth is a concept that both organizes and gives form to the thinking, feeling and action of people. Truth is therefore historical. This has two consequences. First, truth is provisional and transient. It is difficult under the given conditions for our common sense to bare the idea that there is no 'world out there' outside of our praxis. It is equally difficult for our common sense to grasp the idea that truth should be transient, and yet still hold true. Concepts are not just words, they don't just designate elements of knowledge our consciousness has attained. They are specific social relations in which the thinking, perception, and feeling operate. Truth is modified through the practice of its own concepts; the concepts being moved by the objects they apprehend. As such they only let themselves be fixed for a short time. This historicity of every world and life view and its concepts, the historicity of all that holds and is true, also applies to the philosophy of praxis itself. The philosophy of praxis is also bound to the existence of specific social antagonisms; it organically deploys the theoretical concepts of these contradictions and – as the struggles within bourgeois society are fought – also changes as a philosophy. The philosophy of praxis doesn't correspond to the realm of freedom. This would see the abolition of the philosophy of praxis and of a specific type of world view and intellectual, as well as the abolition of a thinking based on contradictions. The provisional character of the philosophy of praxis can, as Gramsci himself is aware, lead to dramatic upheavals in the consciousness of the proletariat as there is no longer anything absolute which one can hold on to. In contrast, Gramsci tells us, the great intellectuals assume an Olympic posture, a posture of superiority and moral scepticism (Gramsci 1975, *Notebook* 11: 62).

Second, with these historically provisional ways of thinking, concepts and truths; the masses become aware of their situation and take up the fight around these very concepts and truths. The concepts are therefore anything but arbitrary. They are universalized in a complex cathartic process. This process takes place in broad social conflicts between social classes where the world view of a group becomes universalized transforming itself from a mere egoistic-passional moment, to an ethical-political one (Gramsci 1975, *Notebook* 10: II: 6). These concepts are a stake in the social struggle; they embody collective practice. As the process through which concepts become binding and give shape to collective thinking and action, this process of social catharsis is central to Gramsci's understanding of the philosophy of praxis. Concepts become historical in the second sense of the term: they form a unity with collective practice, which itself becomes grasped, thought, experienced, perceived and felt in exactly these concepts. These concepts are part of a concrete historical way of life, they embody the social conflicts. As the starting point for further collective action, thinking and feeling they appear determining and necessary. Truth is not historical because it might, as knowledge, only appear fleetingly on the surface of history, but on the contrary, because it determines the collective action of the people and imprints itself deeply in their way of life. Consciousness and collective action are organically connected to a specific superstructure, a specific historic bloc, and therefore with the whole society at a specific historical moment. Truth can and must therefore – despite its relative character – be seen as binding. The struggle around truth and the status of truth changes the relation between the concepts and the collective practices themselves. This leads Gramsci to a radical political conclusion. Politics in the name of the philosophy of praxis can't be allowed to assume a distant, tactical and instrumental relation to truth. Politics must much rather be fully aware of the negative consequences of not standing up for truth seriously, consciously and consistently:

> There is a very widely held view in certain circles (and the dissemination of this view is indicative of the political and cultural stature of these circles) that lying, knowing how to conceal astutely one's true opinion and objectives, knowing how to make people believe the opposite of what one really wants, etc., is of the essence in the art of politics. … In politics one may talk of circumspection, not of lying in the mean sense held by many; in mass politics, telling the truth is, precisely, a political necessity. (Gramsci 2007: 17)

Gramsci is very clear on this point: it is the very historicity of truth which makes it necessary to speak the truth, also in everyday politics. One should not – for some tactical reason – use 'truth' instrumentally (Gramsci 1974: 116). Gramsci is not making a moral argument here. The argument is a truth-political and truth-ethical one. For in the critical challenge to the historically concrete practice of our common sense, it is not just our common sense which is transformed but new forms of work, intellectuality and superstructures are prepared. The philosophy of praxis is aware that the truth it deploys is a provisional one. This however doesn't lead to scepticism, but leads to a new emancipatory way of life: a way of life which stands up for truth, and yet is aware of truths historically transient character. A way of life which, aware of the provisional character of truth and all that it entails, is also self-critical regarding the very power of the truth it strives to abolish.

Concluding Remarks

I have tried here to look at Foucault and Gramsci's work as contributions to problems for which they shared an interest such as the critique of the power of knowledge and its history, the relationship between the sciences and the knowledge of the subaltern, the critique of philosophy and specific approaches to history prevalent in the social sciences, a shared interest in a new conception of the State and in social struggles and emancipation.

A comparison between Foucault and Gramsci regarding their conception of truth shows up both points of agreement and disagreement. Their arguments also show themselves to be complimentary in a number of ways.

1. Points of agreement: firstly we see a shift of focus away from epistemology, away from the great philosophers and thinkers of the past and their way of looking at – and professing truths about – the world. Instead the focus shifted towards practices and ways of life of the subaltern. The subaltern and the power they are subject to become the fulcrum for the analysis of dominant knowledge and the dominant intellectual. Secondly, truths are understood as historically relative practices which nevertheless determine the subsequent social and intellectual processes. Thirdly, concepts and feelings form a unity; they become two moments of a world-view which either fosters or blocks engagement and practice. Fourthly, knowledge is seen by both as bound to specific fields of knowledge, hegemonial apparatuses of civil society. Fifthly, both are concerned with a universal truth practice and see emotional and intellectual practices as one. Sixthly, truth is related to the separation of manual and intellectual labour, meaning truth becomes related to a concrete practice of intellectuals. Out of this a politics and ethics of truth emerges, through which truth itself – its very status and power – can be changed.
2. In a number of aspects these two writers can be read complimentarily. Gramsci wanted to understand knowledge as a concrete discursive field on which the struggle between social groups is carried out. Here the concern is whether power is maintained or whether subaltern groups are able to free themselves from the thinking of those in power and to become autonomous. He developed terms such as catharsis, hegemony, organicity, structure and superstructure to help analyse the process through which critical thinking, knowledge and feeling emerge from social work processes and universalize themselves. Gramsci gives the example of a number of bigger and smaller intellectuals and mentions many of their concrete activities within newspapers, publishing houses, the Catholic Church, the sciences or parties. But he doesn't pursue this cathartic process – through which the ruling class (or subaltern) universalizes itself – through a detailed analysis of discursive practices. For example how exactly – and through which compromises and alliances – does the ruling class (or subaltern) form social power bases

> and attains leadership? Foucault on the other hand reconstructs specific historical constellations of knowledge, rationality and power technologies, only to mostly ignore the intellectuals and the historic constellations which participate in this knowledge. He thus avoids falling back on class theory as an explanation, or ending up with trivial causal assumptions based on some overarching theory of power. Foucault studies the discursive practices, but not the intellectuals active within civil society. He equally ignores the power relations and contradictions which run through discourses and the many compromises which reveal themselves in the form of specific concepts, ways of arguing and text genres. It is only when he takes up the analysis of the Cynics – when he discusses the carnivalesque relationship between the Cynical ethics of truth to the otherwise dominant philosophy – that such internal contradictions are analysed. Gramsci wants to understand the conflicts within civil society and the conflicts between intellectuals. From his point of view the intellectuals, as servants of the superstructure, develop the concepts with which the subaltern are dominated by the bourgeoisie. Gramsci is therefore not so interested in the all-encompassing rationality of a power technology or in the contingent coherence of a discourse and its internal power effects. What interests him more, is the way in which such a discourse can bring very different ruling powers to a compromised and yet precarious unity with those they rule. Gramsci is to a certain extent 'more historical' than Foucault. Foucault often asserts that a certain discursive practice – examination of conscience and pastoral power, ethical Parrhesia, psychiatric or pedagogic practices – becomes operant over the centuries or decades and subsequently becomes determining for our thought and actions. But the analysis of how and why this happens – that power and leadership emerge in this way and which conflicts emerge between the hegemonic powers and the subaltern – is either not pursued at all or only sketchily outlined. The studies of cynical veridiction however can be seen as an attempt to grasp and analyse a resistant intellectual practice.

There are also clear differences between the two thinkers. Foucault focuses more on the ethics of truth as an individual posture. The connection between truths and both the social production apparatus and the collective practices of the subaltern are not something he studies. Nor does he study the connection between world view and the sciences. Gramsci by contrast is more concerned with the problem of a politics of truth, and the struggle for the means of learning and knowledge and for the capacity to impose a certain 'objective reality' within a hegemonic struggle. Science constitutes a moment in the formation of a world view. Gramsci is therefore interested in the question of truth as a collective stance and poses the question in the context of a socially apprehended general process. In doing so he ignores the element of true and committed way of life of individuals. Gramsci's interest in a politics of truth and Foucault's interest in an ethics of truth are however not incompatible. Foucault after all worked on both questions. We are left with a problem to which both authors made important contributions: how can we think a way of life, in which working at the status of truth connects itself with a truth driven passion, in which comprehensive critical social theory and world view are deployed as one; without becoming scientistic, and so that such a unity between superstructure and base exists, so that everyone can – to the same extent and in the same self-determined way – take part in social freedoms and imperatives. It may indeed transpire that the courage of truth is only necessary under those social conditions that Marx refers to as prehistoric.

References

Demirović, A. 2007. Hegemonie und die diskursive Konstruktion der Gesellschaft. In *Diskurs – radikale Demokratie – Hegemonie. Zum politischen Denken von Ernesto Laclau und Chantal Mouffe*, Martin Nonhoff (Hg.). Bielefeld: transcript, pp. 55–86.

Derrida, J. 1969. *Writing and Difference*. University of Chicago Press.

Donzelot, J. 1997. *The Policing of Families*. Tr. by Robert Hurley, Johns Hopkins University Press.

Foucault, M. 1970 [1981]. The order of discourse. In *Untying the Text: A Poststructuralist Reader*, edited by Robert Young. London: Routledge.

—. 1974 [2002]. Die Wahrheit und die juristischen Formen. In *Dits et Ecrits*, Bd. II. Frankfurt am Main: Suhrkamp.

—. 1977 [2003]. Das Spiel des Michel Foucault. In: *Dits et Ecrits*, Bd. III. Frankfurt am Main: Suhrkamp.

—. 1980a. *Truth and Power, in Power/Knowledge: Selected Interviews and Other Writings 1972–1977*, edited by Colin Gordon. New York: Pantheon.

—. 1980b [1991]. Between 'Words' and 'Things' During May '68. In *Remarks on Marx: Conversations with Ducio Trombadori*. New York: Semiotext(e).

—. 1984 [2011]. *The Courage of the Truth*. New York: Palgrave.

Gramsci, A. 1974 *Per la verità*. Scritti 1913–1926. Roma: Editori Riuniti.

— 1975. *Quaderni del Carcere. Edizione critica dell' Istituto Gramsci*. A cura di Valentino Gerratana. Torino: Giulio Einaudi Editore.

—. 1999. *Further Selections from the Prison Notebooks*, translated and edited by Derek Boothman. London: ElecBook.

—. 2000. *The Gramsci Reader. Selected Writings 1916–1935*, edited by David Forgacs. New York University Press

—. 2007. *Prison Notebooks, Volume III*, edited and translated by Joseph A. Buttigieg. New York: Columbia University Press.

Laclau, E. and Mouffe, C. 1991. *Hegemony and Socialist Strategy. Towards a Radical Democratic Politics*. London: Verso.

Chapter 3

Rethinking the Gramsci–Foucault Interface: A Cultural Political Economy Interpretation Oriented to Discourses of Competitiveness

Ngai-Ling Sum

Introduction

Gramsci and Foucault were, in their different ways, two of the leading critical theorists and political activists of the last century. Although they wrote and struggled in very different conjunctures and were committed to quite different views on the feasibility of revolution in Western capitalism, their work displays interesting, important, and illuminating parallels as well as some obvious tensions. This chapter identifies three main analytical strategies to possible linkages between Gramsci and Foucault and, after commenting on the first two, develops the third approach. This is based on a targeted return to their writings on questions of what Gramsci called the regularities of the determined market and their relation to the state in its integral sense and what Foucault called liberal and neo-liberal economic rationality and their relation to governmentality and statecraft. Also relevant is their work on intellectuals and hegemony and the production of truth regimes respectively. This entry point is only one among several productive ways to construct a doubly posthumous virtual dialogue between the two thinkers. Its interest here is that it connects to cultural political economy, i.e., a combination of critical semiotic analysis and the critique of political economy. After introducing a six-moment heuristic scheme, I present a case study that illustrates the value-added of putting the innovative concepts and historical analyses of Gramsci and Foucault into dialogue. This study concerns discourses of competitiveness and draws on Gramsci's analyses of Americanism and Fordism and Foucault's work on liberalism and neoliberalism respectively. The chapter concludes with some general remarks on the potential contribution of Gramsci and Foucault to the development of the emerging agenda of cultural political economy.

Comparing and Critiquing Gramsci and Foucault

For the purposes of this volume, one could establish the Gramsci–Foucault interface in three ways: (i) review previous attempts to bring Gramsci and Foucault into dialogue, to the extent that commentators have considered this feasible and worthwhile; (ii) consider conventional readings of Gramsci and/or Foucault in the Anglophone literature and whether these indicate the scope for connections and synergies or point; and (iii) re-examine their work for connections and synergies, to the extent that they can be identified.

For the first approach to work, it must treat both thinkers even-handedly and to the same depth where comparison is being made. This has proved difficult for two reasons. For Gramsci this arises because, as Foucault noted, the Italian is someone who is 'more often cited than really known' (Foucault 1984); and, for Foucault, the problem is the extent to which Foucauldian scholarship engages with limited aspects of his overall oeuvre, often in areas where links with Gramsci are limited or less obvious. Where these challenges are overcome, some interesting arguments emerge. An excellent example is Morera's discussion of whether Gramsci can really be read as a precursor of postmodernism (2000). After careful and even-handed identification and interrogation of some substantive areas of overlap between Gramsci and Foucault on issues such as the body, identity, power, truth regimes, and ideology, he concludes that Gramsci is a critical modernist unassimilable to postmodernism but also takes care to distance Foucault from some of his more uncritical postmodern disciples. Other examples that highlight potential overlaps and the possibility of a critical dialogue include: Smart 1985; Kenway 1990; Olssen 2006; Ekers and Loftus 2008; and Stoddart 2005.

The second approach seeks to establish synergies ab initio rather than build on those identified by other scholars. Here, two major obstacles to a rapprochement are culturalist readings of Gramsci as the theorist of the superstructures and/or cultural hegemony; and the dominance of the Anglo-Foucauldian school of governmentality, which rejects Marxism. In the former case, where efforts are made to synthesize Gramsci and Foucault, it tends to occur through a strategy of 'Foucauldizing Gramsci', whereby neo-Gramscian or post-Marxist scholars use Foucault to provide disciplinary and material foundations for the study of cultural hegemony and to break with Gramsci's alleged [residual] class reductionism (e.g., Barrett 1991). Conversely, Anglo-Foucauldian governmentality scholars reject the Marxist tradition, eschew macro-analyses whether class reductionist or not, and seek bottom-up analyses of governmentality (e.g., Burchell et al. 1991; for a critique of the Anglo-Foucauldian approach see Jessop 2010). This leaves little scope for rapprochement on their part, although some heterodox Marxist scholars have sought to show that Foucault's work on governmentality would have benefitted from lessons from Marx (Marsden 1999), Poulantzas (Jessop 1990), or critical realism (Frauley 2007).

This chapter develops the third approach. However, as this exercise requires a reference point, my contribution takes the transformation of political economy as its field of application. The respective examples that shape my interpretation in this regard are Gramsci's work on Americanism and Fordism, and Foucault's studies of the genealogy of capitalist discipline and, later, the development of neoliberalism as one form of economic governmentality. There are many potential synergies here and my chapter will identify these and then illustrate how they can be exploited to develop a more adequate explanation of a recent transformation that can be illuminated through the work of both scholars. This concerns the changing economic imaginaries of competitiveness, the development of competitive subjects, the technologies of competitiveness discourse (and associated truth regimes), and the broader implications for the state in its integral sense, i.e., the state as a major site for the strategic codification of power relations. My analysis in this section proceeds in three steps: first, some key themes in Gramsci, then in Foucault, and, third, identifying possible synergies.

Antonio Gramsci

Gramsci was an innovative Marxist theorist and communist leader who developed a wide-ranging philosophy of praxis that sought to understand the historical specificity of capitalist social formations, their complexity as an ensemble of many kinds and levels of social practices, and the conditions for a successful revolution in the 'West'. It is impossible to do justice to the breadth and depth of this work in a few introductory remarks. Instead I identify five themes that are important for Gramsci and relevant to my case study. These are: the economy as a sphere of social relations, the ethico-political dimension of economic regimes, the complexities of state power, the historical bloc, and the crucial role of intellectuals in social organization. These also provide important cross-reference points for my comments on Foucault's research.

Mercato determinato

Gramsci developed Ricardo's concept of 'determinate market' (mercato determinato) to highlight the historical specificity of different economic forms, institutions, and dynamics in different epochs and in specific economic regimes. Ricardo's concept was 'equivalent to [a] determined relation of social forces in a determined structure of the productive apparatus, this relationship being guaranteed (that is, rendered permanent) by a determined political, moral and juridical superstructure' (Gramsci 1971: 410). It is characterized, to a determinate extent, by a certain automatism, an ensemble of uniformities and regularities, which are always grounded in specific historical and material conditions.

Ethico-political

These regolarità are linked to the formation of a specific type of homo oeconomicus (Gramsci 1995: 167–8, 172), which depends on a wide range of social practices. This social type is reflected in 'popular beliefs' and a certain level of culture (Gramsci 1971: 279–318, 400n, 413; 1995: 167). In the case of Americanism (the American system of manufacturing) and Fordism, for example, this involves new forms of factory discipline suited to assembly-line production, achieved in part through high wages, social benefits, and ideological and political propaganda (1971: 285); and, outside the factory, at least in Ford's factory towns, it was coupled with rigorous discipline of sexual instincts, the strengthening of the family and household unit, and training workers to spend their high wages rationally (1971: 300–303).

The state in its inclusive sense

Although Gramsci argued that hegemony in US Fordism originated in the factory (1971: 285; cf. 1995: 260), its overall organization also involved the 'integral state', i.e., 'political society + civil society', 'hegemony armoured by coercion'. His focus was not on the state in its narrow, juridico-political sense but in the broader, more inclusive meaning of 'the entire complex of practical and theoretical activities with which the ruling class not only justifies and maintains its domination but manages to win the active consent of those over who it rules' (1971: 244). He adds that

> every State is ethical in as much as one of its most important functions is to raise the great mass of the population to a particular cultural and moral level, a level (or type) which corresponds to the needs of the productive forces for development, and hence to the interests of the ruling classes. (1971: 258)

The historical bloc

This comprises the necessary, reciprocal correspondence of the ensemble of the social relations of production (economic structure or mercato determinato) and 'the complex, contradictory and discordant ensemble of the superstructures'. This reciprocal relation is not determined by a one-sided economic determination through quasi-natural laws but through the organization of hegemony, which operates by creating appropriate forms of 'economic man' (and, of course, women) and through the direct, active conforming of all social relations to the economic (and extra-economic) needs of the economic structure. In other words, it depends on entrepreneurs' ability to organize 'the general system of relationships external to the business itself' (1971: 6) through a range of economic, political, and ideological apparatuses. In this sense, the necessity emerges ex post, through social practices, reciprocal interdependence and co-evolution.

Intellectuals and hegemony

Intellectuals have a key role here both in specific fields of social practice and at the level of the wider social formation. In addition to the work of specific intellectuals, one or more strata of intellectuals must also 'give the dominant class a certain homogeneity and an awareness of its own function in the social and political as well as the economic fields' (1971: 410–14). While certain key individuals can play a leading role here, it is the activities of organic intellectuals, considered as a social category, that are crucial to the reproduction of this hegemony. Securing the reciprocity between structure and superstructure depends on specific intellectual, moral, and political practices that translate narrow sectoral, professional, or local (in Gramscian terms, 'economic-corporate') interests into broader 'ethico-political' ones. Only thus does the economic structure cease to be an external, constraining force and become a source of initiative and subjective freedom (1971: 366–7).

Michel Foucault

Michel Foucault's early work was mainly epistemological and methodological and critiqued, inter alia, humanism and orthodox Marxism. After May 1968, he addressed more substantive issues. *Discipline and Punish* (1977) and *La Volonté de savoir* (1976) were major initiatives in exploring, rather unsystematically, the nature of power in modern societies. Foucault treated power as a social relation that has no privileged origin and no a priori essence. At this stage, he focused on the micro-physics of power, adopting a bottom-up approach that implied an agnostic position on whether different sites and forms of power were linked together to produce an overall pattern of social domination. Resisting any attempt to provide a total or totalizing interpretation of social events, Foucault adopted two principal methods of investigation: the archaeological and genealogical. His more structuralist archaeology of discourses reconstructed the rules of formation that lead specific discourses to generate particular patterns of thought; and his anti-essentialist genealogical method explored the complex, contingent, and non-linear origins of institutions and events. All of this seems quite far removed from Gramsci (although Morera (2000) does establish some interesting points of articulation).

Just as there are many ways to interpret Gramsci's work, so are there many ways to interpret Foucault. He has been presented as a poststructuralist, as a discourse theorist, as an anti-Marxist (e.g. Sheridan 1980), as someone engaged in a tactical alliance with Marxist analyses in politics and history (Balibar 1992), and as having taken Western Marxism to a higher stage (Poster 1984). Given the concerns of this chapter, however, my remarks focus on his contributions to the critique of political economy. While Foucault rejected 'official Marxism' and the Soviet experience, he did not reject the insights or methods of Marx – indeed, he once claimed that he delighted in using Marx' concepts, phrases, and texts without citing him (Foucault 1980: 52–3). Conversely, as noted above, he also suggested that Gramsci is more often cited than really understood, which implies a degree of sympathy to the Italian thinker and activist when he was properly understood (on Foucault and Marx, see Jessop 2007; Marsden 1999; Nigro 2008; Paolucci 2003; Schärer 2008). Taking up themes in political economy, during the 1970s he argued that capitalism had penetrated deeply into our existence, especially as it required diverse techniques of power to enable capital to exploit people's bodies and their time, transforming them into labour power and labour time respectively to create surplus profit (see, for example, Foucault 1977: 163–4, 174–5, 218–23; 1979: 37, 120–24, 140–41; 2003: 32–7; 2008a: 338, 347; 2008b: 220–22). These comments already indicate the scope for initiating a doubly posthumous, virtual dialogue between Gramsci and Foucault based respectively on the *Prison Notebooks* and Foucault's scattered *dits et écrits*.

I now identify some core themes in Foucault's critique of the general economy of power and of political economy. Key reference points here are *Discipline and Punish* (1977), the first volume of the *History of Sexuality* (1979), and three early series in the Collège de France lectures (Foucault 2003; 2008a; 2008b). Foucault started to explore the nexus among the production of particular conceptions of human nature (as a free agent of exchange and/or as a competitive subject), a particular formation of subjectivity (homo oeconomicus, the entrepreneurial self), and a particular political ideology (liberalism, neoliberalism). Based on these texts, other lectures, and various articles, interviews, and journalism, I will consider five important themes: the economic as a field of exchange relations and/or competition; disciplinary practices and subject formation; governmentality; the state as the site of the strategic codification of power relations; and the production of truth regimes.

The economic field

Foucault's first three series of lectures at the Collège de France address 'government, population, political economy', which 'form a solid series that has certainly not been dismantled even today' (Foucault 2008a: 108). In this context he traced the development of state projects and economic agendas of government over four centuries, noting how these agendas pose different problems at each turn about the limits of state power as well as about the rationales and mechanisms of such (self-)limitation.

Disciplinary practices and subject formation

While *Discipline and Punish* had already explored questions of disciplinary normalization in areas like the prison, garrison, school, and factory, the *Birth of Biopolitics* explores the constitution of the liberal economic subject as the bearer of exchange relations and, later, the transformation of homo oeconomicus into an active entrepreneurial subject (2008b: 225–94 passim). In short, liberalism and neoliberalism depend on different economic subjectivities, which, when they are successfully created, disciplined, and reproduced lead, in Gramscian terms, to the economic structure ceasing to be an external, constraining force and becoming a source of initiative and subjective freedom (1971: 366–7). This is precisely the meaning of Foucault's work on self-responsibilization.

Governmentality

Foucault was interested in the self-reflexive art of governing or 'the conduct of conduct'. This had three aspects: (i) government as a relatively new and certainly more important mode of exercising power than sovereignty, discipline, etc.; (ii) population as the specific object of governmental practices (in contrast to the body as the anatomo-political object of disciplinary power); and (iii) political economy as the overarching object of inquiry and reference point for veridiction that frames governmental rationality in state formation and transformation from the early modern administrative state through to the contemporary neo-liberal era.

Statecraft

Foucault is well known, especially in Anglo-Foucauldian circles, for his abjuring of the state as a sovereign subject and of state theory as an autonomous field of inquiry. This does not mean that he rejected all concern with state power. On the contrary, he proposed an alternative account based on the state's role in the strategic codification and institutional integration of power relations at different sites and scales of social organization. Compared to his earlier work on the micro-physics of power, Foucault presents this later work on (neo-)liberalism as a scaling up of his previous micro-analytics of power to macro-level questions about the cumulative effects of the exercise of private and public power within and beyond the state (2008b: 186). This is translated into concern with the statification of government and the governmentalization of the state (2008a: 109). This process is both intentional and non-subjective. It is intentional because no power is exercised without a series of aims and objectives, which are often highly explicit at the limited level of their inscription in local sites of power (Foucault 1979b: 94). But it is also non-subjective because the overall outcome of the clash of micro-powers cannot be understood as resulting from the choice or decision of an individual, group, or class subject (cf. Foucault 1979b: 94–5).

Truth and power

Foucault is well known for his account of power/knowledge relations and these are, indeed, crucial not only in scientific discourse but also in many other sites where power is exercised. Power/knowledge relations vary between the sedimented (where their contested origins are forgotten and they have become part of what Gramsci calls 'common sense') to the heavily politicized (which are often crucial to struggles over hegemony). Foucault remarked that '[e]ach society has its regime of truth, its "general politics" of truth – that is, the types of discourse it accepts and makes function as true' (1980: 131). He elaborated various sites, mechanisms, techniques, procedures, apparatuses, and gatekeepers through which 'true' statements were distinguished from 'false' ones. The 'political economy of truth' works across sites ranging from the micro- through to a few great economic and political apparatuses (university, army, writing, media). A key role is played not only by grand intellectuals but a wide array of 'specialist intellectuals'. Foucault's lectures on neoliberalism illustrate this in his account of how the neoliberal regime of truth came to be established (2008b).

Gramsci and Foucault: Hegemony, Truth, Power and Intellectuals

Gramsci and Foucault share an anti-economistic theoretical position that regards the emergence of the economic field and its transformation as the product of discourses, subjectivization, and practices that derive in part from outside the socially constituted boundaries of the economy and that depend on the mobile play of private and public powers. For Gramsci, the state in its inclusive sense comprises 'political society + civil society'; by analogy, we could describe Foucault's account of statecraft as based on tactics of 'government + governmentality in the shadow of hierarchy' such that governing is 'conceptualized both within and outside government' (Foucault 2008b: 2; cf. 2008a: 109). Drawing on these and other themes, we can explore the birth of a new economic regime in terms of material transformation in the technical and social relations of production but also in terms of three further issues. These are: (i) the production of a new common sense that conforms individual action and different social fields to the alleged imperatives of an extra-discursive economic order (e.g., Americanism and Fordism, liberalism, neoliberalism); (ii) the emergence of a new hegemonic vision (Gramsci), a new regime of truth (Foucault) and new hegemonic form of subjectivization; and (iii) the roles of intellectuals in both respects. This is not an exhaustive set of conditions, of course, but will serve to organize the following heuristic device and case study on cultural political economy.

Towards a Cultural Political Economy

Cultural political economy (CPE) builds on parallels, explicit and implicit borrowings, convergences, and potential synergies in the work of Marx, Gramsci, and Foucault, among others, to develop a distinctive approach to the contingently necessary nexus among mercato determinato, statecraft and governmentality, and hegemony and governmental rationality as the contingent, provisional, partial, and unstable effect of the micro- and macro- dimensions of 'realities'. Gramsci and Foucault each bring something distinctive to this synthesis in terms of discursive, structural, technological, and agential selectivities. The Italian philosopher of praxis has a more explicit affiliation to Marx in the critique of political economy and this is reflected in his value-theoretical account of mercato determinato and the historical bloc (on Gramsci as a proto-regulation theorist, see Jessop and Sum 2006: 348–73). Both show great interest in the changing economic and political imaginaries and governmental rationalities respectively that provide the aims and objectives of economic performance and different forms of governmental intervention. The French philosopher of discursive and extra-discursive practices has more to offer in regard to the specific technologies of structuration and power. Conversely, Gramsci offers a richer vocabulary for thinking about the shifting agential forces and the scope for alliances in a changing but unstable equilibrium of compromise compared to Foucault's emphasis on the dispersion of micro-revolts and the particular forms of resistance. The resulting synthesis, which remains to be completed, can be described in terms of the Marxianization of Gramsci and Foucault (based on a return to the critique of political economy), the governmentalization of Gramsci (based on Foucault's insights into the complex mechanisms of disciplinary normalization and governmentalization, already anticipated in some of Gramsci's work on Americanism and Fordism), and the Gramscianization of Foucault (based on Gramsci's greater insights into the character of common sense, the crucial role of intellectuals and hegemonic apparatuses, and the challenge of building an historical bloc and the social bases for a durable economic regime).

Accordingly, CPE sees the 'economy' from a discursive as well as material perspective or, better, examines it in discursive and extra-discursive properties as the emergent product of various economic imaginaries and/or their translation into hegemonic strategies and projects. This involves examining the 'economy' in terms of 'economic imaginaries' that are discursively constituted by agency and materially reproduced on many sites and scales (on 'competitiveness' as one such object/subject, see Sum 2009). These discursively constitute economic imaginaries and their associated objects/subjects and can be studied in terms of their role alongside material mechanisms in reproducing and/or transforming economic and political domination. The translation of diverse economic, political, and social interests into effective agency in this regard depends not only on material resources and capacities but also on the ability to define and articulate identities and interests into specific accumulation strategies, political projects, and hegemonic visions in and across different scales. These projects and their bearers play a bigger role than Foucault seems to have comprehended. They have both material and discursive bases and, although economic power is grounded in control over economic resources and state power is grounded in its constitutionalized monopoly of organized coercion, struggles among competing forces and interests in these domains are normally waged as much through the battle for ideas as through the mobilization of primarily material resources and capacities. Success in these struggles typically depends on the capacity to articulate compelling visions that combine political, intellectual, moral and self-leadership abilities with a flow of material rewards and institutional support.

One way to develop this approach is by exploring the interrelations among different kinds of selectivity in social relations: structural, discursive, technological (in the Foucauldian sense of techniques of governance), and agential. The first has been theorized in Jessop's strategic-relational approach (hereafter SRA). In its early stages (1982; 1990), this focused on the strategically selective nature of the structural contexts in which agents exist and act and argued that structures always privilege some strategies over others. Thus the SRA treats structures analytically as strategic in their form, content and operation; and actions are treated analytically as structured, more or less context-sensitive, and structuring. It examines what Jessop terms 'structurally-inscribed strategic selectivities and structurally-oriented strategic calculation'. The former concept refers to how a given structure may privilege some actors, some discourses, some identities, and some strategies over others. The latter highlights how actors orient their strategies in the light of their understanding of the current conjuncture, engage in strategic calculation about their 'objective' interests, and recursively select strategies through reflection, learning, and, indeed, forgetting. The SRA is especially useful in addressing the dialectic of path-dependency and path-shaping in hegemonic transformation. For, the reflexive reorganization of structural configurations is subject to structurally-inscribed strategic selectivities; and the recursive selection of strategies depends in turn on individual or organizational learning capacities and on the 'experiences' resulting from the pursuit of different strategies in different conjunctures. This suggests that forces seeking to establish successful hegemonic projects should analyse the strategic contexts for their actions, engage in a stepwise transformation of the structural selectivities that may obstruct and/or facilitate the realization of the project, and promote individual and collective learning on the part of potential hegemonic subjects and subaltern forces so that they will share its values and objectives. It also identifies some of the basic structural and discursive mediations that affect the success of such hegemonic projects. Some of these concepts, arguments, and insights are elaborated in my own model below.

More recently Jessop has integrated discourse and discursive selectivities into the SRA schema. Arguing that the real world is too complicated to be understood in all its complexity in real time, he emphasizes the importance of complexity reduction through meaning-making as a condition of actors being able to go on in the world. He uses the generic concept of imaginaries (with its links to lived experience) to describe the interpretative frameworks that oriented agents to the world. Building on the three basic evolutionary mechanisms of variation, selection-elimination, and retention, he presents three broad substantive arguments that are directly relevant to this chapter. First, imaginaries and their associated objects/subjects should be seen as socially constructed, historically specific, more or less socially (dis)embedded in broader networks of social relations and institutional ensembles, more or less embodied ('incorporated' and embrained), and need continuing social 'repair' work for their reproduction. In this context, he emphasizes that, while subjects and objects are often co-constituted, there is no simple one-to-one correspondence between them such that subjects always reproduce objects and/or objects always find appropriate subjects. Second, while eschewing reductionist approaches to social analysis, a discursively-sensitive SRA should still stress the materiality of social relations and highlight the constraints involved in processes that operate 'behind the backs' of the relevant agents. Third, he argues that only imaginaries that correspond, albeit partially, to real material forces in the existing or emerging political economy will become hegemonic. Other imaginaries will be silenced, surviving, if at all, on the margins of the dominant economic, political, and social order (Jessop 2004; 2009).

The hegemony of economic imaginaries is reinforced where they involve discursive chains and networks that link many potentially mutually reinforcing forces, fields and genres of discourse. The emergence of the social agenda in (late) neoliberal discourse, for example, stems from their promotion by powerful actors on many sites and scales, their combination of different but complementary discursive genres, and their reliance on different fields of knowledge and intervention. I elaborate this approach in terms of six interrelated discursive-material moments below.

Developing this six-fold approach further, I explore how actors on different sites and scales are (self-)mobilized in support of regimes of truth that offer cultural glue in mediating the emergence of transnational historic blocs.

Selectively combining Gramsci's and Foucault's approaches is useful here because both stress the capillary and contingent nature of power – for Gramsci in the complex ensemble of civil society, for Foucault in the micro-physics of power. Foucault and a neo-Foucauldian perspective (Rose and Miller 1992; 2008; Dean 1999) enable us to open the black box of hegemony. Of particular importance are the disciplinary bodies of knowledge that normalize and render particular imaginaries/strategies 'knowable' and calculable (Higgins 2001: 312).[1] Foucault identifies two complementary sets of mechanisms in this regard. First, his analysis of the disciplinary society focuses on how power/knowledge circuits and matrices produce 'normalized' individuals through the combination of legal and moral norms with very detailed, highly structured, and tightly supervised training techniques and assignments. This external gaze is reinforced by the mutual gaze of the population as its members monitor conformity to existing standards and systems of power/knowledge. Second, Foucault's analysis of the control society focuses on governmentality as the 'conduct of conduct', i.e., the inculcation of self-observation and self-discipline. A key aspect of this is the acceptance of ethical standards that inform the sense of self independently of external standards and systems. Although some authors read Foucault's work on disciplinary and control societies as a periodization of power/knowledge relations (e.g., Hardt and Negri 2000), this chapter interprets it in terms of alternative techniques for exercising power that can be variously combined in different conjunctures.

Insights from these approaches suggest a heuristic possibility of Gramscianizing Foucault to map our understanding of the production of hegemonies in terms of six nodal 'discursively-selective' moments, i.e., analytically distinct but empirically interrelated discursive and structural aspects that are subject to the evolutionary mechanisms of variation, selection and retention. Three particular aspects of this process in the social world, which are worth exploring here, are embodiment, institutionalization of economic imaginaries, and possible resistance to this discursively and extra-discursively co-constitutive processes (see the six discursively selective moments below). Even when hegemonic projects seem to create social unity and consensus, these are always partial, unstable, and temporary. For hegemonies, which are multifaceted composite, are vulnerable to de-stabilization at the personal, institutional, and macro-structural levels. The multiple subjectivities of individuals and the gap between discursive justifications and actual practices open space for alternative conceptions of society and counter-hegemonic subjectivities. Similarly, on the institutional and macro-structural levels, because hegemonic projects in capitalist social formations exclude, marginalize, or suppress some identities and interests in creating an 'illusory community', space opens for subaltern forces to engage in tactics of resistance, demands for reform, and counter-hegemonic strategies.

1 These include sciences, administrative techniques, and normative criteria.

Six Discursively Selective Moments in Production of Hegemonies: Locating Social Relations within Meaning-Making (A Heuristic Schema)

1. *Discursive-Strategic Moment of Economic Restructuring*
   - Faced with political and economic challenges (e.g., falling growth, rising debt) and pressures to restructure, actors at different scales and sites may rethink their opportunities for economic and political actions;
   - This often involves struggles and/or cooperation to (re-)make objects of governance and/or introduce new ones (e.g., competitiveness, corporate social responsibility, poverty reduction, austerity, green new deal, etc.);
   - These objects of governance involve the construction and/or appropriation of discursive frames, storylines; these discursive frames have their spokespersons and followers to acquire discursive lives;
   - This entails a repertoire of conflicting and complementary discourses that map different paths and strategies of restructuring; and
   - This occurs in part through inter-discursivity (see moment C) and, in part, through the mobilization of (inter-)discursive networks of actors across different sites and scales.

2. *Structurally-Inscribed Agential Selective Moment*
   - The differential embedding of actors in social relations affects their capacities to deploy (inter-)discursive networks to build new objects of governance through the selective articulation of diverse discourses and signs;
   - Some agencies in the (inter-)discursive networks find it easier to privilege and limit what symbols or signs can be articulated, what meanings can be fixed upon a set of signifiers, and what relations can be established across different discourses to support or reinvent objects, imaginaries and projects; and
   - These (inter-)discursive networks are mediated through key sets of economic, political and intellectual forces. Currently these include IMF, World Bank, WTO, OECD, World Economic Forum, states, political parties, think tanks, consultancy firms, philanthropic bodies, government bureaucracies, MNCs, business federations, chambers of commerce, standard-setting agencies, financial organizations, service-oriented NGOs, business schools, consultancy firms, banks, schools, business media, cinemas, celebrities, etc.

3. *(Inter-)Discursive-Selective Moment in the Ordering of Discourses*
   - These actors problematize, negotiate, and co-construct discourses and discursive chains related to the objects of governance/strategies;
   - Their contents often involve the articulations between and among genres (ways of interacting), discourses (ways of construing) and styles of representation;

- The selectivities of these 'word orders' (or 'number orders') operate (in part) via knowledging technologies that discipline, normalize and governmentalize judgements;
- These technologies involve a set of knowledge, expertise, techniques and apparatuses that construct authority and/or otherness:
  - Economic, social, managerial and norm-based knowledge on market, competitiveness, globalization, development, poverty reduction, sustainability, etc.;
  - Modalities of expertise of significant agents (those occupying key positions as economists, management gurus, IMF/WTO officials, standard-setting agencies, politicians, opinion makers, etc.);
  - Knowledging techniques (invoking logics of inevitability, linearity, classification, performance, metaphors, etc.);
  - Apparatuses (e.g., consultancy reports, blueprints, guidelines, standards, codes of conduct, best practices, numbers, indexes, targets, scorecards, etc.); and
- These micro-technologies of control discipline, normalize and governmentalize thoughts, aspirations and decisions partly through their recontextualizations in civil society and interstices of everyday life.

4. *Moment in the Remaking of Subjectivities and Identities (Constituting Subjects)*
   - Under the actual or imagined gaze of an authority or truth regime, subjects are engaged in the process of identity formation more or less actively;
   - Agents may refashion subjectivities by appropriating (adopting for the agent's own purposes) and/or resisting (rejecting opening or subtly) these knowledge and standards;
   - They perform, repeat, mimic and/or reject these neo-liberal subjectivities in mundane institutional events (e.g., training sessions, report writing, attending seminars) and everyday practices (e.g., working, managing, discussing, debating, consuming);
   - Such disciplining by external- and self-regulation extends/disperses the range of governing to multiple sites and settings (e.g., guidelines, codes, indexes) and settings (e.g., offices, families, schools);
   - These forms of governing common sense at a distance are multifaceted, composite and contradictory; and
   - This 'contradictory consciousness' means that agencies view the world from a perspective that both contain hegemonic modes of thinking and forms of critical insights. This mix varies across individuals, some participate more in maintaining the hegemonic modes of thinking whilst others are more ambivalent.

5. *Moment in Conditioning and Re-Regularizing Social Relations*
   - These subjectivities and everyday practices help to condition the reproduction of uneven and contradictory social relations;
   - They become regularized through strategies, institutions and governance;
   - The greater the range of (sub-)hegemonic sites in which these resonant discourses and practices are selected and strategies are promoted, the greater is the scope for effective institutionalization based on 'unstable equilibrium of compromise' between groups and class fractions; and
   - These 'moving equilibria' may result in temporary modes of governance that are continuously challenged by marginal/subaltern groups.

6. *Counter-Hegemonic Resistance and Negotiations*
   - The existence of 'contradictory consciousness' and the numerous sites and scales that these processes encompass are bound to involve surpluses of meaning and unevenness with regard to class, gender, ethnicity, nature, place, etc.;
   - This shows that hegemony is not a cohesive and singular relationship of leaders and led; it is riddled with tensions, contradictions and the suturing of difference;
   - This opens up the possibility of counter-hegemonic struggles and the building of solidarity networks (e.g., movement-oriented NGOs, World Social Forum, etc.) and alternative knowledge;
   - These networks may disrupt/subvert dominant cultural symbols and practices in the forms of:
     - 'Branding from below' (e.g., 'Another World is Possible');
     - Use of strategies by unions and social movements (e.g., strikes, walk-outs, political demonstration, name and shame, etc.); and
     - Use of tactics by the weak/subalterns (e.g., political theatre, insurrectionary art, resort to lies/secrets/fictions, refusal to speak, etc.); and
   - Hegemonic forces have to negotiate and constantly shift grounds in order to accommodate these challenges through depoliticization, repoliticization and remoralization of particular (dis-)order.

The Production of Hegemonies: 'Competitiveness' Discourses as a Knowledge Brand

A short chapter cannot show how all six moments can be applied in concrete cases. For illustrative purposes, this section examines the making of 'competitiveness' as a hegemonic discourse across different sites and scales since the 1980s. In this regard, the aim is to show, in an admittedly partial manner, how moments A to D can be applied to how some actors (and their networks) become nodal in the making of particular discourses not as knowledge but as 'knowledge brand' that is specific to particular structural conjuncture.

Discourses on 'competitiveness' date back centuries and they involved a mix of theoretical and policy paradigms (Sum 2009). With the structural crisis of Fordist accumulation regimes, the USA and UK were experiencing low growth, rising unemployment, high inflation and techno-economic decline vis-à-vis Japan and East Asia since the 1980s. Faced with these challenges, economic and political actors were searching for new economic imaginaries to guide economic renewal. Among other initiatives, various national and regional commissions and organizations reflected on geo-economic strategies for transition. Reagan set up the Commission on Industrial Competitiveness in 1983, the Organisation of Economic Cooperation and Development (OECD) stressed the importance of the relationship between competitiveness and 'national system of innovation' (see Miettinen 2002), and the EU published its White Paper on Growth Competitiveness and Employment (1993) and the Lisbon Strategy for Competitiveness (2000), and so on.

This rise of policy accounts of competitiveness was reinforced and supported by developments in parallel knowledge fields (e.g., management theories, business studies and consultancy outputs). More specifically, these were articulated by 'organic' intellectuals occupying positions in prominent business school professors (e.g., Michael E. Porter), consultancy firms, think tanks. These had become an important part of the transnational knowledge-policy circuit and constructed 'saleable' meaning-making models bundled with claims to problem-solving competencies on growth and development. Porter's account is an exemplary case of such development with a simple model (Porter's 'diamond'), best-selling books (e.g., *The Competitive Advantage of Nations* 1990), and iconic policy ideas (e.g., cluster building to boost productivity, growth, employment and, hence, competitiveness). Porter's account has provoked debates, criticisms and support. Some business and management scholars (e.g., Gary 1991; Stopford and Strange 1991) criticized it for lack of formal modelling, while others (e.g., Thurow 1990; Rugman 1991; Dunning 1992) challenged its originality. Nonetheless, his cluster approach is widely discussed and has often been repeated within policy circles as one of the leading ideas that frame regional development and proposals for local development. While Foucault's work reminds us that power is something that is exercised rather than possessed and not attached to agents, Porter is well positioned as a node in the consultancy-policy circuit of capitalism.

One indication of such hegemonic position can be seen in a local government website. The UK government's Improvement and Development Agency for local government (IDeA) has a special website page on Porter's ideas, noting that 'despite (the) plethora of competing but similar ideas, Porter's theory became, for some time, the established "industry standard"'.[2] This status as an 'industry standard' indicates that not all knowledge is equal. Some knowledge is selected and even

2 For a detailed account of the implications of Porter's model for regional development, see http://www.idea.gov.uk/idk/core/page.do?pageId=8507296, accessed 31 July 2010.

transformed into a brand as the 'standard' in the knowledge-policy-consultancy circuit. Its prominence can partly be explained by: (i) the cliché and quality guarantee that comes with Harvard University and the Harvard Business School (HBS); (ii) the appointment of Professor Porter as a member of Reagan's Council of Competitiveness in 1988 and to other, subsequent bodies at urban, regional, national, and international levels; (iii) the generality, simplicity, and flexibility of 'competitiveness' which allows diverse interpretations, frequent renewal, and building of possible alliances among actors involved in economic strategies (Thomas 2003); (iv) the promotion and circulation of this body of knowledge by diverse institutions across the global, regional, national and local scales (see Table 3.2); (v) the accumulation of credibility as it echoes within and across idea-policy networks – especially when backed by celebrity-guru-academics (e.g., Porter) and high-profile conferences, business media and journals;[3] (vi) the offer of ready-made policy advice (e.g., cluster-building strategies) as national/regional reengineering solutions in the face of growing pressures for fast policy and the fear of economic restructuring in a global information age; and (vii) the popularization of the 'cluster approach' by HBS-related institutions (e.g., the Institute for Strategy and Competitiveness) and associated strategy firms (e.g., Monitor Group and ontheFRONTIER Group). Through the joint claims to academic-managerial expertise by these actors and institutions, Porter's cluster-based strategy is flexibly applied to quite different countries (e.g., Canada, Denmark, New Zealand, Portugal, Sweden, and Switzerland) and regions/cities (e.g., Atlanta, Rhône-Alpes, Baltic Sea, Singapore, and Hong Kong/Pearl River Delta). Strategy firms like ontheFRONTIER Group have also adapted it to so-called 'emerging markets' (e.g., Mexico, Peru, Bolivia, and Rwanda).[4]

Apart from the Harvard-associated organizations, this body of knowledge – albeit not always purely Porterian in content – has also been adopted/adapted on different scales by international authorities (e.g., World Economic Forum and United Nations Industrial Development Organization), regional banks (e.g., Asian Development Bank), national agencies (e.g., United States Agency for International Development and Asia Competitiveness Institute) and city governments/development agencies (for example, see Table 3.2). Complementary sites in these knowledge networks in the civil society include other business schools, consultancy firms, chambers of commerce, think tanks, research institutes, business and mass media, town hall meetings, luncheon gatherings and public performances (e.g., conferences and speeches by consultants). The presence of celebrity consultant-

3 Hindle, who compiled the *Economist Guide to Management Ideas and Gurus* (2008), described Porter as the guru on cluster building.

4 For further information on the diverse objectives, projects and cluster initiatives, see The Competitiveness Institute website (http://www.competitiveness.org/article/archive/1/), the Asia Competitiveness Institute (http://www.spp.nus.edu.sg/ACI/home.aspx), the Monitor Group (http://www.monitorgroup.com.cn/en/) and ontheFRONTIER Group (http://www.otfgroup.com/home.html). All these websites were accessed on 29 July 2010.

gurus magnifies the impact of such media and events (Huzynski 1996; Jackson 2001). In turn this body of management knowledge circulates widely and resonates strongly in policy networks in developed and developing countries, gaining credibility (even consent) from its promotion by idea entrepreneurs, strategists and consultants, opinion-forming journalists, leading policy-makers and executives who recontextualize, package and market related discourses. Such production of hegemonies is also objectified and constituted by ways of other micro-level techniques and apparatuses such as reports, indices, scoreboards, databases, development outlooks, cluster plans, best practices, training courses, manuals, etc. (see Tables 3.1 and 3.2).

These institutions, agencies, and actors have quite heterogeneous conceptions and produce multiple and localized regimes of truth. Any 'coherence' they have in contributing to the circulation of competitiveness as neoliberal discourses

Table 3.1 Examples of institutions and discourses related to competitiveness at different scales

Scales	Examples of Institutions Involved	Examples of Competitiveness Discourses/Instruments
Global/ International	World Economic Forum Institute for Management Development The Competitiveness Institute United Nations Industrial Development Organization (UNIDO)	• Global Competitiveness Report and Global Competitiveness Index • World Competitiveness Yearbook and World Competitiveness Scoreboard • The Cluster Initiative Database • The Cluster Initiative Greenbook 2003 • Clusters and Networks Development Programme 2005
Regional	Asian Development Bank African Union Inter-American Development Bank	• Asian Development Outlook 2003: III Competitiveness in Developing Countries • Pan African Competitiveness Forum 2008 • Competitiveness of Small Enterprises: Cluster and Local Development 2007
National	United States Agency for International Development (USAID) Japan International Cooperation Agency (JICA)	• African Global Competitiveness Initiative 2006 • Strategic Investment Action Plan (Competitiveness/SME) 2005
Local/City	Numerous (inter-)city competitiveness projects and plans	• The Hong Kong Advantage 1997 • OECD 's International Conference on City Competitiveness 2005 • Remaking Singapore 2008

Source: Author's own compilation based on website information of these institutions, accessed on 29 July 2009).

Table 3.2 Two knowledge apparatuses and knowledging technologies in the construction of 'competitiveness'

Knowledge Apparatuses/ Instruments	Knowledging Technologies and Practices in Meaning-Making	Major Institutional Sites/Actors
Benchmarking reports and indices constructed in:		
Global Competitiveness Report Growth and Business Competitiveness Indices and Global Competitiveness Index	Technologies of performance and judgement (Index)	*World Economic Forum*
Cluster metaphor constructed in:		
Cluster-Based Industrial Development Workshop (2006) Cluster building in Vietnam: software/ICT, fruit, ceramics, and agricultural products (rice, coffee, pepper, rubber, etc.)	Technologies of agency (Policy seminars, workshops, courses, pilot projects, technical assistance, etc.)	*Asia Development Bank Institute* (and *Institute for Industrial Policy and Strategy in Vietnam*)

Source: Author's own compilation.

and practices is the result of contingent convergence, structural coupling, skilful recontextualization rather than attributable to a singular and predetermined project. For this very reason its reproduction and effects are fragile and require continuing suturing, negotiation or 'repair work' at many sites and scales.

Given their pervasiveness across different scales and sites, Porter-inspired ideas about competitiveness gradually acquired prominence and even brand status in policy-consultancy circuits. Like commercial brands (Lury 2004; Schroeder and Morling 2005), knowledge brands address the rational and irrational aspects of human nature. Cognitively, a brand like Porter's competitiveness 'diamond'/'cluster' model is rationalized and legitimated by its association with HBS, its circulation among policy elites, its distinctive policy advice, re-engineering solutions and individual career benefits. Emotionally, it addresses pride, anxieties, threats, and social tensions linked to growth or decline, development, and the intense pressures of economic restructuring in globalized information age. These rational and irrational effects shape struggles to make a brand hegemonic. In this context, a knowledge brand can be defined as a resonant hegemonic meaning-making device promoted by 'world-class' guru-academic-consultants who claim unique knowledge of the economic world and pragmatically translate this into transnational policy recipes and tool kits that address social tensions, contradictions, and dilemmas and also appeal to pride, threats, and anxieties about socio-economic restructuring.

In circulating transnationally, such brands offer stable but flexible templates that can be developed and recontextualized to changing global, regional, national and local conditions. For illustrative purposes, this chapter now examines the recontextualization of the 'competitiveness' brand in two sites – the construction of benchmarking reports and indices by the World Economic Forum for global application and cluster building programme in Vietnam. Each knowledge apparatus has its own evaluative-regulative rules and micro-technologies of power that discipline individuals and governmentalize countries and their population.

'Competitiveness' narratives are linked to the development of knowledging apparatuses such as benchmarking reports and indices. The two best-known series of reports, which have been published since the 1990s, come from international private authorities. The *Global Competitiveness Report* is issued by the World Economic Forum (WEF) in Geneva and the *World Competitiveness Yearbook* is published by the Institute for Management Development (IMD) in Lausanne. The *Global Competitiveness Report* produces the Global Competitiveness Index, which is connected to Porter (and associates); whereas the *World Competitiveness Yearbook* forwards the World Competitiveness Scoreboard. After cooperating to produce the *World Competitiveness Report* in 1989, these bodies published separate reports after 1995. This chapter concentrates on the WEF not only because of its connection with Harvard Business School but also because of its wide influence. From a CPE viewpoint, this report functions as a discursive apparatus that frames the understandings of 'competitiveness'. Its 2004–05 version presented the report as a 'unique benchmarking tool in identifying obstacles to economic growth and assist (*sic*) in the design of better economic policies'.[5] It achieves this partly through its use of knowledging instruments such as 'indices' and 'best practices' that construct countries as competing market actors. These instruments combine disciplinary and governmental power in one set of evaluative-performance discourses.

More specifically, instruments such as indices are dominated by the principles and language of competition. This knowledge apparatus relies on assigning numbers to countries. As a 'number order', it ranks and scores countries in terms of evaluative rules scoring the presence/absence of certain factors of competitiveness (see Table 3.3). Notwithstanding their relatively short history, these indices are becoming part of a global statistical instrumentarium produced by international private authority. This does not mean that they are not questioned (Krugman 1994; Lall 2001; Kaplan 2003) but their circulation and recognition in the policy-consultancy world reinforce their hegemonic potential within and across many economic and political spaces. As a largely exogenous and constraining body of economic discourse, it is dominated by the language of competition in and through which indices serve to benchmark countries by visibilizing their competitive strengths and weaknesses. Countries are located in a number order which then

5 Palgrave-Macmillan was the publisher of the *Global Competitiveness Report* 2004–05. In its website material, the report is described as a 'unique benchmarking tool', see http://www.palgrave.com/products/title.aspx?PID=270902, accessed on 6 August 2010.

operates as a disciplinary tool (or paper panopticon) with surveillance capacities over them. Its draws (more and more) countries into its number order and countries are compared in terms of economic performance to each other and/or over time (see Table 3.3). It deploys numbers and tables to rank them. Annual revisions create a cyclical disciplinary art of country surveillance that institutionalizes a continuous gaze through numbers that depicts countries' performance via changing rank and score orders. Its power operates through the hierarchization of countries and their division into high/rising and low/falling economies in the competitive race.

Table 3.3 World Economic Forum and its global competitiveness rankings of the USA and selected Asian countries, 2004–2012

	Index 2011–12	Rank 2011–12	Rank 2004–05
United States	5.47	7	2
Singapore	5.67	2	7
Japan	5.40	9	9
Hong Kong	5.41	11	29
South Korea	5.12	24	21
Taiwan, China	5.28	13	4
Malaysia	5.06	21	31
China	4.83	26	46
India	4.32	56	55
Indonesia	4.40	46	69

Source: World Economic Forum, *Global Competitiveness Reports* 2007–12.

As Table 3.3 shows, such performance and judgement technologies are used to subject countries to the treadmill of competitiveness and open them to pressures to change economic and social policies in line with specific recommendations and 'best practices'. Countries with a low or slipping position in the rank order are visibilized and targeted to become more competitive. Such ranking discourses are frequently used by government officials, think tanks and journalists to communicate pride, needs, desires and even panics over economic restructuring. For example, actors may narrate a fall within this index order as threatening and/or a sign of 'hollowing out'. This generates pressures on governments, firms, communities and, indeed, some individuals to refashion themselves to become competitive subjects and economic categories (e.g., entrepreneurs and clusters) in the race to aspire to a world-class ranking or, at least, do better than their immediate comparators.

There is more to this discourse, however, than its disciplinary power. Cox, Mann and Samson (1997: 290–91) distinguish benchmarking (as competition) from benchmarking (as collaboration) and argue that, whereas the former is more externally imposed and top-down, the latter is more joint and responsive. But the notion of benchmarking in this report is ambivalent insofar as it combines both aspects. On the one hand, the benchmarking elements of the discourse on indices disciplines countries in terms of an annual number order; on the other, its benchmarking qualities see countries as sharing some 'bench' space with others and each country acts upon its own conditions of competitiveness in the hope of enhancing them and acquiring greater capacities for self-guidance. Thus, in terms of technologies of power, the WEF's benchmarking report combines disciplinary and governmental power in that countries are externally regulated by indices and also governmentalized into becoming more competitive by building clusters, enhancing FDI, promoting SMEs/education/catch-up development, etc. Devices such as strategic plans, cluster programmes, training workshops, technical assistance schemes, manuals and handbooks are said to contribute towards 'capacity building'. It is beyond the scope of this chapter to examine the particular details of Asia Development Bank Institute and related cluster-based programmes/best practices; but the discursive practices of cluster training recall what neo-Foucauldians term the technology of agency (Cruikshank 1999), which combines participation and capacity-building in the processes of governing as well as controlling the exercise of agency. This array of discourses and practices on regional development produce 'participatory' actors equipped to perform their constructed but eventually self-guided role in promoting catch-up competitiveness. Despite their capacitating aspects, they also control the organization of regional space, the policy for exercising agency and types of agency.

More specifically, actors are encouraged to treat regional spaces as (potential) clusters in which firms, suppliers, service providers, and associated institutions interact to form export-led production- and/or service-oriented nodes (e.g., software, fruit, rice, electrical/electronic products, etc.) that are opened to foreign direct investment and multinational-dominated global value chains. It also self-responsibilizes public and private agencies to become competitive, entrepreneurial and world-market-oriented in their journey towards catching up with competitiveness. Depending on their locations and related interests, individual subjects may reorganize themselves through training and affective-pragmatic identification with the competitiveness project; whilst others are ambivalent and even resistant in the institutional and everyday life of neoliberal competitiveness (Birkenholtz 2009).[6]

6 In the case of India, resistance is rampant especially when cluster-building initiatives (e.g., Special Economic Zones) involve the appropriation of land that affects the livelihood of farmers.

Concluding Remarks: Production of Hegemonies and Hegemonies of Production

Two sets of remarks are in order to highlight the potential of examining the Gramsci–Foucault interface especially the links between hegemony, truth, power and intellectuals and the articulation between the discursive and the extra-discursive levels. At stake here is creatively combining Gramsci and Foucault (and scholars inspired by one or other) to formulate a cultural political economy approach. More specifically, this governmentalizes Gramsci and Gramscianizes Foucault and suggests a series of what, who and how questions in the examining the production of hegemonies. It focuses on: (i) what kind of economic imaginaries (e.g., competitiveness) are selected and how they develop; (ii) who gets involved in the discursive networks that cut across diverse institutional orders and civil society (e.g., business schools, strategy firms, think tanks, international organizations, private authorities, regional organizations, aid agencies, business press, etc.); (iii) how policy ideas are being turned into transnational knowledge brands; (iv) how the brands are being recontextualized at every site and scale; (v) how and through what mechanisms (e.g., knowledge apparatuses and technologies) they are (re-)produced as part of the hegemonic logics via micro-practices; (vi) how this hegemonic constellation of policy discourses and practices comes to be challenged and (re-)negotiated in specific conjunctures; and (vii) how these mediate the rebuilding of social relations.

This necessarily brief chapter could only give a glimpse of the richness and potential of this approach. In a fuller analysis, the CPE approach would examine the interaction among policy discourses, governmentalities and structure in the production of hegemonic policy discourses and practices. The concept of 'knowledge brand' is just one illustration of how CPE scholars approach knowledge and power especially the challenge of moving between actual events and processes and real, underlying mechanisms in order to develop a critical understanding of production of hegemonies. For a 'knowledge brand' can be seen as a transnational manifestation and condensation of institutional, organizational and discursive power in the knowledge-consultancy-policy circuits. After all, not all knowledges are equal; some are more brandized than others. In this regard, knowledge is at the same time diffused and condensed along specific nodal points, the location of which is extra-discursively as well as discursively conditioned. While this chapter has focused on the production and the recontextualization of one Harvard-related knowledge brand, a fuller CPE account would analyse its intertwining relations with the hegemonies of production and their effects. These include the capacities to construct, select and recontextualize these discourses; the specific structural (and agential) selectivities that are involved in hegemony making; the ways these changes mediate alliance-building in particular sites, their uneven impact on class, gender, place, and nature. As illustrated in the case study, hegemonies of neoliberal competitiveness are pervasive across different sites and scales with the effects of remaking personal, institutional subjectivities that mediate changes. These need to be analysed also in conjunction the hegemonies of production and related forms of capitalist accumulation (e.g., the removal of social protection built-up under the era of Keynesian welfare states, land use projects favouring particular clusters and the identities/interests of particular groups, depoliticization of labour and gender issues as entrepreneurialism and catch-up development, etc.) are all part of the major concern of CPE.

Acknowledgement

Research for this chapter was supported by a grant from the British Academy (BARDA-48854). It also draws in part on Sum and Jessop (2013) and has benefitted from comments by Bob Jessop.

References

Balibar, E. 1992. Foucault and Marx: The question of nominalism. In *Michel Foucault: Philosophe* translated by T. Armstrong. London: Routledge, 38–57.
Barrett, M. 1991. *The Politics of Truth: From Marx to Foucault*. Cambridge: Polity.
Birkenholtz, T. 2009. Groundwater governmentality: Hegemony and technologies of resistance in Rajasthan's (India) groundwater governance. *Geographical Journal* 175(3): 208–20.
Burchell, G., Gordon, C. and Miller, P. (eds) 1991. *The Foucault Effect: Studies in Governmental Rationality*, translated by C. Gordon. Hemel Hempstead: Harvester Wheatsheaf.
Cox, J., Mann, L. and Samson, D. 1997. Benchmarking as a mixed metaphor: Disentangling assumptions of competition and collaboration. *Journal of Management Studies* 34(2): 285–314.
Cruikshank, B. 1999. *The Will to Empower*. Ithaca: Cornell University Press.
Curtin, B. 2002. Foucault on governmentality and population. *Canadian Journal of Sociology* 21(3): 505–33.
Donzelot, J. and Gordon, C. 2008. Governing liberal societies – the Foucault effect in the English-speaking world. *Foucault Studies* 5: 48–62.
Dreyfus, H. and Rabinow, P. 1982. *Michel Foucault: Beyond Structuralism and Hermeneutics*. Chicago: University of Chicago Press.
Dunning, J. 1992. The competitiveness of countries and the activities of transnational corporations. *Transnational Corporations* 1(1): 135–68.
Foucault, M. 1977 [1975]. *Discipline and Punish: The Birth of a Prison*, translated by A. Sheridan. London: Allen Lane.
—. 1979. Introduction. In *History of Sexuality: Volume 1*, translated by R. Hurley. London: Allen Lane.

—. 1980. *Power/Knowledge: Selected Writings and Other Interviews 1972–1977*, translated by C. Gordon, L. Marshall, J. Mepham and K. Soper. Brighton: Wheatsheaf.

—. 1984. Personal letter to Joe Buttigieg, 20 April. Cited in: J. Buttigieg, Introduction. In *Prison Notebooks, Volume 1*, by A. Gramsci, edited by J. Buttigieg. New York: Columbia University Press.

—. 1991 [1978]. Governmentality. In *The Foucault Effect*, edited by G. Burchell et al., 87–104.

—. 2001. *Power: Essential Writings*, translated by R. Hurley. London: Allen Lane.

—. 2003. Society must be defended. In *Lectures at the Collège de France 1975–1976*, translated by D. Macey. New York: Picador.

—. 2008a. Security, territory, population. In *Lectures at the Collège de France, 1977–1978*, translated by G. Burchell. Basingstoke: Palgrave.

—. 2008b. The birth of biopolitics. In *Lectures at the Collège de France, 1978–1979*, translated by G. Burchell. Basingstoke: Palgrave.

Frauley, J. 2007. The explosion of Foucault from governmentality studies: Towards an archaelogical-realist retrieval. In *Critical Realism and Social Sciences*, edited by J. Frauley and F. Pearce. Toronto: Toronto University Press, 258–72.

Gary, H. 1991. International competitiveness: A review article. *International Trade Journal*, 5(5): 503–17.

Global Competitiveness Reports 2004–12. http://www.weforum.org/en/initiatives/gcp/Global%20Competitiveness%20Report/index.htm, accessed on 16 January 2013.

Gramsci, A. 1971. *Selections from the Prison Notebooks*. London: Lawrence & Wishart.

Gramsci, A. 1985. *Further Selections from the Prison Notebooks*. London: Lawrence & Wishart.

Hardt, M. and Negri, A. 2002. *Empire*. Cambridge, MA: Harvard University Press.

Higgins, V. 2001. Assembling restructuring: Governmentality, economic regulation and the historical emergence of the 'enterprising farmer' in Australian agricultural policy. *Review of International Political Economy* 8(2): 311–28.

Huczynski, A. 1996. *Management Gurus: Who Makes Them and How to Become One*. London: Routledge.

Jackson, B. 2001. *Management Gurus and Management Fashions*. New York: Routledge.

Jessop, B. 1990. *State Theory*. Cambridge: Polity.

—. 2004. Critical semiotic analysis and cultural political economy. *Critical Discourse Studies* 1(1): 1–16.

—. 2005. Gramsci and spatial theory. *Critical Review of International Social and Political Philosophy* 8(4): 421–37.

—. 2007. From micro-powers to governmentality: Foucault's work on statehood, state formation, statecraft and state power. *Political Geography* 26: 34–40.

—. 2010. Another Foucault effect? Foucault on governmentality and statecraft. In *Governmentality: Current Issues and Future Challenges*, edited by U. Bröckling, S. Krasmann and T. Lemke. New York: Routledge, 56–73.

Jessop, B. and Sum, N-L. 2006. *Beyond the Regulation Approach*. Aldershot: Edward Elgar.

Kaplan, D. 2003. Measuring our competitiveness – Critical examination of the IDM and WEF competitiveness indicators for South Africa. *Development South Africa* 20(1): 75–88.

Kenway, J. 1990. Education and the Right's discursive politics. In *Foucault and Education*, edited by S. Ball. London: Taylor and Francis.

Krugman, P. 1994. Competitiveness: A dangerous obsession. *Foreign Policy* 73(March): 342–65.

Laclau, E. and Mouffe, C. 1985. *Hegemony and Socialist Strategy*. London: Verso.

Lall, S. 2001. Competitiveness indices and developing countries: An economic evaluation of the Global Competitiveness Report. *World Development* 29(9): 1501–25.

Lury, C. 2004. *Brands: The Logos of Global Economy*. London: Routledge.

Marsden, R. 1999. *The Nature of Capital: Marx After Foucault*. London: Routledge.

Morera, E. 2000. Gramsci's critical modernity. *Rethinking Marxism* 12(1): 16–46.

OECD 1962. Minutes of the 4th Session, Committee for Scientific Research, SR/M (62). Paris: OECD, 2.

—. 1991. *Technology and Productivity: The Challenges for Economic Policy*. Paris: OECD.

Olssen, M. 2006. *Michel Foucault: Materialism and Education*. London: Paradigm Publishers.

Miettinen, R. 2002. *National Innovation System: Scientific Concept or Political Rhetoric*. Helsinki: Edita.

Nigro, R. 2008. Foucault, reader and critic of Marx. In *Critical Companion to Contemporary Marxism*, edited by S. Budgen and S. Kouvelakis. Leiden: Brill, 647–62.

Paolucci, P. 2003. Foucault's encounter with Marxism. *Current Perspectives in Social Theory* 22: 3–58.

Porter, M. 1990. *Competitive Advantage of Nations*. Basingstoke: Macmillan.

Read, J. 2009. A genealogy of homo-economicus: Neoliberalism and the production of subjectivity. *Foucault Studies* 6: 25–36.

Rose, N. and Miller, P. 1992. Political power beyond the state: Problematics of government. *British Journal of Sociology* 42(3): 173–205.

—. 2008. *Governing the Present*. Cambridge: Polity.

Rugman, A. 1991. Diamond in the rough. *Business Quarterly* 55(3): 61–4.

Schärer, A. 2008. Theoretisch keine Brüder: Marx und Foucault als Antagonisten. *Prokla* 151: 221–36.

Schroeder, J. and Morling, S. (eds) 2005. *Brand Culture*. London: Routledge.

Smart, B. 1985. *Foucault*. London: Tavistock Press.

Stoddart, M. 2005. The Gramsci–Foucault nexus and environment sociology. *Alternative Routes* 21: 26–40.

Stopford, J. and Strange, S. 1991. *Rival States, Rival Firms.* Cambridge: Cambridge University Press.

Sum, N-L. 2004. 'Towards a cultural political economy: Discourses, material power and (counter-)hegemony', http://www.lancs.ac.uk/cperc/research.htm, accessed on 14 January 2010.

—. 2009. The production of hegemonic policy discourses: 'Competitiveness' as a knowledge brand and its (re-)contextualizations. *Critical Policy Studies* 3(2): 184–203.

—. 2010. A cultural political economy of transnational knowledge brands: Porterian 'competitiveness' discourse and its recontextualization in Hong Kong/Pearl River delta. *Journal of Language and Politics* 9(4): 184–203.

Sum, N-L. and Jessop, B. 2013. *Towards a Cultural Political Economy.* Cheltenham: Edward Elgar.

Tellman, U. 2009. Foucault and the invisible economy. *Foucault Studies* 6: 5–24.

Thomas, P. 2003. Recontextualization of management. *Journal of Management Studies* 40(4): 775–801.

Thurow, L. 1990. Competing nations: Survival of the fittest. *Sloan Management Review* 32(1): 95–7.

Chapter 4

Power and Resistance: Linking Gramsci and Foucault

Marcus Schulzke

Introduction

Gramsci and Foucault are often interpreted as taking contrary perspectives on central philosophical issues, making their work appear incompatible, if not contradictory. However, although the two theorists draw on different theoretical presuppositions, employ different analytical methods, and have very different perspectives on the future of political and social life, their theories can be reconciled. When the two theorists are analysed together, in reference to specific problems, they can be seen as filling in the gaps of the other's work and raising new challenges to be overcome. This chapter will argue that Gramsci and Foucault are especially well suited for theorizing resistance that is capable of overcoming the myriad forms of power that shape modern life. It will show that Foucault's theory of power can incorporate Gramsci's thoughts on political action, and that Gramsci's social transformation can be further developed with the help of Foucault's work.

Interpretations of Foucault tend to describe his theory of power in terms of social control, oppression, and surveillance. His theory of power seems deeply threatening to individual agency. Some of his most famous examples to characterize these forms of power, such as the panopticon, are examples of power being used by an agent intent on domination. This has led some commentators to argue that Foucault makes resistance impossible (McCarthy 1990; Dews 1987; Schrag 1999; Taylor 1985; Fraser 1985; 1989). Others have challenged this interpretation, arguing that, because power is ubiquitous and infused in everyday discourses, people may be able to use sites of power for their own purposes (Hoy 2004; Ruti 2006; 2009; Pickett 1996). The element missing from the affirmative readings of Foucault is a convincing account of how individuals can become conscious of disciplinary constraints and take action against them when they are unable to use power intentionally. Gramsci provides a strong theory of resistance through the political party, which can be read as filling in this gap in Foucault's analysis of power. Gramsci's description of the political party explains how activists can appropriate power for their own purposes even when power is beyond intentional control. Foucault's theory of power also raises questions about the internal power dynamics of the political party, as Gramsci describes it.

The first section of this chapter will provide a brief overview of Foucault's theory of power and of the work of several commentators who have argued that Foucault makes resistance either impossible or pointless. The second section will discuss whether an affirmative reading of Foucault's theory of power is possible. I will argue that while affirmative interpretations of Foucault are correct in maintaining that Foucault's theory of power can be read in ways that promote resistance, they fail to adequately explain the agent of resistance, the tactics of resistance, and how the goals of resistance can be established. The third section will explain Gramsci's theory of hegemony and point out some of the important similarities and differences between it and Foucault's theory of power. The similarities between their theories will help to establish how Gramsci's theory of resistance might be adapted in order to respond to the forms of power Foucault describes. The fourth section will discuss Gramsci's theory of resistance through the political party. It will show that Gramsci's theory of the political party raises potential solutions to the limitations of Foucauldian theories of resistance by recasting the agent of resistance as a collective, rather than an individual. The final section explains how Foucault's theory of power can modify Gramsci's theory of resistance to make it responsive to more varied sources of power, especially power operating within the political party.

The Many Dimensions of Power

Although Foucault writes on a broad range of subjects and addresses topics that span the social and natural sciences, he is best known as a theorist of power. Foucault's studies of the relationships of power are among his most original and important contributions to contemporary social theory. These studies also appear to be deeply pessimistic, as Foucault describes myriad forms of power that are so pervasive and difficult to contest that they often seem to preclude any hope of resistance. The most basic type of power Foucault describes is overt, coercive domination by a single person or a group of people. Foucault identifies this type of power as that of a sovereign, who has personal control over government and the administration of justice (1979; 1997). Although coercive power has existed throughout history and continues to exist, Foucault shows that the sources of power and uses of power have shifted over the past three centuries, and that other types of power have become more prominent. Whereas authority figures of the past often chose to exercise power through force and violence, authorities of the modern world generally prefer to adopt less direct means of asserting their control.

The most famous example of the modern form of control is Foucault's example of the panopticon. This type of prison, originally designed by Jeremy Bentham, is structured so that the guards can watch all of the prisoners in their cells but remain unseen (Foucault 1979: 200). In this setting, the source of power and relationships of power are clear, but the authority exercising the power is nevertheless elusive. Because the prisoners cannot see the guards, they are under constant threat of observation, even when they are not actually being watched. The prisoners learn to live in constant fear of being seen by the guards, so they learn to discipline themselves. Foucault argues that the basic power structure of the panopticon is reproduced in many different contexts, as a way of permitting authorities to monitor those subject to their authority, whether in prison, the military, at work, or at school.

The panopticon is an important entry point for understanding Foucault's theory of power, but it is only one of the many expressions of power Foucault describes. In a 1976 lecture, Foucault distinguishes four elements of disciplinary power: selection, normalization, hierarchalization and centralization (1997: 181). The panopticon illustrates selection, as those subjected to observation are selected to be administered by a prison or some other institution employing this model of control. It also shows hierarchalization and centralization, since those being observed are neatly arranged in space and are monitored by a central authority. Normalization is a more difficult process to capture, as it operates even when there is no clear relationship between those administering power and those subjected to it. Ubiquitous observation creates a constant threat of an authority figure seeing and punishing behaviour that is deemed unacceptable. Those subject to the possibility of observation internalize the relations of power as their fear of being observed leads them to discipline themselves. The process of normalization forces individuals to be complicit in their own control and therefore complicit in the suppression of resistance.

The panopticon is a strong illustration of Foucault's theory of how power operates in the modern world, but it is also somewhat misleading. The panopticon metaphor suggests that there is an authority figure exercising power, but such an authority figure may not exist. Usually Foucault describes power as a force that is diffused among multiple actors, institutions, and relationships. Foucault also describes this type of power as being non-intentional; it is something that individuals cannot deliberately wield over one another, which means its source cannot be an individual or a group. As Foucault explains:

> Power is not something that is divided between those who have it and hold it exclusively, and those who do not have it and are subject to it. Power must, I think, be analyzed as something that circulates, or rather as something that functions only when it is part of a chain. It is never localized here or there, it is never in the hands of some, and it is never appropriated in the way that wealth or a commodity can be appropriated. (Foucault 1997: 29)

Thus, Foucault describes power as an expansive concept that appears in so many different locations and in so many different forms that it becomes inescapable. It is impossible to think or act in ways that transcend relations of power. This moves Foucault's analysis of power beyond the panopticon or any other specific instantiations of power to his theory of how power operates through knowledge and discourse.

A recurring point in Foucault's studies of the historical development of discourses and institutions is that truth is not a matter of correspondence to facts about the world. Truth is created and transformed by power (Foucault 2010: 36). The power of a regime of truth is largely defined based on its ability to constitute the world according to its needs. As Foucault says, 'power produces knowledge', (1979: 27) and 'determines the forms and possible domains of knowledge' (1979: 28). Foucault's historical studies show many examples of power manufacturing knowledge (1976; 1979; 1988). He pays close attention to shifts between regimes of truth, as these disruptions provide the best view of what constitutes the truth of a particular era (Foucault 1982). The normalizing discourses that regimes of truth produce are widely accepted because they take on the false appearance of necessity. People become so embedded in social relations based on these discourses that it becomes exceedingly difficult to see how they create and reproduce relations of power, much less to resist these relations of power.

Power that is not rooted in a controlling agent and that is not used intentionally raises significant barriers against resistance. Given the pervasiveness of power, and the ways in which it constitutes identities, social relations, and knowledge itself, it is difficult to account for how people can be capable of any kind of autonomous action. Many interpretations of Foucault's theory of power describe Foucault as a pessimistic theorist who emphasizes the myriad ways in which individuals are subjected to power and domination without providing a basis for critique or action.

Dews argues that Foucault describes individuals as being passive recipients of the narratives and disciplinary apparatuses that structure their lives (1987: 161). McCarthy maintains that Foucault employs a reductionist view of the individual, which casts the individual as nothing more than an object of power, incapable of expressing agency (1990). According to McCarthy, this conclusion follows from the way Foucault describes power forcing people into patterns of behaviour. Schrag states this even more forcefully saying that 'individual human actors and human choices can play little or no role' in society as Foucault describes them (1999: 379). According to these readings, individuals are largely powerless. They have little, if any, ability to transcend power and therefore no hope of carrying out genuine acts of resistance.

Taylor criticizes Foucault for developing an incoherent theory that fails to acknowledge the possibility of freedom from power and that provides no grounds for preferring one system of domination over another. 'There can be no such thing as truth independent of its regime, unless it be that of another. So that liberation in the name of "truth" could only be the substitution of another system of power for this one' (Taylor 1985: 178). Thus, Taylor's point is that based on Foucault's theory of power, even if individuals do have the capacity for resistance, resistance has no value. It cannot serve any purpose beyond leading to the establishment of an alternative system of power that cannot be judged better or worse than the one that preceded it. Similarly, Fraser questions why Foucault promotes acts of resistance against power since he provides no reason to prefer freedom to domination (1985; 1989). As she sees it, Foucault does not provide an adequate basis for his normative claim that power should be resisted.

Finding Routes of Resistance

Some commentators have attempted to respond to interpretations of Foucault that characterize him as a pessimist by showing how power might serve as a means of activism or self-expression when it is no longer seen as simply a means of elite domination (Hoy 2004; Ruti 2006; 2009; Pickett 1996). When power is localized in the hands of a ruling class, as it is the overt domination of a sovereign over a subject population, it is in some ways easier to contest than the diffuse power of modernity. The source of domination can be clearly located and its exercise can be monitored. Resistance can be carried out directly against those who dominate others. By contrast, if power is, as Foucault argues, not something with a single source, then it is difficult to locate and difficult to contest. This is what is so threatening about power as Foucault theorizes it. However, by dislocating power and making it pervasive, Foucault makes it potentially accessible to those who are outside of the dominant political and economic classes. This raises the possibility that activists could be able to manipulate power for their own ends even if they lack the ability to directly challenge the dominant social classes or to seize control of civil or political institutions.

Even the prison, which epitomizes disciplinary control, gives rise to resistance. Foucault argues that the modern prison is supposed to be a place in which prisoners learn to respect the law, but that this project fails because the structure of prison life produces unintended consequences. The experience of being subjected to punishment makes prisoners resent the government, its legal system, and even society as a whole (Foucault 1979). Resentment increases when inmates leave the prison to find that their criminal past has made it impossible for them to find good jobs or to have full rights of citizenship (Foucault 1979: 265–6). This is an example of the exercise of power producing a backlash of dissatisfaction, which in itself raises the possibility that exercises of power could inadvertently give rise to resistance activities. Foucault goes on to argue that prisons actually encourage inmates to organize themselves into groups for protection against their harsh conditions. Upon release, they have networks of trusted accomplices to assist in their crimes. In other words, the inmates become more powerful through associational links and a shared sense of resentment that was created by the judicial system acting as a constraint. The example of inmates becoming empowered to commit more crimes may not seem like a very promising model for substantive acts of resistance. Nevertheless, Foucault's discussion of the unintended consequences of the exercise of power at least serves as an example of how those who seem to be most constrained and repressed may still be capable of acting in ways that challenge the status quo.

Commentators attempting to develop Foucauldian theories of resistance have explored ways in which people might be able to contest power or use it for creative purposes. Hoy argues that people may engage in 'critical resistance' by 'using the very mechanisms of power to destabilize and subvert domination' (2004: 82). This kind of resistance relies heavily on genealogical critique to expose discourses of power, and is primarily concerned with liberating the body, as the body is the central object of disciplinary power. Pickett argues that Foucault has a well-developed theory of resistance, albeit one that deviates from traditional models of resistance. Pickett says that the form of resistance Foucault favours is a continual struggle against any discourses that limit the scope of individual freedom (1996). Resistance must therefore be a continually shifting struggle against hierarchy, inequality, and normalization. Pickett says that such an unlimited struggle is potentially self-destructive because it must reject any form of constraint, yet maintains that this does offer a way of subverting even the most pervasive forms of power.

Mari Ruti offers an affirmative reading of Foucault's theory of self-creation that makes resistance into a personal project (2006; 2009). According to Ruti, Foucault thinks that 'power is actively generative rather than merely prohibitory, restrictive, or negating – that it opens the path to the articulation of meanings even as it delimits the field of discursive possibility' (2006: 60). Individuals have the capacity to contest power by critically assessing their own lives and deliberately constructing their identities in ways that may resist normalizing discourses. Ruti argues that 'Foucault presents a subject who is not merely passively molded by power, but able to dynamically participate in the fashioning of its own subjectivity' (2006: 64). She therefore sees Foucault's theory of the self as permitting individuals to transcend the disciplinary apparatus.

The affirmative readings of Foucault's theory of power offer promising alternatives to the pessimistic interpretations of his theory of power, yet they are difficult to sustain. These theories depend on individuals being creative agents of resistance, but as the previous section showed, Foucault characterizes individuals as being so overwhelmed by various manifestations of power that they have little capacity for independent thought and action. Individuals often seem to be over determined by various modes of disciplinary power acting on them. Their subjectivity is constituted by normalizing narratives. They are constrained by regimes of knowledge, under the constant threat of observation from authorities, and continually tested and judged to ensure that they are not deviant. Those who attempt to derive theories of resistance from Foucault offer strong explanations of how power can be mobilized by ordinary people, but they offer insufficient accounts of how individuals can ever hope to rise above the multiple sources of power acting on them to the extent that they can carry out acts of resistance.

There is also a more serious problem with deriving a theory of resistance from Foucault's work. One of the most serious problems with the critical resistance as Ruti, Hoy, Pickett and others discuss is that deliberate resistance usually depends on individuals being able to use power intentionally. This is impossible given

Foucault's description of power as being beyond individual control. One of the difficulties of resistance, according to Foucault's account is not only that power is pervasive but that it is not something that an individual can control and use at will. Foucault argues that power is not intentional, that is to say, it is constituted by social practices and not subject to the individual will (1978: 94).

There is a hope of recovering a philosophy of resistance from Foucault, but the attempts to do this tend to provide insufficient explanations of how resistance can be reconciled with Foucault's strong statements of power. The key to this difficulty lies in recognizing the limits of individual power and theorizing alternative agents of resistance. Because individuals are largely at the mercy of various sources of power, they must be able to form associations that overcome the constraints that individuals experience. Moreover, these collectives must be able to contest power in ways that do not presuppose an intentional view of power. Gramsci's theory of resistance to hegemony can help to provide a basis for resistance.

Hegemony and Control

There are important similarities between Foucault's theory of power and Gramsci's theory of hegemony. At the most basic level, Foucault and Gramsci are both concerned with describing the exercise of power in ways other than through the use of force or violence. As Bates puts it, 'the basic premise of the theory of hegemony' is 'that man is not ruled by force alone, but also by ideas' (1975: 351). Gramsci deviates from the traditional Marxist view that the superstructure is simply a means of reproducing and transmitting the ideology of the dominant economic class. By Marx's account, power is a relatively simple concept, in the sense that it has a clear source and follows predictable patterns. Those who hold the dominant positions in the system of production wield power by virtue of their control of the means of production (Marx 1978; 1990). They solidify their position by taking over civil and political institutions and using these to protect their economic interests. Under capitalism, this means using the state as a tool for maintaining control of subordinate classes and taking control of foreign markets. Marx describes power as overt domination, especially when it is manifest under a bipolar class structure such as the one he thinks exists in a developed capitalist economy. Such a model is ideally suited for guiding revolutionary activities, as it clearly locates the source of power, explains the restrictive function of power, and identifies disempowered revolutionary actors that can challenge the dominant class.

Gramsci's theory of power is more complex than the traditional Marxist theory, as Gramsci maintains that the political and ideological superstructure has some level of autonomy from the economic base (1992d). He argues that civil and political institutions, as well as the culture they help to create, may act in ways that are influenced by, but not determined by, the economic relations. This means that power can be expressed by the superstructure as well as by the base and that it can follow different patterns depending on its source and the interests it serves. According to Gramsci, power is manifest in the many institutions that make up political and civil society. State political institutions, including the military, police, courts, and prisons all represent dimensions of state coercive power. These political institutions employ violence and threats of violence in order to express the will of the state. However, Gramsci draws attention to how infrequently these institutions have to assert their power. Except in times of crises, most people accept the legitimacy of the state without being forcibly compelled to do so. The tacit acceptance of the state has much do to with the institutions of civil society, including schools, civic associations, and religious groups, which sustain themselves as well as political and economic institutions through the exercise of power in covert ways. This aspect of power is captured by Gramsci's concept of hegemony.

Gramsci considers hegemony, rather than overt domination, to be the primary mode of power in the modern world (1992d: 265). Hegemony helps to constitute individuals, acting on them in myriad ways as individuals interact with the institutions that constitute hegemony. Individuals' identities are inextricably linked to their place within the institutions of the state and civil society. They tend to accept their status and the roles that go along with it as being natural. Hegemony operates through securing consent. It must satisfy people's needs in order to retain control, but it only does this to a limited extent. People must be satisfied, yet only to the extent that they are content with their position and become complacent. Like Foucault's disciplinary power, hegemony raises new barriers to resistance. Hegemony is not a unified system, nor are hegemonic values always coherent. Rather, hegemony is a diverse assemblage of institutions and values that can be both complementary and contradictory. Because of its diverse form and its various instantiations, it is difficult to challenge hegemony, especially through force. Hegemony can incorporate attempts at resistance, depriving them of their force and even transforming them into affirmations of the status quo.

Thus, much like Foucault, Gramsci is concerned with the way institutions exert power through invisible mechanisms. Both hope to expose the apparent necessity of the institutions and discourses that shape people's lives as illusory and consider this to be an essential component of resistance. However, Gramsci remains much closer to the Marxist view of power than Foucault. Gramsci never goes as far as Foucault in theorizing power as a diffuse entity existing in relationships of surveillance or in normalizing discourses. Moreover, unlike Foucault, Gramsci typically links power to a set of interests and intentions. He considers it to be an instrument of class domination and a potential means of liberation. The similarities and differences between hegemony and disciplinary power are important to bear in mind. Gramsci's theory of action is directed at challenging a concept of hegemony that bears important similarities to the type of power Foucault theorizes. It is therefore a promising candidate for a theory of resistance that can be extended to also operate against the type of power Foucault describes.

The Political Party

Gramsci and Foucault face similar problems. They attempt to theorize resistance and social transformation when faced with systems of hegemony or disciplinary power that make it exceedingly difficult to think or act in critical ways. One of the great strengths of Gramsci's theory when compared against Foucault's is that Gramsci has a far more developed account of the agents that are capable of carrying resistance and the strategies they should employ. Whereas Foucault and commentators on Foucault tend to give inadequate explanations of who can mobilize power for liberation, Gramsci provides a detailed account of the party structure and explains how political parties can become more powerful than lone individuals.

In his essay *The Modern Prince* Gramsci appropriates Machiavelli's famous work of statecraft and adapts it as a guide for resisting hegemony. Machiavelli describes power in ways that coincide with Foucault's sovereign mode of power. Machiavelli's prince wields a direct, intentional form of power and uses it to maintain personal control over a subject population. The strategies Machiavelli describes for maintaining power fit perfectly with those Foucault describes in his examples of sovereign displays of power. For example, Machiavelli writes about the importance of fear and argues that it is better to be feared than loved because one can control fear by deliberately intimidating others. As Machiavelli says, 'men love at their convenience and fear at the convenience of the prince' (1998: 68). In other words, fear is a form of intentional power that the sovereign personally embodies. This type of control through intimidation is one of the central objectives of the rituals of punishment that Foucault associates with sovereign power in *Discipline and Punish* (1979). Foucault alludes to this in his lectures on Machiavelli, as he considers Machiavelli to be the exemplar of the view of sovereignty that treats the sovereign as a transcendental figure that stands outside of, and above, the society he rules (1991).

Machiavelli's strategies may be successful in the context of taking and using coercive power, but they are poorly suited for resisting power as it is described by Gramsci and Foucault. Thus, Gramsci appropriates *The Prince* as a foundation for a new theory of social transformation. Gramsci makes a point of declaring that his interest in *The Prince* is not simply a matter of academic curiosity. Rather, he sees the book as a living document that can serve as a guide to political action. 'The basic thing about *The Prince* is that it is not a systematic treatment, but a "live" work, in which political ideology and political science are fused in the dramatic form of a "myth"' (Gramsci 1992b: 125).

Gramsci thinks that in the modern world no single person could be the prince. Hegemony shapes the totality of modern social life, and is therefore far too strong and pervasive for any individual to challenge. The contemporary prince must be a collective agent, which is embodied by the political party.

The modern prince, the myth-prince, cannot be a real person, a concrete individual. It can only be an organism, a complex element of society in which a collective will, which has already been recognized and has to some extent asserted itself in action, begins to take concrete form. History has already provide this organism, and it is the political party – the first cell in which there come together germs of a collective will tending to become universal and total. (Gramsci 1992b: 129)

The modern prince Gramsci theorizes is not simply an organization akin to other types of social groups. It is a collective that is so unified in structure and goals that it can be imagined as a single person. The party represents a single economic class and manifests that class' interests, but it is composed of several distinct parts. The leaders of the party maintain the party's commitment to a unified purpose, and must guard against conservative or reactionary impulses from within its ranks. The bulk of the party's membership is made up of ordinary people who support the party and participate in its struggles, but who cannot devote all of their time and energy to the party. Finally, there is an intermediary group that maintains contact between the various party levels, organizing and teaching members of the base, while also conveying their needs and wishes to the leadership. Thus, the party Gramsci describes 'is an institutional structure that binds together intellectual and political leaders with a mass base that can be a fundamental economic class ' (Augelli 1997: 31). For these groups to work collectively each part must perform its respective function. Boggs calls Gramsci's party a compromise between Leninist vanguardism and anarchist voluntarism, since it attempts to establish a strong leadership without allowing leaders to dominate other members of the organization (Boggs 1976: 109). Hobsbawm sees it as representing an improvement on the Leninist vanguard ideal, which is better suited to facilitating mass engagement (Hobsbawm 1977).

Like Foucault, he recognizes the limits of interpreting power as an intentional concept and considers the ways in which it operates without being deliberately used by one class against another. However, Gramsci thinks that resistance depends on being able to exercise some measure of deliberate use of power. By basing his theory on *The Prince*, a work that purports to show how an individual prince can seize control of the state and wield intentional power, Gramsci signals that his own goal is to exercise deliberate control over hegemony. The party's goal is to carry out this struggle in every sphere of political and civil life in which hegemony is manifest. As Aronowitz puts it, 'under the best of circumstances where the party has sufficient resources, especially cadres, it contests bourgeois hegemony on all fronts, not merely in the sphere of electoral politics' (Aronowitz 2009: 10). This gives Gramsci's party a far more expansive role than political parties typically take on. Although liberal political parties may go beyond political action and attempt to shape cultural norms, this is done for the purpose of achieving political goals, such as winning elections. Gramsci argues that in addition to pursuing political goals the party must also work to establish hegemony from below, or counter-hegemony, that can replace the hegemony of the ruling class. Gramsci envisions the party performing cultural and political functions, thereby contesting hegemony at multiple points. It is essential for a modern prince to be able to do this, as challenging political institutions may require first challenging the civil institutions that legitimize and sustain them. The civil and cultural functions are so important that Gramsci thinks there are times when this element of the party's struggle takes precedence.

At each level of the party hierarchy, members perform vital roles in challenging hegemony and developing counter-hegemony. To put this in terms of Foucault's philosophy, the party is a collective that constantly works to overcome normalizing narratives through the collective efforts of its members acting according to their respective capacities. It also creates new narratives that remake relations of power in more liberating ways. It is not necessary for every member of the party to be fully aware of these discourses or how they operate, only that each one is capable of performing a role that allows the party to collectively escape hegemony and create opposition to it. As Gramsci emphasizes, the members of the party are unified in such a way that they can act as if they were a single person, yet they are more efficacious and resistant to domination and control than any single individual could be.

Collective Resistance

Applying Gramsci's theory of the modern prince as a model for resistance helps to overcome some of the challenges facing affirmative readings of Foucault's theory of power: determining the agent of resistance and the means of carrying out acts of resistance. The central task when locating an agent of resistance is explaining how any agent can become conscious of disciplinary control and begin thinking about ways to contest that control even as they are subject to it. In order to engage in resistance, according to Foucault, one would have to be able to discover the existence of hidden relations of power, to critically assess the regimes of truth responsible for establishing these relations of power, and to challenge the limits prevailing institutions and values impose. This is a daunting task for a single person. Individuals might have the desire to contest some of the more overt forms of surveillance, normalizing narratives, and examination that order their lives, but Foucault describes power as being so pervasive that most individuals would lack the ability to discover each of its sources.

Gramsci's pronouncement that 'the modern prince, the myth-prince, cannot be a real person, a concrete individual' (1992b: 129) shows that he recognizes the impossibility of resistance against hegemony being carried out by a lone individual. He maintains that resistance is only possible when it is part of a collective activity. This is why he emphasizes the structure of the party as an intensely unified collective body. Gramsci's new prince has the advantages of maintaining a level of unity and purpose akin to that of an individual while having the capacity of an entire organization. A sufficient number of individuals unified in this way might be capable of uncovering the various mechanisms of power acting on them and of overcoming these through an effort of collective will.

Gramsci's descriptions of collective resistance carried out with a unifying purpose and structure provides a strategy for overcoming the myriad expressions of disciplinary power by displacing the agent of resistance. Foucault is primarily concerned with how power constitutes individuals. The power is largely based on categorizing individuals, locating them in space, and quantifying their actions. This power depends on being able to disaggregate collectives and to see individuals as interchangeable parts. In other words, it depends on the Enlightenment abstraction of the autonomous individual, which coincided with the widespread implementation of disciplinary power. By rejecting the idea that individuals are the agents of resistance and describing collectives as being like individuals, Gramsci distances himself from the Enlightenment view of individuals as independent agents. He also moves beyond the system of disciplinary power Foucault describes, which is established based on the Enlightenment model.

The political party is ideally suited for overcoming the limitations individuals face when confronted with normalizing discourses. Organic intellectuals draw attention to relations of power and expose their false necessity (1992a). In doing so, they can build political consciousness. Party leadership maintains the organization's shared purpose and chooses the most effective ways of enacting it. The mass base of the party, operating as a unified body, can more successfully refuse to submit to the institutions that create relations of power than isolated individuals.

As the previous section showed, Gramsci and Foucault both describe the ways in which power acts even when it is not being used intentionally. Gramsci's hegemony is initiated by elites and supports their interests, but hegemonic institutions and values take on their own existence and are usually not directly controlled by elites. However, Gramsci hopes to reintroduce intentionality. He critiques the economist belief, which was widespread during his time, that revolution might be achieved through passively waiting for the contradictions of capitalism to bring about economic and political transformation (Gramsci 1992c; 1992b). Instead, he argues that revolutionaries must act to bring about revolutionary change. They must deliberately use existing institutions, which serve elite interests, but that can operate to undermine the ruling elite and the system they created.

Gramsci's theory of action is pragmatic. He is willing to make some concessions to traditional institutions, such as the Catholic Church, as a means of producing counter-hegemony (1994b). Gramsci views traditional institutions and values not simply as impediments to social progress, as other Marxist thinkers tend to do, but as ways of appealing to people and building support for revolutionary change. For example, the Catholic Church is a conservative organization that has often worked to stifle social change, yet Gramsci sees it as a potential forum through which to contact oppressed people and to mobilize them (1994b). It may therefore be instrumental in attacking the status quo that it so often defends.

Rather than simply resisting the status quo and opposing all facets of it as being part of the system that must be destroyed, Gramsci describes ways of using the existing institutional structure against itself. He therefore employs a dual strategy of appropriating existing institutions and values while also establishing new institutions, such as factory councils and trade unions (Gramsci 1994a; 1994c).

Gramsci's strategy is to find the kinds of contradictions in the institutions that create relations of power that Foucault describes in his example of the prison system generating unintended consequences by building associational links between inmates. This type of resistance, as it is described by Gramsci and by Foucault, does not presuppose an intentional control over power. It only requires that activists may be able to direct power in ways that produce contradictions and unintended consequences.

Gramsci and Foucault agree that resisting hegemony or normalizing narratives depends on recognizing dominant norms and values as being contingent and as reflecting the interests of certain members of society. They also seem to agree that the best way of contesting power is through indirect means, such as using institutions that manifest power against each other or aggravating these institutions' internal contradictions. However, the way in which Gramsci proposes to do this is more plausible. The forms of power he and Foucault describe operate through institutions, narratives, and value systems – phenomena that act at a high level and that are highly resistant to individuals' efforts to change them. By establishing the party as a collective force of resistance Gramsci introduces an agent of resistance that may more plausibly contest power operating at this level. Organizations are in a much better position to challenge institutions and values because of their greater resources and their capacity for large-scale direct action. Thus, Gramsci theorizes ways in which revolutionaries acting within an organization can deliberately strike against these internal contradictions without assuming that activists are capable of reaching a level of individual autonomy that is at odds with Foucault's theory of power.

The Party's Self-Critique

Thus far, this chapter has focused on reading Gramsci's theory of the party as a model for resistance against the forms of power he and Foucault describe. However, Gramsci should not be seen as simply offering a corrective to Foucault's theory of power. Gramsci's theory of actions suffers from its own shortcomings that need to be addressed. There are risks associated with making political parties the agents of social transformation, which can best be assessed by considering party organization from the perspective of Foucault's theory of power.

The party Gramsci theorizes is an agent developed for a specific mode of political engagement. It is established along the model of democratic centralism, which helps to make the party a unified body, and also puts leaders in a strong position to exert control of the party. This model of the party is potentially dangerous, as it raises the possibility that the party could become an elite institution that falls under the complete control of its leaders. Foucault's theory of power shows that any political party, even one with an organic connection to its class, must have its own internal relations of power. Gramsci acknowledges that this raises the potential problem that charismatic authority figures might attempt to seize power within the party and theorizes other forms of cultural association that could potentially guard against this (1992d). Moreover, Gramsci seems to think that even if a strong party were to constrain its members, it would still be preferable to the hegemony of the capitalist ruling elite (1992b). However, Foucault might challenge Gramsci's belief that a strong party could be sustained without also giving rise to coercion. Any party capable of acting with such a high degree of unity that it can be described as being like an individual is doubtless one that would create new limits that members might feel compelled to resist. The challenge for members of the party is building an organization capable of acting like a modern prince but that is not so centralized that it simply becomes a new institution for disciplining its members. This is the point at which Foucault's comments on resistance can contribute to Gramsci's party model.

Whereas Gramsci says that the party's goals must be relatively stable and that leaders must keep the organization on course, Foucault would maintain that any organization hoping to carry out genuine acts of resistance would have to allow its goals to shift and change based on the changing power structures it confronts and its members' changing interests. Foucault thinks that the form of resistance must continually change in order to respond to new limits on individual freedom. The goals of resistance are likewise not fixed and determinate. Rather, they must be dynamic, constantly changing to fit new circumstances. Moreover, Foucault emphasizes that resistance must also include some degree of self-criticism; individuals must be capable of challenging their own consciousness in order to uncover beliefs and modes of thought that impose control from within. Gramsci's party incorporates internal mechanisms for self-critique, but he places far more weight on the importance of party unity. A party attempting to guard against imposing new constraints on its members would have to devote much of its attention to self-critique and self-creation to locate power it may have internalized or created. Its goals and methods would need to be more open to change based on the shifting relations of power that it would have to contest.

Gramsci considers the party's unity to be a virtue and worries that excessive internal conflict may lead to factionalism or corporatism (1994b; 1992b; 1992d: 226). However, such factionalism may be unavoidable if organizations are to remain unified while also preventing the forms of power they initiate from becoming new modes of oppression. In order for the party to function as a single agent, while also being capable of resistance, it would have to give greater attention to its internal dynamics and ensure that they can permit conflict and competition within the boundaries of a party structure. According to Gramsci's model, this task of self-critique is probably a function that would be best performed by intellectuals.

Intellectuals lead the effort to challenge hegemony and to establish counter-hegemony (Gramsci 1992a: 12). Although Gramsci describes intellectuals as individuals, he says that they only achieve their status by virtue of their connection to others. Being an intellectual is not a matter of intelligence but of performing a particular social function (Gramsci 1992a: 9). This means that intellectuals are necessarily connected to others, and that they therefore naturally fit into the type of party structure Gramsci describes. In fulfilling their party function, intellectuals also have the responsibility for mediating between different levels of the political party and ensuring that the party continues to function as a unified entity. This places them in the best position to lead the effort to guard against the emergence of oppressive relations of power within the party itself. Such a project of self-critique would draw on the same skills as those intellectuals display when challenging hegemony and disciplinary power outside the party.

Conclusion

As this chapter has shown, Foucault's theory of power can be interpreted in ways that permit resistance. However, it is difficult to account for how this resistance might be carried out by individuals, given the extent to which their subjectivities are produced by existing power structures. Gramsci's theory of collective resistance in the model of the modern prince offers a way around this challenge. First, Gramsci shows that even when individuals are subjected to a strong disciplinary apparatus, they may be able to exercise power through collective action. Second, Gramsci's strategies for contestation are ones that can operate within the system of power that Foucault describes, as they are based on using existing institutions and values against themselves.

Foucault's theory of power can also be used to challenge Gramsci's political party, as the party risks becoming too rigid and centralized. Foucault's theory suggests that any political party engaged in resistance would have to devote much of its energy toward self-critique and reassessing its goals. Any political party capable of genuine acts of resistance must maintain the tenuous balance between the high degree of unity that collective action in pursuit of a common objective requires and the internal freedom to dissent that has to be protected to prevent the party itself from becoming a source of power that restricts individual freedom.

References

Aronowitz, S. 2009. Gramsci's concept of political organization. In *Perspectives on Gramsci: Politics, Culture and Social Theory*, edited by J. Francese. New York: Routledge, 7–19.

Augelli, E. and Murphy. C.N. 1997. Consciousness, myth and collective action: Gramsci, Sorel and the ethical state. In *Innovation and Transformation in International Studies*, edited by Stephen Gill and James H. Mittelman. New York: Cambridge University Press, 25–38.

Bates, T.R. 1975. Gramsci and the theory of hegemony. *Journal of the History of Ideas* 36(2): 351–66.

Boggs, C. 1976. *Gramsci's Marxism*. London: Pluto Press.

Dews, P. 1987. *Logics of Disintegration: Post-Structuralist Thought and the Claims of Critical Theory*. New York: Verso.

Foucault, M. 1976. *Mental Illness and Psychology*, translated by A.M. Sheridan-Smith. New York: Harper and Row.

—. 1978. *History of Sexuality, Vol. 1: An Introduction*, translated by Robert Hurley. New York: Pantheon Books.

—. 1979. *Discipline and Punish: The Birth of the Prison*. New York: Vintage.

—. 1982. *The Archaeology of Knowledge and the Discourse on Language*. New York: Pantheon.

—. 1988. *Madness and Civilization: A History of Insanity in the Age of Reason*. New York: Vintage.

—. 1991. Governmentality. In *The Foucault Effect: Studies in Governmentality*, edited by G. Burchell, C. Gordon and P. Miller. Chicago: University of Chicago, 87–104.

—. 1997. Society must be defended. In *Lectures at the Collège de France 1975–1976*, translated by D. Macey. New York: Picador.

—. M. 2010. The birth of biopolitics. In *Lectures at the Collège de France, 1978–1979*. New York: Picador.

Fraser, N. 1985. Michel Foucault: A 'young Conservative?' *Ethics* 96(1): 165–84.

—. 1989. Unruly practices: Power, discourse, and gender. In *Foucault on Modern Power: Empirical Insights and Normative Confusions*, edited by N. Fraser. Minneapolis, MN: University of Minnesota Press, 17–34.

Gramsci, A. 1992a. The intellectuals. In *Selections from the Prison Notebooks of Antonio Gramsci*, edited by Q. Hoare and G.N. Smith. New York: International Publishers, 3–14.

—. 1992b. The modern prince. In *Selections from the Prison Notebooks of Antonio Gramsci*, edited by Q. Hoare and G.N. Smith. New York: International Publishers, 123–204.

—. 1992c. Notes on Italian history. In *Selections from the Prison Notebooks of Antonio Gramsci*, edited by Q. Hoare and G.N. Smith. New York: International Publishers, 44–120.

—. 1992d. State and civil society. In *Selections from the Prison Notebooks of Antonio Gramsci*, edited by Q. Hoare and G.N. Smith. New York: International Publishers, 206–75.

—. 1994a. The factory council. In *Pre-Prison Writings*, edited by R. Bellamy. New York: Cambridge University Press, 163–7.

—. 1994b. Some aspects of the Southern question. In *Pre-Prison Writings*, edited by R. Bellamy. New York: Cambridge University Press, 313–37.

—. 1994c. Unions and councils. In *Pre-Prison Writings*, edited by R. Bellamy. New York: Cambridge University Press, 115–20.

Hobsbawm, E.J. 1977. Gramsci and political theory. *Marxism Today* 21(7): 205–13.

Hoy, D.C. 2004. *Critical Resistance: From Poststructuralism to Post-Critique*. Cambridge, MA: MIT Press.

McCarthy, T. 1990. The critique of impure reason: Foucault and the Frankfurt school. *Political Theory* 18(3): 437–69.

Machiavelli, N. 1998. *The Prince*, translated by H.C. Mansfield. Chicago: University of Chicago Press.

Marx, K. 1978. The manifesto of the Communist Party. In *The Marx-Engels Reader*, edited by R. Tucker. New York: Norton & Company.

—. 1990. *Capital Vol. 1*, translated by B. Fowkes. New York: Penguin Books.

Pickett, B.L. 1996. Foucault and the politics of resistance. *Polity* 28(4): 445–66.

Ruti, M. 2006. *Reinventing the Soul: Poshumanist Theory and Psychic Life*. New York: Other Press.

—. 2009. *A World of Fragile Things: Psychoanalysis and the Art of Living*. Albany: State University of New York Press.

Schrag, F. 1999. Why Foucault now? *Journal of Curriculum Studies* 31(4): 375–83.

Taylor, C. 1985. Foucault on freedom and truth. In *Philosophy and the Human Sciences*. New York: Cambridge University Press, 152–83.

Chapter 5
Building a Gramsci–Foucault Axis of Democracy

Jean-Paul Gagnon

Introduction

This chapter is a work of comparisons and contrasts. It aims to meet the need for carefully built conciliatory ontologies from works within the corpuses of Gramscian and Foucauldian thought. This chapter explores how Gramsci and Foucault thought of democracy. For me it appears that both had interesting things to say about the individual. Her behaviour as a citizen, her role as a member of a society, and the expectations that she must fill are focuses. And they led me to build the argument that Gramscian and Foucauldian theory support a democracy focused on citizen-experts who actively resist power.

As Kreps captured so eloquently in his introduction to this volume, when the existing commentary on the confluence of Gramsci and Foucault is summarized, we are given three options. The first two options can be presented as follows: Gramsci is right and Foucault is wrong or vice versa. It looks to be clear at this stage of critical social theory that this ostensibly antimonious contrast has not, in the nascent moments of the twenty-first century, met with its expected grounds.

We are left then, once more as Kreps described, with a third option. He asks for us to analyse Gramsci and Foucault for union. This last and novel option is transcendental to the extent that it seeks not to dispel the existing Gramsci–Foucault antagony as there is some utility therein.[1] Gramsci and Foucault are, for instance, not the only ones in contestation with each other. There are numerous similar contestatory pairings such as between Gramsci and Norberto Bobbio; Foucault and Gilles Deleuze or Foucault and Jean-Paul Sartre. These sometimes artificially constructed antagonisms are useful for advancing debates and putting ideas into relief.

---

1 Although there are numerous examples to justify this argument, hegemony will be used as it is central to this chapter. It was in the almost combative, and certainly at times heated, debates between 'who got hegemony right' that contributions were made toward recognizing the heterogeny of hegemony. It went for example from the analogous condition of 'one correct' understanding of power to 'several correct' understandings. See Ougaard (1988), Khan (2008) and Grebe (2009) who each argue an ontology of hegemony similar to the one outlined in this note.

As Schulzke made obvious in this volume, it is in the way that we frame the differences between these two thinkers that the commonalities permitting union emerge. That is why this chapter builds two distinct, if only tenuous, conceptions of democracy. They are each built on what are arguably to be the most relevant selections from the corpus of works from Gramsci and Foucault. This has its difficulties. How do we understand 'the corpus' of one particular thinker? And how do we categorize what is most relevant? Although there are numerous ways to answer these questions, the method I use is to first collect works written for example by Foucault and to then analyse them for objects relating to the parameters associated with the ontology of basic democracy (Gagnon 2010, 2013, 2014). Examples include how the demos is bounded, the way the sovereignty of a demos is described, and the portrayal of a distinct teleology of a demos. Not all works from Gramsci or Foucault are used because some of them meet the needs of this argument more than others. This method of selecting works is endemic to grounded theory analysis (Charmaz 2006) as the selection of the works is in itself explanatory of what is included and excluded.

The 'why' in this method, however, needs an explanation. As will come to be seen further below, especially in the works listed under both Gramsci and Foucault at the end of this chapter, I focus on their writings about politics, culture, discourse, hegemony and the individual. This is the case because those works have data within them that can be constructed as objects to use for further analysis that will be conducted to achieve the aims of this chapter. That is why those works are included and all other primary works excluded.

This selection of the primary works is then followed by a programmatic investigation of literature written for example about Foucault's contributions to democracy. I have explicitly sought out works on Gramsci and/or Foucault and democracy. By collating my opinion formed during the analysis of primary documents with opinions stemming from secondary documents, it is possible to then construct a conception of democracy.

Once the construction of Gramsci and Foucault's conceptions of democracy is complete, a discussion takes place comparing and contrasting them. In Table 5.1 found nearer the end of this chapter, the clear differences, uncertain differences or commonalities, and clear commonalities between Gramscian democracy and Foucauldian democracy are presented. This leads to a discussion of a prominent and possibly normative desire on the part of both thinkers: individuals, should they expect to have or resist power, must develop expertise in political knowledge. This applies to the level of the individual (Foucault) and to the level of the group, association, class (Gramsci) or ethnicity and nation (Mann 2004).

Clarifying Explanations and Justifications

The overarching ontology framing this chapter needs attention before we can proceed to building the Gramscian conception of democracy. It has to do with post-foundationalism[2] and the thematic uncertainty underlying this work. The expression of Foucault and Gramsci as axis of democracy can only be foundational to the extent of the works drawn upon as well as the systematics behind my argumentation and method. Because of that, each step taken in the argumentation of this chapter has been as careful, capacious, meek and inclusive as possible.

This chapter contributes to the literature that uses Gramsci and Foucault to make theoretical inroads for the study of democracy. There are few if any works that are solely devoted to seeing what democratic theory might emerge through an in-depth study of Gramscian and Foucauldian primary documents.

Some might find my work convincing but it is not, in my understanding, possible nor desirable to come to a positivist and deterministic (rather than heuristic and tenuous) conclusion on the matter. To get to that point it is necessary for many other individuals to run the same gamut which may offer through meta-analysis a convergence point of contingent conclusions. Or, through fictional metaphor, by looking at all of the dozens or hundreds of different paintings about Gramsci and Foucault, the thousands of visiting audience members in the gallery will be able to come to some conclusion over the most common themes across all of the paintings. At the exit, each individual is asked: 'what do you think were the most common attributes between all the paintings?' The median from the aggregate of their opinions will be some type of convergence point. In that convergence we might then find an agreeable foundation for the subject at hand that is less parochial, less subjective, and thus possibly more 'true' – at least in the way we contemporaneously understand 'truth'.

Democracy as Class Power

Gramsci's works offer numerous points of entry into building a conception of democracy. A synthesis across dominant themes that I have constructed as objects is sought out in a selected Gramscian corpus. *In Search of the Educational Principle* (Gramsci 1965), *Religion: A Movement and an Ideology* (Gramsci 2001a) and *Economic Trends and Development* (Gramsci 2001) together offer descriptions about a type of bounded citizenry. Although Gramsci does not use the word 'demos', it appears that he had been picturing a type of tiered proletarian society that we might reasonably call a communist demos. Coutinho's (2000) argument on Gramsci's 'priority of the public' supports this view. So too do Nun and Cartier (1986: 224) and Landy (1990). The way Cammett (1967: 75) highlights how Gramsci tried to relate the factory as the equivalent of the electoral place for the bourgeois also aides in understanding the communist demos that Gramsci framed in his works.

---

2 As defined primarily by Wingenbach (2011: 3–19) and Eckersley (2011), post-foundationalism is a resistance to parochialism, to certainty, and to anthropocentrism. It needs to be inclusive, humble, and embrace complexity.

In *Towards a New Leading Group* (Gramsci 1978b), *The New Orientation* (Gramsci 1978c), and *Towards the Communist Party* (Gramsci 1977c) we see that the proletariat is meant to seize power from the bourgeois, aristocrats and their state. This shows that for Gramsci it is only the worker or labourer who holds legitimate power. He or she is the moral agent that should come to occupy different roles in governance. Government would be through the Communist Party. Sovereignty is his or hers to claim and exercise ostensibly within the framework of the Italian Communist Party. Landy (1990: 156), Mouffe (1979), Sassoon (1987) and Coutinho (2000) back this point. Landy (1990: 178) for example convincingly demonstrates that Bobbio saw the problematics between Gramsci's sovereignty of the group as it appears to be in conflict with certain theories of democracy which emphasize the sovereignty of the individual. This is a tension that Gramsci resolves in his discussion of the future.

> [From *The Prison Notebooks*] I do not think it is correct to say that the physiocrats merely represented the interests of agriculture; they represented the bourgeoisie, which was at an advanced stage of development and was the organizing force of a far more complex future society than the one they lived in – they certainly did not represent mercantilism and the guild system, etc. Historically, the physiocrats did in fact represent the break with the guild system and the expansion of capitalist economic activity into the countryside; theirs was the 'language' of the time, an unmediated expression of the contrast between city and country. (Gramsci 2007, Notebook 13, §13)

Is it too far of a stretch to think that Gramsci might have thought that the proletarian vanguard could have made a break with the capitalist system and moved into a social democratic system in the future? After reading his works it seems that the process would have evolved from an initial forced collective behaviour by the Communist Party to something more democratic.

It is mostly in Gramsci's writings on education, politics, language and culture (see *Politics and Culture* (Gramsci 1985a), *Language, Linguistics and Folklore* (Gramsci 1985b), and *Popular Literature* (Gramsci 1985c)) that he elaborates on the importance for the proletariat to be in command of this form of communication. They must communicate their awareness, their mutual education, and their normative desires to each other to achieve awareness and ascend to a higher culture. Morera (1990: 24), Nun (1987), and Nun and Cartier (1986: 202) support this argument. For the latter, the authors offer insight into Gramsci's ostensible role for political communication: it needed to change 'common sense' in the proletariat so as to make the collective the power-holders and not subjects of the bourgeois. This emphasis on communication and education looks to be the forced measure Gramsci thought was needed to break from capitalism. Hill (2007: 135, 165, 199) is also useful in backing this point. Communication was the foundation for 'neohumanstic reform' through democracy.

Gramsci's code for this break from capitalism comes mainly in the rejection of the existing state, the international order of relations, and in his discussions on the role of the politburo (or party leadership). Leaders must and can only be decided by the proletarian mass – once the mass has of course ascended to Gramsci's conception of 'higher culture'. Nevertheless, there is mention of leadership before the proletariat's cultural ascendency which was needed to force education and political communication. See *Religion: A Movement and an Ideology* (Gramsci 2001a) and *Towards a New Leading Group* (Gramsci 1978b) for more. Fonte's (2000: 50) argument that Gramsci saw the *Modern Prince* (Gramsci 1992b) as the Communist Party itself is helpful. But it seems to cancel out the idea of a leadership decided by the demos. As can be seen across much of his primary works, Gramsci writes that the proletariat must first be made 'aware' and can then act in 'democracy'. Leadership then seems to be modelled on a type of democratic centralism that incorporates both democratic and autocratic elements. That view is supported by Gramsci's writings on the structure of the Communist Party which in itself is a mixture of the two.

It is, for me, clear in *Socialism and Fascism* (Gramsci 1978a) as well as in *Soviets in Italy* (Gramsci 1968) that law or the expression of hegemony is only permitted from the proletarian demos and, more precisely, its governing bodies (such as the party leadership). Nun and Cartier (1986: 224) suggest Gramsci was building his view of legal legitimacy from Rousseau. Law must come from the popular will. It would first have to come from the 'aware' and then come from the 'aware' proletarian mass through the party leadership.

Gramsci discusses, at least implicitly, through his writings on the Communist Party and the justifications for proletarian emancipation the need for the worker mass to have homogeneous visions for the future. It might be argued that this is the removal of class, economic and militaristic oppression. See *Science, Logic and Translatability*, (Gramsci 2001b) *The Philosophy of Benedetto Croce* (Gramsci 2001c) and *Bordiga's Polemic* (Gramsci 1977b) as Gramsci discusses teleology to some lengths across these works. I argue that Nun and Cartier (1986: 204) and Fonte (2000: 51) are in agreement with my observation. Whilst Nun and Cartier rely on evidence from the *Quaderni*, Fonte makes my point in a discussion of G.W.F. Hegel, Richard Rorty, Walt Whitman and John Dewey whose roles in his work are built on a Gramscian foundation.

The discussion above leads to Gramsci's concept of cultural hegemony (Mouffe 1979 is central here). Gramsci's appropriation of Hegelian or Crocean (possibly Nietzschean, see Emden 2005; Katsafanas 2005 for more) thought about the power of consciousness and its expression through language to meet Marxist aims was new for the then European intellectual climate. By having experts change culture through making the individuals composing the proletariat aware of bourgeois and aristocratic dominance, social transformation would, in Gramsci's thinking, occur. To my contemporaries reading this, that may seem rather undemocratic. Gramsci argued that the demos deserved democracy but first had to realize that they needed democracy for their emancipation. The path to this awareness for Gramsci is in some ways autocratic: (forced?) education, specific or different literature, and the overall control by experts in the communist vanguard or party leadership would lead to democracy.

This evidence makes it difficult to reconcile Gramsci with certain conceptions of democracy (e.g. most democracies from the liberal typology). However, there are democratic elements to Gramscian thought and these are the ones I focus on. Even though Gramsci's political ethology is not the same as mine in this chapter (because Foucault is interpreted and synthesized with Gramsci) it is not unreasonable or improper to borrow insights that Gramsci gives about democracy in order to build a Gramscian conception of democracy.

To understand this position further we must first look at how Gramsci appears to bind the demos – or in his case, the proletariat as democratic hegemon. *Analysis of Situations/Relations of Force* (1980) outlines one boundary: it is clear therein that Gramsci saw the world as a place of nation-states that operate a network of international power. This was not in favour of the proletariat but rather, as seen in later works (the 1939–45 blocs), a place for the domination or indoctrination of individuals regarding one capitalist (notably unfriendly to the socialist) system. However, the transnationalism of the proletariat can take this situation and make it into its own system of force.

That binary between the proletariat as demos and the state, inclusive of nations and their international relations, is useful. It helps us to understand that Gramsci contrasted the demos with the bourgeois and aristocratic oppressors backed by militarism, spin and capital. It reveals a demos bounded by a conception of class and not necessarily restricted by state or national borders. Gramsci appears to have had little sympathy for the more hawkish Italian partisan communists as their emphasis on violence reflected the brutality of nascent fascism in Italy as well as Europe more widely. It was about 'class war' and not 'violent war'. Aside from the fact that destroying the Italian bourgeois or aristocrats would have been highly improbable, it still appears that this was an option not at least readily tabled by Gramsci. His focus was on culture, and not violence, as a definer of hegemony.

Landy (1979: 158–9) brings a strong point to this discussion. Gramsci was for most of his writing years in anxiety over (i) how to unlock the potential for workers to effect social change and (ii) how to defy not only Italian but the more perfidious sort of European fascism. For the latter, this is especially obvious in his *Quaderni del Carcere* or *Prison Notebooks* (1992a). For the former, a lot of attention is given to this question possibly due to his entrepreneurial role in helping to establish the Italian Communist Party. For the reasons of needing to be practical and politically effective, Gramsci had to grapple with hegemony. It is his cleverness and his willingness to engage with contemporaries (Nun 1986: 199) that led to his arguments for culture and language as being the frames of hegemony enacted by the unknowing consent of the workers. The solution for Gramsci and one that I still think is convincing in method today (apart from its autocratic leanings), was or is creating awareness in the proletariat through education and expert leadership.

As can be seen in what the literature appears to have configured as Gramsci's 'cultural writings' (see, for example, Gramsci 1985 and 2001) he places great emphasis on the need for communication as a means to empowering the demos.

Language, journalism and literature shape the contours of culture and thus structure power relations. Here there is certainly agreement with Foucault, but more on that later. This may help to explain why Gramsci places as much importance as he does on the proletariat realizing itself (awareness), educating itself (not being educated by the bourgeois system), and enacting itself (not being influenced by power through dominant bourgeois culture). By either seizing communication or denying communication from the bourgeois or aristocracy, the proletarian demos logically gains hegemony.

There are difficulties in the way Gramsci contemporaneously framed the demos. For him, it was about mass. There are few instances where he gives a philosophy of the self as a dialectic in relation to the proletariat. For example, in *Towards the Communist Party* (1977c) or *The Young Socialist* (1977a) there is that sense of dialectic between individual and institution or individual and the self (for the latter especially in *The Young Socialist* (1977a)). There is too the sense that these writings are at the same time normative and personal but still looking at the individual from above. In other words it is about what the individual should be doing to strengthen the hegemony of the proletariat.

Overall, Gramsci's theory of democracy is predicated on formulating the demos as the working mass separate to capitalist culture and its bourgeois acolytes. We know today that words like 'the people', 'mass' and 'the proletariat' are myths. But they were not myths it seems for Gramsci as generalizing individuals in this way was common across most political spectrums in Europe during the early twentieth century. There are nevertheless nuances that deserve attention. The hierarchies and different roles in the Communist Party as well as working class organizations could play a role in how Gramsci viewed the demos. My portrayal of the Gramscian demos is not a homogeneous mass but rather a collection of workers inhabiting different, changeable roles.

Gramsci places sovereignty in this demos. He tries to figure out ways of exercising this sovereignty or even shifting it from illegitimate locales like the bourgeois state to his demos. That is where Gramscian praxes become most apparent: it is the need to realize this theoretical condition that drives Gramsci towards a 'democratic' stump regarding education, communication, and, eventually, leadership. This one way of constructing Gramsci's democracy culminates in the belief of the expert intellectual. This type of person is aware of hegemony. She is enlightened with philosophy, and through that controls or affects culture and thus power. It is Gramsci's desire for workers to have such power as this, collectively, will then lead to the Gestalt switch that he was after. No longer would the bourgeois, or capitalism, or the state monopolize the power of norm setting. Power would be the sole prerogative of the expert proletarian demos. This is one way of explaining what Gramsci's 'higher culture' may have been.

It is here specifically that a major contrast appears between Gramscian and Foucauldian hegemony. Foucault, as will be seen in the next section below, rejects the proletariat and the view that sees politics as only the struggle between classes. Hegemon is the individual – all else is dominance over the individual being human.

Democracy as Person Power

In comparison to Gramsci, Foucault's writing is much more nuanced regarding democracy. It may even be argued that democracy was not really part of Foucault's intellectual mandate. And this is reflected in the secondary literature. Although there is a substantive body of literature on Foucault's contributions to liberal democracy there is still far more writing available on Gramsci and democracy than there is on Foucault and democracy. Indeed, aside from liberal theory, Foucault seems to only be linked to radical conceptions of democracy.

It is mainly in the conception of biopolitics that Foucault builds throughout his three (and almost four) volumes of *The History of Sexuality* (Foucault 1978) that we can construct some idea of citizenship. Boundaries of 'we' are also discussed in *Kant on Enlightenment and Revolution* (Foucault 1986). Biebricher (2007: 235–6) supports this point with his discussion of Foucault's 'resisting individuals'.

I argue that Foucault is both suspicious of the sovereignty of reason and desirous to have sovereignty more dispersed among heterogeneous individuals in *Madness and Civilization* (Foucault 1988). This is elaborated further in *Society Must be Defended* (Foucault 2003) where we see, especially in relation to biopower, Foucault's refutation of socialism due to its abuses of the individual. Olssen (2002: 486) supports this point in his argument that Foucault wanted a balance between the power of the individual and the power of society. Foucault leaned more towards the complexity and difference inherent in the human being and her history when arguing how this constructs layered societies.

The Subject and Power (Foucault 1982) offers insights into the function of communication: it is both an actant and changer of existing power. This is elaborated upon in *Orders of Discourse* (Foucault 1971: 3). Walter (2008: 537–8) supports this point in his critique of mainly John Dryzek and Iris Marion Young's conception of deliberative democracy. Expert knowledge often determines the ontology of communication in any given society.

The Subject and Power (Foucault 1982) offers insights into Foucault's conception of leadership. It (leadership) was not something decided by the demos as the demos is populated by subjects. We may argue then that he sees the demos selecting leadership in a way that avoids subjectifying the human being. *The Archaeology of Knowledge* (1969, especially page 176) plays a central role here too. Biebricher (2007) and Olssen (2002) are in support of this point. Schrift (2000: 155) is also important especially his discussion of how Mouffe and Laclau's conception of radical democracy synthesizes with Foucault's unfinished project of the 'hermeneutic of the self'. Schrift's discussion points to the need for leadership to be fluid, dynamic, and non-dominant in the autocratic and totalitarian sense.

Across *Madness and Civilization* (1988), *The Birth of the Clinic* (1963), and *The Order of Things* (1966), especially in the dualism of the self (body/self), I argue that law has to come not entirely from outside but also from within the person. See also *Spaces of Security* (1978a) *Alternatives to the Prison* (2009), and *The Archaeology of Knowledge* (1969). Walter's (2008: 534) discussion of Dryzek's critique of legal expertise helps to make this point. But it also helps to highlight the resistance that Foucault had to being foundational. Anyone can be an expert so long as they have power within discourse through knowledge which was Dyrzek's point.

I think that for Foucault the only certainty is resistance to power. The heterotopy of the 'resisting individual' appears to be the teleology of his conception of democracy if one existed. It is in the *Orders of Discourse* (Foucault 1971: 7–8) that this point is made clear. Foucault himself is expressing the tension between the individual resisting power and the institution establishing the dominance of power over the individual for the individual to be subject within. Although Weymans (2009) supports the point in his discussion of Marcel Gauchet and Gladys Swain's result showing that individuals were resisting in asylums during French 'modernity', I needed to leave the secondary literature to further back this point. Grant (2010), Wisnewski (2000) as well as Yates and Hiles (2010) can together make the point that the 'resistant self' is a constant in Foucauldian teleology.

Before moving into the summative description of Foucauldian democracy, it would be good to discuss his first three books: *Madness and Civilization* (1988), *The Birth of the Clinic* (1963), and *The Order of Things* (1966). Foucault delivers a useful heuristic for thinking about the individual (down-up) and the mostly illegitimate hegemon (top-down). In *Madness and Civilization* for example and his later positions on the anti-psychiatric movements of the '50s and '60s onwards, mental illness is not considered a fabrication: it is possibly there as a medically determined condition. But the individual being labelled as 'mad' or 'ill' too has the freedom not to be punished because of, for example, a lack of conformity to supposed rational culture. So on the one hand there is technocratic medical advance with its own legitimate hegemony but on the other hand there is also the advance of the rights of the individual to not be forced into 'treatment' or 'confinement'. In short, this is a foundation for Foucault's biopolitics and reflects the balance that Olssen (2008) opined was present in the way Foucault saw the critical or resistant self in relation to societies.

This foundation is revelatory to the extent that it is also in some sense a treatise for the emancipation of the self. I interpret it as a call for the explosion of the heterotopy of individuals in contestation to how Foucault saw modernity and its logos of false uniformity and order. That position does not deviate much from Dahl's (1989) pluralism, Keane's (2009) pluriverse, or Latour's (1993) hybrids[3] (also Haraway's (1991) cyborgs) which points to Foucauldian democracy as something capacious, inclusive, and complex. In *the Order of Things* (1966) it is especially clear, in his placement of the individual, that Foucault is speaking to discourse framed by historicism as the structural determinant of power.

3 For coverage of Latourian hybridity, see Blok and Jensen (2011).

Foucault does not readily give a boundary to a demos. But this does not mean that we cannot construct a conception of a Foucauldian democracy. In his work on governmentality and biopolitics it is possible to see that the demos is fabricated by the state. Although Foucault does not argue this, I feel that his critique leads us to the view that for the individual to exist this must happen outside of hegemonic structures. These include the institutions of the state or the cultures of reason superimposed over individuals or that individuals impose over themselves. Togetherness, in the sense of individuals forming associations, led to an exponential increase in the power of biopolitics from down-up. But these will invariably form different discursive power relations and possibly – only rarely – an actual majority derived from the heterotopy of power formed when people associate through the affinity of choice.

For Foucault, one type of sovereignty exists in the nation-state and its institutions (see *Security, Territory, Population* 1977) but that it is not the sole legitimator of power. There is a heterotopy of power which is expressed in the way Foucault explores the self, others, and governing institutions. That, under this logical frame, supports the argument that the individual might be viewed as the only legitimate sovereign in Foucauldian democracy. Then there is the exercise of sovereignty which is fundamentally based on the act of complex, heterogeneous individuals resisting not only the power of state, institutions or nature, but also the power of each other and themselves. This is one reason why 'Marxists' have typically attacked Foucault because they mistakenly placed his thinking as supportive of liberal understandings of democracy that uphold the capitalist bourgeois system. Foucault, in my opinion, supports nothing other than the emancipation of the self and the fundamental distrust of power. Open and inclusive critique free of violence democratizes discourse and, through that, dilutes power.

The position on the self, summarized above, is the foundation for Foucault's thoughts on political communication, law, leadership and long-term societal goals. As Foucault argued in *The Subject and Power* (1982: 780–82), his works to that date were not predicated on studying power but rather the resistance if not contradiction to power. Taking note that this was written but two years before his death it is striking that the democracy literature is not more emphatic about this point. Indeed, the focus on resistance is relegated to radicalism in politics and the protest against the few dominant contemporary forms of democracy in practice. This is not a bad thing, but it is limiting. The act of the self in contradiction if not dialectic to the power of the state-prescribed conception of the 'citizen' might in itself be a recipe for future democratic change. Although this point will be contentious, Foucault's 'resisting self' could be looked for by democratic theorists in re-readings of history to come up with a new theory of democracy in action across time and space: the theory of resistance democracy.

Table 5.1 Commonality and difference in Gramscian and Foucauldian democracy

	Foucault		
	Clear Difference	*Uncertain Difference or Commonality*	*Clear Commonality*
Gramsci	Foucault does not allow for what I agree as being the 'myth of the people' or other categories like the proletariat. As Gramsci relies on these myths, it is a clear difference.	The effects of culture and language on power seem to be both easily agreeable and disagreeable. The difference is in first order statements from both thinkers. The telos is the commonality.	The individual is subject to fabricated power. This is sometimes the result of the individual's ignorance, sometimes the fault of history, or culture, or discourse, or economy.
	Foucault places legitimate sovereign power within the individual whilst Gramsci places it first with the expert vanguard in the Party leadership and then with the proletariat.	Experts are the educated elite for Gramsci. It is their responsibility to make individual workers 'aware'. Expertise is knowledge held by those who care to access it for Foucault. It is needed to resist the dominance created by experts (politicians, technocrats, etc.) who claim authority.	The State and its international relations is a container of power. There are divisions of populations within the State, or the province, town, etc., and power is held in different ways and by different groups but mostly those above the peasantry/proletariat or individual. For Foucault this is apparent concerning any subalterns.
	Gramsci sees sovereignty of the proletariat and the transcendence of class politics as the end result of socialist democracy. Foucault sees only the continuation of individual heterotopies resisting power through critique no matter how that manifests democratically. The first sees democracy as a means to an end. The second sees multifarious democracies (or other politics) as means to constant ends.	Individuals have the capacity to change culture or discourse. For Gramsci this is emancipatory: the culturally heightened individual leads the vanguard of 'simple people' (see Nun and Cartier 2000: 206). For Foucault, individuals escaping subjectivity appears impossible unless discourse or historicism changes through constant resistance.	Citizens require expert knowledge. This knowledge should be about diluting power. They must also understand their role as selves in dialectic to the role of citizen. Finally, this expertise will allow for an emancipated politics for the self, association and demos. Awareness, in other words, will rescue democracy and flip the Gestalt switch that Foucault and Gramsci were possibly after: the equitable sovereignty of individuals.

Discussion – Expert Democracy?

Throughout the evidence and discussion presented in the two earlier sections of this chapter, where Gramscian and Foucauldian conceptions of democracy are constructed, there has been both commonality and difference between the two thinkers. Following the method used by Mann (2004) to make heuristic-based arguments clearer I have in Table 5.1 categorized 'clear difference', 'uncertain difference or commonality', and 'clear commonality' between Gramsci and Foucault.

Both agree that language or discourse is a determiner of hegemony in the given society that uses this discourse. History as shaped by discourse and discourse as shaped by history is a circular device of some use to both thinkers. Culture, as a container of power, also seems to be a point of agreement between the two thinkers although it is clear that they differ on first order principles. For Gramsci, culture is the determiner of discourse whereas for Foucault it appears that discourse is the determiner of culture. To me the symbiosis is apparent: discourse and culture affect each other. They might even be one and the same as culture can be the expression of discourse which means that a change in discourse can affect culture.

In *The Order of Things* (Foucault 1966) it becomes instantaneously clear that Gramsci's work on culture and Foucault's work on episteme are commensurable. They both speak to the possibility of a paradigm shift in human societies. Foucault describes these changes throughout his studies of medical and scientific history. Epistemological shifts happened in history. They can happen again. It then follows that Gramsci was not incorrect in his thinking that changing culture through education, language and literature (i.e. popular discourse) was possible. It still is possible.

As can be seen in Table 5.1, Gramsci and Foucault substantively differ in their first order arguments as well as moral philosophies. And although my ultimate argument built from Gramscian and Foucauldian thought – that citizen experts are needed – was given at the beginning of this chapter, it was by no means a fait accompli when research for this work was undertaken. Indeed, it was of significant surprise to find the agreements between the two thinkers that permitted me to build this axis of democracy: the axis of expert-citizens and resistance to power.

Conclusion – Paths Leading Elsewhere

It pays to note that Gramsci was an advocate of a 'democratic road to socialism' (Morera 1990: 23). This was a position formed probably due to his distaste for fascism and its version of the 'dictatorship of the people'. Although Gramsci does not explicitly detail his conception(s) of democracy, he has left enough for the convergence to form through numerous contingent readings by others of his writings. When collating my readings of Gramsci's primary works with the arguments formed in the secondary works, the synthesis seems to support a compassionate, equitable, but inescapably foundational and thus flawed conception of democracy. Democracy was the route for Gramsci to attain the emancipation of the working masses. It flew in the face of the need to recognize that Marx and Lenin were not right about everything and that the party leadership would not be able to meet his utopian vision of benevolent expertise. Nevertheless, although democracy was a means to an end for Gramsci, his heuristics were contemporaneously important to counter fascism. When taken with the required amount of salt as post-foundationalists do, many of his normative and more equitable desires are still of importance today.

Foucault approaches the conclusions of Gramsci from his own points of departure. My chapter highlights the differences of origins in argumentation between the two thinkers but in the end highlights the view that they seem to come to agreement over empowering the individual (or citizen) with expertise. It was Foucault's way of questioning the structures and origins of discourses that led to his criticisms of forms of governmentality and dominance. The focus on the complexity of the individual and its societies in his historical as well as contemporaneous works (circa 1960s, '70s and '80s) can be established as an emancipation of the self. I am uncertain if Gramsci would have reached this point. Nevertheless, I reason that both support the argument that the individual must have hegemony and must be an expert on the transmutations of power and how it affects human beings.

In the end, the conclusion of this chapter reached in the final row of the last column in Table 5.1 points invariably to an unfinished project affecting the politics of today. From studies into the diffusion of political knowledge (Rapeli 2014 and 2013), or a citizen's knowledge of politics, and of a practitioner's (i.e. politician's or bureaucrat's) knowledge of normative expectations from political philosophers, it is critically clear that the majority of individuals populating those categories are failing to reach variously constructed bottom parameters.

The Gramsci–Foucault axis of democracy is based on the need for each individual to have expertise in politics. This I think would today encompass the expectations experts have for democratization, democracy practices, and the way that power within democracy and power exercised by the individuals and associations composing the demos occurs. The two thinkers and my interpretation of their thoughts in this chapter, point to the need for a turn in human knowledge: a turn towards politics, philosophy, social theory, and in the end, knowledge of democracy.

References

Biebricher, T. 2007. Habermas and Foucault: Deliberative democracy and strategic state analysis. *Contemporary Political Theory* 6(2): 218–45.

Blok, A. and Jensen, T.E. (eds) 2011. *Bruno Latour: Hybrid Thoughts in a Hybrid World*. London: Routledge.

Cammett, J.M. 1967. *Antonio Gramsci and the Origins of Italian Communism*. Stanford, CA: Stanford University Press.

Coutinho, C.N. 2000. General will and democracy. In *Rousseau, Hegel, and Gramsci. Rethinking Marxism* 12(2): 1–17.

Dahl, R. 1989. *Democracy and Its Critics*. New Haven: Yale University Press.

Eckersley, R. 2011. Representing Nature. In *The Future of Representative Democracy*, edited by S. Alonso, J. Keane and W. Merkel. Cambridge, UK: Cambridge University Press.

Emden, C.J. 2005. *Nietzsche on Language, Consciousness, and the Body*. Urbana: University of Illinois Press.

Fonte, J. 2000. Gramsci's revenge: Reconstructing American democracy. *Academic Questions* 13(2): 49–62.

Foucault, M. 1961. *Histoire de la Folie* à *l'Âge Classique* [or, in 2006, *Madness in Civilization: A History of Insanity in the Age of Reason*]. Paris: Plon.

—. 1963. *Naissance de la Clinique: Une Archéologie du Regard Medical* [or, in 1973, *The Birth of the Clinic: An Archaeology of Medical Perception*]. Paris: PUF.

—. 1966. *Les Mots et les Choses: Une Archélogie des Sciences Humaines* [or, in 1970, *The Order of Things: An Archaeology of the Human Sciences*]. Paris: Gallimard.

—. 1969. *L'Archéologie du Savoir* [or, in 2002, *The Archaeology of Knowledge*]. Paris: Gallimard.

—. 1970. The Archaeology of Knowledge. *Social Science Information* 9(1): 175–85.

—. 1971. Orders of Discourse. *Social Science Information* 10(2): 7–30.

—. 1976. *La Volunté de Savoir* [or, in 1978, *The Will to Knowledge*]. Paris. Gallimard.

—. 1977. Security, territory, population. In *Lectures at the Collège de France*, Volume 4, edited by M. Senellart, translated by G. Burchell. New York: Picador.

—. 1978a. Spaces of security: The example of the town. Lecture of 11 January 1978. *Political Geography* 26(1): 48–56.

—. 1978b. *History of Sexuality, Vol.1: An Introduction*, translated by R. Hurley. New York: Pantheon Books

—. 1982. The Subject and Power. *Critical Inquiry* 8(4): 777–95.

—. 1984a. *L'Usage des Plaisirs* [or, in 1985, *The Use of Pleasure*]. Paris: Gallimard.

—. 1984b. *Le Souci de Soi* [or, in 1988, *The Care of the Self*]. Paris: Gallimard.

—. 1986. Kant on enlightenment and revolution. *Economy and Society* 15(1): 88–96.

—. 2003. Society must be defended. In *Lectures at the Collège de France*. NY: Picador.

—. 2009. Alternatives to the prison: Dissemination or decline of social control? *Theory, Culture and Society* 26(6): 12–24.

Gagnon, J.P. 2010. Democratic theory and theoretical physics. *Taiwan Journal of Democracy* 6(2): 1–22.

—. 2013. *Evolutionary Basic Democracy: A Critical Overture*. Basingstoke: Palgrave Macmillan.

—. 2014. *Democratic Theorists in Conversation: Turns in Contemporary Thought*. Basingstoke: Palgrave Macmillan.

Gramsci, A. 1965 [circa 1929–35]. In search of the educational principle. *New Left Review* 32: 55–62.

—. 1968 [circa 1920]. Soviets in Italy. *New Left Review* 51: 28.

—. 1977a. The young socialist. In *Selections from Political Writings 1910–1920*. London: ElecBook.

—. 1977b. Bordiga's polemic. In *Selections from Political Writings 1910–1920*. London: ElecBook.

—. 1977c. Towards the Communist Party. In *Selections from Political Writings 1910–1920*. London: ElecBook.

—. 1978a. Socialism and fascism. In *Selections from Political Writings 1921–1926*. London: ElecBook.

—. 1978b. Towards a new leading group. In *Selections from Political Writings 1921–1926*. London: ElecBook.

—. 1978c. The new orientation. In *Selections from Political Writings 1921–1926*. London: ElecBook.

—. 1980 [circa 1929–1935]. Análisis de las situaciones. Relaciones de fuerzas [Analysis of situations: Relations of force]. *Nueva Antropología* 4(15–16): 7–18.

—. 1985a [circa 1916–35]. Politics and culture. In *Selections from Cultural Writings*. London: ElecBook.

—. 1985b [circa 1916–35]. Language, linguistics and folklore. In *Selections from Cultural Writings*. London: ElecBook.

—. 1985c [circa 1916–35]. Popular literature. In *Selections from Cultural Writings*. London: ElecBook.

—. 1992a. *Selections from the Prison Notebooks of Antonio Gramsci*, edited by Q. Hoare and G.N. Smith. New York: International Publishers, 123–204.

—. 1992b. The modern prince. In *Selections from the Prison Notebooks of Antonio Gramsci*, edited by Q. Hoare and G.N. Smith. New York: International Publishers, 123–204.

—. 2001a [circa 1916–35]. Religion: A movement and an ideology. In *Further Selections from Prison Notebooks*. London: ElecBook.

—. 2001b [circa 1916–35]. Science, logic and translatability. In *Further Selections from Prison Notebooks*. London: ElecBook.

—. 2001c [circa 1916–35]. The philosophy of Benedetto Croce. In *Further Selections from Prison Notebooks*. London: ElecBook.

Grant, J. 2010. Foucault and the logic of dialectics. *Contemporary Political Theory* 9(2): 220–38.

Grebe, E. 2009. Contingency, contestation and hegemony. *Philosophy and Social Criticism* 35(5): 589–611.

Haraway, D. 1991. A cyborg manifesto: Science, technology, and socialist-feminism in the late twentieth century. In *Donna Haraway's Simians, Cyborgs and Women: The Reinvention of Nature*. London: Routledge.

Hill, D.J. 2007. *Hegemony and Education: Gramsci, Post-Marxism and Radical Democracy Revisited.* London: Rowman and Littlefield.

Katsafanas, P. 2005. Nietzsche's theory of mind: Consciousness and conceptualization. *European Journal of Philosophy* 13(1): 1–31.

Keane, J. 2009. *The Life and Death of Democracy*. New York: Simon and Schuster.

Khan, G.A. 2008. Pluralisation: An alternative to hegemony. *The British Journal of Politics and International Relations* 10(2): 194–209.

Landy, M. 1990. Review essay on socialism and/or democracy: Gramsci and/or Bobbio? *Boundary 2* 17(3): 154–89.

Latour, B. 1993. *We Have Never Been Modern*. Cambridge, MA: Harvard University Press.

Mann, M. 2004. *The Dark Side of Democracy: Explaining Ethnic Cleansing*. Cambridge: Cambridge University Press.

Morera, E. 1990. Gramsci and democracy. *Canadian Journal of Political Science* 23(1): 23–37.

Mouffe, C. (ed.) 1979. *Gramsci and Marxist Theory*. London: Routledge and Kegan Paul.

Nun, J. 1987. Elementos para una teoría de la democracía: Gramsci y el sentido commun [Elements for a theory of democracy: Gramsci and common sense]. *Revista Mexicana de Sociología* [*Mexican Review of Sociology*] 49: 21–54.

Nun, J. and Cartier, W. 1986. Elements for a theory of democracy: Gramsci and common sense. *Boundary 2* 14(3): 197–229.

Olssen, M. 2002. Michel Foucault as 'thin' communitarian: Difference, community, democracy. *Cultural Studies <=> Critical Methodologies* 2(4): 483–513.

Ougaard, M. 1988. Dimensions of hegemony. *Cooperation and Conflict* 23(2): 197–214.

Rapeli, L. 2013. *The Conception of Citizen Knowledge in Democratic Theory*. London: Palgrave Macmillan.

—. 2014. What Should the Citizen Know about Politics? Two Approaches to the Measurement of Political Knowledge. *Democratic Theory*, 1(1): 58–93.

Sassoon, A.S. 1987. *Gramsci's Politics*. Minneapolis/St. Paul: University of Minnesota Press.

Schrift, A.D. 2000. Nietzsche, Foucault, Deleuze, and the subject of radical democracy. *Angelaki: Journal of the Theoretical Humanities* 5(2): 151–61.

Walter, R. 2008. Foucault and radical deliberative democracy. *Australian Journal of Political Science* 43(3): 531–46.

Weymans, W. 2009. Revising Foucault's model of modernity and exclusion: Gauchet and Swain on madness and democracy. *Thesis Eleven* 98(1): 33–51.

Wingenbach, E. 2011. *Institutionalizing Agonistic Democracy*. Farnham, UK: Ashgate.

Wisnewski, J.J. 2000. Foucault and public autonomy. *Continental Philosophy Review* 33(4): 417–39.

Yates, S and Dave, H. 2010. Towards a 'critical ontology of ourselves'? Foucault, subjectivity and discourse analysis. *Theory and Psychology* 20(1): 52–75.

Chapter 6
Subalternity In and Out of Time, In and Out of History

Sonita Sarker

Subalternity

In these times, which have come to be known in the United States of America as the era of the 99 percent, the crisis that comes immediately to attention has two main features: political disenfranchisement and stark economic disparity. The 99 percent appears to include a cross-section of at least two distinct identities. In one such group are peoples that have been historically marginalized and continue to experience the same, if not aggravated, conditions of disenfranchisement. In another such group are peoples who appear to have gained and enjoyed access to political voice and economic stability but find themselves 'newly' marginalized – we experience the gap between the symbolic nature and the actual manifestation of these rights (Boydston 2012; Moore 2012; NACLA 2012; Schneider 2012). On closer examination, these two groups are not homogeneous; there are conflicts and contestations about this global movement's moral foundations and representation of minority issues such as those of women and people of color (Haidt 2012; Pollitt 2012; Campbell 2011). Yet, the diversity and range of the movement against exploitative hegemonic economic and political conditions depicts not only a critical mass of resistance but a contemporary formation of what Antonio Gramsci calls 'subaltern' which is at once derived from sociocultural identity and manifested in 'wars of position' (Gramsci 1971: 88).

In this dialectic of ethnicized/racialized identities and the experience of structural minoritization, particularly as that unfolds in the context of neocolonial globalization today, the two groups described in the opening of this chapter can be said to signify both the 'subaltern ' (identified as a specific group) and 'subalternity ' (a condition that many beyond such groups experience). In his early writings (*Oppressed and Oppressors* 1911), Gramsci is aware of the colonial and colonizing dimensions globally, even as he focuses on the local ramifications of Sardinia and Sicily in relation to the Italian nation-state (Rosengarten 2009). In his later writings, Gramsci moves the definition of 'subaltern' from the literal to the figurative (Green 2002). So while 'subaltern' could refer to a particular group such as the proletariat, and not always in the context of colonialism, subalternity as a condition may encompass a larger group, as it does today, one that experiences subordination/oppression in their lack of access or power to control their labour, production, and capital (Prakash 1994; Srivastava and Bhattacharya 2012). In the two groups described in the opening paragraph, there are the 'subaltern' in the sense that they are identified as 'the oppressed' who experience a coloniality of power (Mignolo 2001). Even though the term 'subaltern' has been equated with the word 'people' (Mignolo 2005; Guha 1988), it can also refer figuratively to territories in a subordinate position, such as Sardinia (Gramsci's own cultural origin) and Sicily (Gramsci's preoccupation with the Italian South).

If either part of the dialectic were emphasized at the expense of the other, thereby eliminating the dialectic effectively, the result would be structural analysis evacuated of identity or essentialist identities devoid of context. In analyses of 'subaltern' groups, identitarian/identity politics (i.e., ascribing the term 'subaltern' to specific groups) or focus on one part of the dialectic maintains hegemonic hierarchies of 'the powerful' and 'the powerless,' ironically often in anti- or postcolonial historiography (Spivak 1988). Even 'subalternity' as a condition signifies to some degree that it is inherent, thus naturalized, in group identities. To the extent that 'subaltern' in particular but also 'subalternity' essentialize powerlessness and lack of agency, I agree with Spivak that subaltern should indicate 'a position without identity' (2005: 476). Spivak's view also draws attention to the systemic and systematic nature of how this identity is enforced and maintained. To make visible this structural nature of the experience of the two groups above, I make a distinction between 'subaltern' and 'subalternized'— I use the latter to mean that being subaltern is not an inherent, natural condition but made to appear as such as an historically understood position. This distinction becomes significant in the analysis, later in this chapter, of the work of groups such as the Indigenous Women's Network (IWN) and the Feminist Dalit Solidarity Organization (FEDO), since the dialectic of identity and position becomes a core issue. In other words, on the one hand, groups that are positioned as the disadvantaged caste/class in terms of citizenship derive their very grounding from belief in this historical identity of subordination; on the other hand, their struggles of political empowerment are motivated by the desire to surpass the disenfranchisement based in this very identity.

Time and History

The discussion below seeks to make visible the matrices in which this dialectic of subalternity is lodged, namely, those of time and history. This section surveys the Western European trajectory of thinking about time and history in and against which Antonio Gramsci and Michel Foucault write. Following that, I map a lineage of thought across the twentieth century, from Gramsci (on 'subaltern') through Foucault (on 'subjugated knowledges') to the present moment. I argue that a foundational part of those matrices is the interpretation of history as distinct from time, as emerges from my reading of Gramsci's and Foucault's writings. In my view, this distinction creates the grounds on which the positions of the marginalized are marked.

To contest perceptions about these 'times' and 'peoples' as homogenous or unique, the discussion marks the changes in the contexts in which 'time,' 'history' and 'subaltern' gather meaning, i.e., in the movement from modernity to postmodernity and, in conjunction, from colonialism to postcolonialism.

It may seem surprising to draw from a distant past in order to connect the first of three delineations of time/history to the twentieth-century theorizings of Gramsci and Foucault. The intention is not only to demonstrate the long-standing views on time and history, but also to mark the different directions that Gramsci and Foucault both take. The first view evident in Western European theory and philosophy is of time as absolute, objective, and neutral, as seen in Isaac Newton's *Principia Mathematica* (1687). Time is a 'frame of reference' (Christian 2011: 357) to organize rhythms of the natural world that are also seen as repeated and unitary, even though they are also changing. What in Newton's view is 'God's time' (Ermarth 2010: 321) becomes an a priori form of perception in Immanuel Kant's understanding of time or 'world time' (Braudel 1984; Eberhard 1965). The concept to have the most impact, even indirectly, on Gramsci's and Foucault's analysis of modernity is that of time as linearity in Hegel's thinking, a concept that underlays the epistemology of colonialism. It is this notion of linearity that allows not only for a teleology of 'progress' (Adam 1994; Gell 1992; Giddens 1979) but makes room for anthropologists, among others, to present the 'un-modern' (native, subaltern, indigenous) as living in cyclical time or even in an absence of time (Perrett 1999; referring to James Mill's *The History of British India*, Banerjee 2006; Berman 2006).

As Friese observes:

> The predominant theoretical edifices of sociological reasoning about time attach the hegemonic concept of time to the (industrial-capitalist) organization of the economy, they see it as founded in the division of social labour and in the exigencies of coordination that are its consequence; or they relate it to the increasing complexity and differentiation of social systems in the course of social evolution.
>
> Accordingly, the predominant temporal consciousness of modernity is a result of the decisive break with traditional modes of action, values and norms … time becomes an ordering device that is to express the separation of 'life-time' [the world of peasants] and 'world-time' [the world of the modern], the precarious relation between finite life-time and infinite possibilities which are to emerge with modernity. (Friese 2010: 412)

The second reconceptualization of time and history pluralizes it, in an effort to combat this dichotomy of linear vs. cyclical (or even static) time. Eisenstadt (2000), Therborn (2003) and Christian (2011), among others, argue that various cultures organize time differently, that there is even 'a hierarchy of temporalities ranging from human time to the timeless' (Fraser 1980: 143; Gurevich 1976), and that an accounting of this difference serves effectively to break the hold of hegemonic and homogeneous organizations of time. My point in this discussion of Gramsci's and Foucault's conceptualizations is that this hegemonic form has been designated as history and claims not to be open to interpretation, refusing other narratives' claims to modernities. This is the struggle of postcolonial epistemologies, to claim modernity and to be recognized *as* modernity.

The third position that enables the possibility that time is not only pluralized, but that various concepts derive from and mutually inform each other, is that of the constructedness of time and history as distinct. Pletsch (1977) and Smail (2011) posit time and history as distinct entities while Bourdieu (1992) suggests that time is produced in the acts through which it produces itself (112); Paul Ricoeur (1983), Clifford Geertz (1973b: 448), Hayden White (1978) and de Certeau (1988) have argued the same, that time is the given template for, but then also the consequence of action.

My contribution to this conversation, as I show below in my reading of Gramsci's and Foucault's work, is that hegemonic forms become mechanisms and methods to co-opt history as the domain of modernity (activity, progress) and relegate those deemed un-modern to the realm of time (static, cyclical). So, rather than pluralize time, I posit that hegemonic forces attempt to eliminate opposition by consigning potential insurrection to a different category of time-space. In other words, pluralization can function as a form of colonialism in which diversity can be controlled by hegemonic forces that either by subsume it or relegate it to a disempowered zone.

A related, and equally significant, aspect of those matrices is how positions are defined—this chapter reveals the ways in which the intersection of class-identity with gender and nation is latent in Gramsci's and Foucault's writings and why it is crucial to consider it more explicitly today. In looking at the ways that particularized identities appear in some of Gramsci's and Foucault's analyses, this chapter considers what kind of identities are implicated in 'wars of position' (Gramsci 1971: 88) and what difference they make to our visions of positive social change.

The discussion below arrives into the present moment with a study of the Indigenous Women's Network (Texas, USA) and the International Dalit Solidarity Network (Copenhagen, Denmark) as well as its branch organization, the Feminist Dalit Organization (Lalitpur, Nepal). A study of these organizations reveals that the economic, sociocultural, and political conditions today call not only for a redefinition of 'subaltern' in Gramsci's view through 'subjugated' in Foucault's, but also for their sustained viability. In other words, this latter issue of viability raises two questions: how is subalternity to be understood in twenty-first-century neocolonial globalization? And, in relation to that subalternity, what is the role of the State and how is that similar to, or different from, Gramsci's and Foucault's times?

I wish to present caveats before proceeding into the discussion: the first is that while the terms 'marginalized' and 'subaltern' overlap, they also carry distinct connotations. It can be said generally that all subaltern are marginalized, and that not all marginalized identities are subaltern. The second is that while the analysis focuses on political voice and economic stability, one assumption in this discussion is that these aspects are mutually informed by social and cultural identity-production.

From Gramsci to Foucault: Time, History and Subalternity

The title of this section could imply that there is a direct and teleological line from Gramsci to Foucault. It indicates rather that the concern with 'subaltern' in Gramsci's texts continues with the focus on 'subjugated knowledges' in Foucault's analyses. The common preoccupation, in Gramsci and Foucault's writings, is with the notion of power as it is organized and the nature of resistance to dominant forces. The similarity in their approaches is that history, as distinct from time, remains the overarching issue. The difference is in the context—Gramsci writes from within the context of Mussolinian dictatorship and Italian colonial nationalism, in which identities fall into categories that are apparently clearly demarcated, and that fit into a structural analysis of the class struggle. Foucault writes from the context of Fifth Republic French postcolonial democracy in which identities challenge not only established categories but also contest 'class' as the only struggle in which they are defined.

Morera (2000) posits that Gramsci 'did indeed prefigure many current arguments and that he entertained thoughts that may be characterized as either explicitly or implicitly postmodern' while he also presents arguments for the modernist Gramsci (16). Morera, on this basis, goes on to relate Gramsci to Foucault in particular, through the connection between hegemony and the truth regime, on the resistance of subjugated knowledges to universalizing history, on the body, the place of religion, and conflict. Swanson (2009) also sees similarities in Gramsci's approaches to poststructuralism in that he rejected the idea of a non-subjective world.

I argue that issues may have been similar but their critical frames and methodologies were significantly different. I would tend to agree more with Morera's assessment that Gramsci was 'cautiously and critically modern, though not a rationalist (in the narrow sense) or a positivist' (16). Nowhere is Gramsci's particular contribution more germane than in the issue of the distinction between time and history, especially because of the ways that these two critical concepts were projected by the Futurists and the Mussolinian regime. In *The Prison Notebooks*, Sardinian-Italian political activist and theorist Gramsci invokes subalternity not in a vacuum but immediately connects it to the force by which they are marked as such, viz. hegemony, the 'protagonists of History' (1971: 52). In his 'History of the Subaltern Classes: Methodological Criteria' (in the section 'Notes on Italian History'), he makes this observation: 'The historical unity of the ruling classes is realized in the State, and their history is essentially the history of States and of groups of States' (197: 52). He does say immediately that this unity is not formal, juridical, or political in nature but 'results from the organic relations between State or political society and 'civil society' (1971: 52). It is significant that the state is the entity that becomes the organizer of history as well as time, in the senses that I have delineated above.

Numerous critical analyses of this treatise on subalternity have focused on, and continue to emphasize, the roles of 'the ruling classes' (the dominant powers), the state, and subaltern identity (Green 2002; Mignolo 2005; Spivak 2005; to name some). Those are indeed the most prominent agents in Gramsci's view. In fact, in the paragraph following the one quoted above, Gramsci reinforces the primacy of these elements—history and the state: '[t]he subaltern classes, by definition, are not unified and cannot unite until they are able to become a "State"; their history, therefore, is intertwined with that of civil society, and thereby with the history of States and groups of States' (Gramsci 1971: 52). Immediately after, Gramsci makes the case that it is

> necessary to study [among 6 elements]: 1. The objective formation of the subaltern social groups ... 2. Their active or passive affiliation to the dominant political formations ... 4. The formations which the subaltern groups themselves produce, in order to press claims of a limited and partial character 5. Those new formations that assert the autonomy of the subaltern groups but within the old framework. (Gramsci 1971: 52)

It is evident in this chapter that the word 'history ' not only begins the treatise but also continues to prevail as the operative word and primary focus. It is mentioned in almost every paragraph of Gramsci's analysis. The state is the symbol as well as structure of political legitimacy and power, and Gramsci's idea is that subalternity must or should aspire to this hegemonic condition. To return to the opening statements, the emphasis is on history as the reason for aspiring to this unity, and the arrival into statehood marks the arrival into history and, by extension, acknowledgment as an entity.

The elements that remain relatively unaddressed translate into the two questions that propel this discussion—the first is that, if subalternity is, by definition, yet to arrive at unity/statehood/history, then in what dimension does it exist prior to that arrival? In contrast to the 'unity' of the dominant state, the 'history of subaltern social groups is necessarily fragmented and episodic' (1971: 54–5) and one of the primary reasons for that is the interruption and intervention by 'ruling groups' (1971: 55). Most of the energy of subaltern groups is spent in defending themselves and only eventually, if occasionally, in rising to '"permanent" victory' (Gramsci 1971: 55). This last statement about victory, permanent victory, in the context of Gramsci's preceding comments, would mean statehood. Below, I ask whether statehood is indeed what subalternity seeks to achieve, and whether there is a dilemma for organizations such as FEDO (Feminist Dalit Organization) and IWN (Indigenous Women's Network) in attempting to arrive at a hegemonic status.

While Gramsci does use the word 'history' in talking about 'subaltern social groups' to signify dominant history, one connotation merits deeper exploration—

that there are simultaneous histories with different valencies, that Johannes Fabian calls 'heterosynchronous structures' (1983). It is at these disjunctures that I read Gramsci's analysis to convey latent distinctions between history and time. In Gramsci's own words, subaltern history is 'fragmented and episodic' which, by implication, does not rise to the unity and integrity of statehood (dominant history). 'History' in this context, then, carries a different connotation; it is distinct in nature from dominant history and, by definition, because of its fragmentariness and episodic nature, participates in modernity on an unequal basis.

Above, I indicate Gramsci's own ethnicity, an aspect that has not been given much attention by scholars of his work. While Gramsci does indeed construct the figure of the subaltern as a general figurative reference, I draw attention to his focus on Sardinian and Sicilian subordination in order to connect it to the minoritization of ethnicities that is a significant element in the discussion of subalternity, in my view, and is in focus below in this chapter. In other words, who is made subaltern matters just as much as how subalternity is located in political structures, as I attempt to indicate in the discussion of the dialectic above. Subaltern groups, in the Italy of Gramsci's era, are represented as marginal, primitive, pre-industrial, lagging behind in the projects of modernity, and most distinctly, as politically un-viable and unintelligible by hegemonic standards. These representations are not only projected as intrinsic features of subalternity but are based in differing valencies of history, as I note above, in Gramsci's text. The history of the 'protagonists' is what we are given to understand as normative, as the unified narrative past, present, and future of those who have achieved statehood and political intelligibility.

The history of subaltern groups is adjacent to this narrative and consigned to time – eternal, abstract, unchanging, un-linear, outside material structure. In other words, subaltern groups may have internal histories but, in their inability to participate or actualize, exist in the a-historical. See, for example, Gramsci's depictions of Sicilians (Grasmci 1978) and Sardinians. Subaltern groups, in this aspect of inhabiting time rather than history, are characterized by their paradoxical inclusion in, and exclusion from, statehood. It can be said that this paradox is founded on, and justified by, the paradigm of more than one history in which the dominant power legitimizes its version and the 'other' (subaltern groups) are represented as living in an-other history, which I call 'time' above.

Connected to the question under discussion thus far, namely, in what dimension does the subaltern group exist prior to an arrival into history?, is the question about the nature and role of such particularized groups/peoples. In 'History of the Subaltern Classes: Methodological Criteria' (Gramsci 1971), the main text in focus in this chapter, Gramsci lists six elements that constitute the actions of subaltern groups in relation to hegemonic history in the form of the state. Among them and worth noting is the fact that the history of subaltern groups, 'fragmentary and episodic,' is not structured as the history of modernity, and also that their claims to that history are 'limited and partial.' This leads him to point out that '[e]very trace of independent initiative on the part of subaltern groups should therefore be of incalculable value for the integral historian' (Gramsci 1971: 55).

Who is this integral historian? Can the organic intellectual of a subaltern group be one? And who is part of the group that is to be studied? Throughout his writings, Gramsci appears to maintain his focus on a structural analysis of subaltern groups in the 'wars of position.' In his essays on Sardinian and Sicilian subalternity, group formation predominates; yet, on a closer look, ethnic/cultural identification is important to the paradoxical position of inclusion and exclusion, and its positioning in time rather than history. In other words, Sardinian or Sicilian subalternity is related to perceptions not of their abstract group status but of their ethnic/cultural affiliation with, and disaffiliation with, the nation-state. By juxtaposition and in contrast, the hegemonic Italian nation-state, the protagonist of history, is not identified in terms of ethnicity, but as 'national culture' (Stacul 2005).

In short, normative (in Gramsci's vocabulary, hegemonic) identity universalizes itself as the possessor of history and invests itself with the power to particularize its 'others' (of which 'subaltern' is one) as non-normative and living outside history, in the unstructured stream called time. These 'others' are particularized in terms of their ethnicized, gendered, sexualized, or class category, e.g., the Sardinian, the woman, the worker, to name some.

In many of Gramsci's analyses of these 'others,' an industrial modernity intersects with a resurgent Italian masculinism. Gramsci refers explicitly to the first since his focus is on the prevailing material conditions of the class struggle. The second remains implicit but ever-present, the closest reference that is often invoked being Italian nationalism and statehood. The two – Italian statehood and masculinism – overlap or can even be perceived as substituted or conflated, and converge ultimately in the figure of Benito Mussolini.

The transition from Italian dictatorship in the 1940s to French Fifth Republic in the 1960s is not a directly linear history of thought, as we move from the notion of 'subaltern' in Antonio Gramsci's texts to 'subjugated knowledges' in Michel Foucault's analyses. The most significant similarity in both critics' writings is the preoccupation with history and the position as well as role of 'other' narratives of peoples who have not attained political and cultural legitimacy within hegemonic conditions. An interviewer, asking Foucault about geography, points out that Foucault privileges time—see issue about periodization and layers of events (*Questions on Geography*, Foucault 1980: 67).

Gramsci's view of subaltern histories as 'fragmented and episodic' appears in Foucault's analysis of power in 'Two Lectures on Power' (Foucault 1980: 78), but with a marked difference. Hegemonic history itself is not intrinsically coherent but presents a 'functionalist coherence or formal systematization' ('Lecture One,' Foucault 1980: 81). This history creates singularities through 'the tyranny of globalizing discourses with their hierarchy and all their privileges of a theoretical avant garde' (83). These observations imply the constructed nature of dominant history, to a degree that was not articulated in Gramsci's analysis. This, to me, marks the shift from modernity to postmodernity; an unavoidable caveat is, of course, that Foucault distances himself from the latter, identifying himself as a critic of modernity. It is worth noting that being a critic of modernity does not exclude the relevance of postmodernity.

Whether the unity of hegemonic history is perceived as innate or constructed, both Gramsci and Foucault are concerned with what the latter calls 'a historical knowledge of struggles' that involve the contestations between 'erudite' and 'disqualified knowledges' (83). Gramsci refers to the difficulties of knowing or collecting subaltern histories, because of their episodic nature; those challenges for the integral historian is not that there is a lack of subaltern histories but that their fragmented nature leads one, from the hegemonic perspective, to mis-recognize them as such. According to Foucault, dominant history generates the 'effects of the centralizing powers which are linked to the institution and functioning of an organized scientific discourse' (84). In 'Lecture One', he continues to call this systematic, hierarchically structured project a 'science' of power. As outlined above, the narrative of time and history in the genealogy of Foucault's observations signifies the 'scientific ambitions' of Western European historiography itself. Cynthia Coe observes, in *Domesticating Time: Two Contemporary Continental Critiques of History*:

> Distinguished from myth, ritual, superstition, visions, and reminiscence, history is able to model itself on scientific projects. In this way, historical methods reflect an Enlightenment preoccupation with dogmatism … [Hegel's] work manifests in an extreme case a more recognizable form of historical domestication, which makes an event intelligible by integrating it into a larger narrative, interiorized in a subject defined by autonomy. It is only through this form of representation that the Subject (with a capital 'S') surpasses the passing of time and comes to occupy a place beyond the limitations of perspective, mortality, and uncertainty imposed by that passing. In the fusion of historical representation and suprahistorical commitments, freedom from the unauthorized authority and influence of the past is not only an element of autonomy but its primary meaning. (Coe 2001: 419–20)

It would appear that this power is monolithic and all-encompassing in its character and its reach; in other parts of his two lectures on power, Foucault offers an exposition of his theory of power (dominant history) that also takes a different direction from Gramsci's theory about the nature of political change.

The significance of the 'insurrection of subjugated knowledges ' (81) can only be understood in the context of such overwhelming effects of a dominant history. As the 'Occupy movement' of the 99 percent demonstrates today, this insurrection is not the 'passive revolution' (Gramsci 1971: 105–20) of the bourgeoisie that Gramsci describes, but a tangible, active, direct initiative through grassroots solidarity that Gramsci also envisions. The dilemma that hounds this direct action is one of establishing self-articulated identities and positions while participating through and with hegemonic discourses which have historically distorted these identities, as I show below in the case of organizations such as the Feminist Dalit Organization (FEDO) and the Indigenous Women's Network (IWN). In other words, the battle for these 'local, discontinuous, disqualified, illegitimate knowledges' is that much greater because 'science' attempts to 'filter, hierarchise and order' such knowledges, i.e., incorporate them into the order of things – 'to annex them' (Foucault 1980: 86) – or annihilate them. It should be underscored that 'subjugated knowledges' are not disqualified or illegitimate by nature, but rendered or interpreted or represented as such by prevailing powers. It is only from the perspective of hegemonic discourses that subjugated knowledges are read as 'naïve knowledges, located low down on the hierarchy, beneath the required level of cognition or scientificity' (Foucault 1980: 82). It is also worth emphasizing here that Foucault is delivering a critique of modernity's blind spot.

The paradigms and parameters of political, economic, social, and cultural legitimacy themselves are determined by 'the inhibiting effect of global, totalitarian theories' (Foucault 1980: 80), in relation to which subjugated histories create not a 'general commonsense knowledge' but 'a differential knowledge' (Foucault 1980: 82). The choice of the word or phrase 'common sense' resonates with Gramsci's theorizing of the same (Gramsci 1971: 419–25; Green and Ives 2009). In both instances, the term gestures towards hegemonic powers that have not only become dominant but have attained the transcendental as well as immanent status of being normalized. In both instances, in Gramsci's and Foucault's texts, the inordinate power of dominant history resides in its being (constructed as) unitary and as 'normal.' The constraints facing subaltern group advocacy, as in the case of FEDO and IWN, are based in the fact that the 'normal' is at once the ground of struggle and also its object – that is, subaltern groups struggle to stake a claim in the 'normal' while attempting to re-define that ground as well as to expose its constructedness at the same time.

Then where does this 'differential knowledge' reside and act? It is apparent, from Foucault's words excerpted above, that, since it is the object of annexation, incorporation, or annihilation, that it resides outside, if not adjacent, to dominant history. It is my contention that history, as hegemonic forces seek to define their own version (as 'normal'), is made distinct from the continuum that differential/subjugated knowledge is perceived as inhabiting. This knowledge that is represented, within dominant paradigms, as local, discontinuous (read 'episodic and fragmentary' in Gramsci's vocabulary) and disqualified, occupies the unstructured continuum of time from which it is pulled into prevailing discourses. As Foucault says, the object of both dominant and subjugated identities is the 'historical knowledge of struggles' (Foucault 1980: 83) in which the latter attempt an intervention.

Gramsci's writings posited that subaltern identity could aspire to history by forming a coherent political identity that could intervene in hegemonic discourse and structure; this strain of thought continues in Guy Debord's idea that 'once the running of a state involves a permanent and massive shortage of historical knowledge, that society can no longer be led strategically' (Bunyard 2011: 6). Gramsci's theory about subaltern intervention envisions change through the guidance and leadership of organic intellectuals, and his listing of the six elements that the 'integral historian' must study include the notion that subaltern initiative (action) will result eventually in finding legitimacy 'within the old framework' (Gramsci 1971: 55). Gramsci appears implicitly to hold the idea that power is exercised in action and is not a commodity, since subaltern groups have to take initiative, yet the overall drive is towards validity through statehood. As Aronowitz puts it:

> The organic intellectual is one whose work is that of expression of the world view of the proletariat or of any other class that aspires to power … State colleges and universities are more or less adequate institutions for the education of the organic intellectuals of capital and of the state … [they train to instrumentalize] science and technology on the one hand, and the various bureaucratic skills such as accounting, economics, especially finance, management, public administration occupations such as planning and budget management. (2009: 13)

Foucault's two lectures arrive at a conception of power that poses a different path from Gramsci's, for subjugated knowledges to intervene in the common sense understanding of history. In 'Lecture One,' Foucault outlines first the 'classic, juridical theory, power is taken to be a right, which one is able to possess as a commodity' (1980: 88). In contrast, the new 'power is neither given, nor exchanged, nor recovered, but rather exercised, and that it only exists in action' (1980: 89).

The most distinct difference in Foucault's idea about power and change through subjugated knowledges appears at the end of 'Lecture Two.' He prepares us for the key terms at stake in first observing that 'sovereignty and disciplinary mechanisms are two absolutely integral constituents of the general mechanisms of power in our society' (Foucault 1980: 108). He then goes on to conclude 'the possibility of a new form of right, one which must indeed be anti-disciplinarian, but at the same time liberated from the principle of sovereignty' (Foucault 1980: 108). This principle, in the strict and literal juridico-political sense of territorial ownership, informs the work of the Indigenous Women's Network (USA) – it is not their primary focus but is a dominant element in the historicizing of the identities of its members. In a more figurative sense, the principle of sovereignty, not territorial but legislative and cultural, informs the work of FEDO. As Green comments: 'Ideally, what Gramsci has in mind is a postsubaltern state, a democratic state that disallows the domination of one group by another' (Green 2002: 22).

To return to and emphasize the dialectical relationship between identity and structure presented at the onset of this chapter, and as prelude to the next section in this discussion, I would like to foreground the significance of particularities. In 1977–78, a year or two after the 'Two Lectures,' in *Security, Territoriality,*

Population (Foucault 2007) Foucault uses the notion of 'biopower ' to explore the ways that sovereignty and discipline function through the control of diverse and multiply identified bodies, namely, human population. Above, I have already referred to the points in Gramsci's works where there are specific ethnic and gendered grounds of subaltern identity, even where the primary focus is on class-identification.

In the next section, I attempt two things in the representations of the Indigenous Women's Network (Texas, USA) and the International Dalit Solidarity Network (Copenhagen, Denmark) and its branch Feminist Dalit Solidarity Organization (Lalitpur, Nepal). I take the genealogy of thought regarding particularized bodies and peoples further than Gramsci and Foucault have, considering their relevance in today's history of power struggles. The 99 percent, in the context of transnational neoliberal globalization, does not constitute a homogenous or narrowly identifiable subaltern or even subjugated position. I also explore how disempowerment leads to political and economic de-legitimation, and cuts across identities plurally and unevenly. The ultimate purpose of the section below is to present how the schism between time and history informs self-conceptualization in terms of the intersecting axes of gender, race, and class, and enables positive structural change.

Subalternity in Time and History: A Position with Many Identities

The juxtaposition of 'position' and 'identity' in the title of this section takes on the dialectic embedded in the matter of subalternity that I have laid out in the discussion above. Across the twentieth century, we move from Gramsci's primarily structural analysis to Foucault's somewhat more modified foray into structure in relation to identity, into Gayatri Spivak's stance that subalternity is 'a position without identity' (Spivak 2005: 476). Louai (2011) and Persram (2011) separately outline the genealogy of the concept of 'subaltern' from Gramsci to Spivak to the postmodern condition. I submit that position can be informed but not determined by identity, and vice versa. Above, I indicate briefly that Gramsci's identity as a Sardinian has been under-addressed in the extensive scholarship about subalternity. In this section, I seek to heed Gramsci's own warning to move away from generalizations (Hall 1988: 161).

It is through negotiation with both structural position and identity-ascription that the Indigenous Women's Network (IWN) and the Feminist Dalit Solidarity Organization (FEDO) function and carry out their work. Their self-representation in their webpages demonstrates that subalternity does not make identity and position mutually exclusive but negotiates one through the other in the very act of negotiating between dominant history and indigenous time. Each organization internally holds and transversally mediates between multiple identity-formations that come together under the umbrella name (IWN or FEDO), and qualifiea the notion of subalternity today. In placing this transnational women's work in the context of Gramscian and Foucauldian ideas of time and history, I take a different approach to the analysis of non-hegemonic strategies than are depicted in studies about similar organizations and initiatives (Kuokkanen 2011; Ackerly and Sapra 2006; Shield 2009). I do not assume that IWN and FEDO are located completely outside hegemonic discourse; instead, I read their position as standing in-between the realms of hegemony and counter-hegemony. I also locate the work of IWN and FEDO at the intersection of postmodernism and postcolonialism, in the context of neoliberal globalization.

In terms of time and history, the two organizations featured in this section build upon an interpreted past to signify a future. In that sense, Patomaki's description below captures the ways in which subordinated knowledges interpret a hegemonic linearity of history:

> We rely on future-oriented narratives to describe on-going processes, the (more comprehensive) end of which can only be seen from a vantage point later than the moment of action within that process. Moreover, the future is no more something that just happens but something that can be shaped, even if only in a structurally conditioned way. With increasingly reflexive, holistic and future-oriented self-regulation of systems, the temporality of human existence is being transformed … When put together, lesser-scale stories may presuppose or constitute, at least in effect, a grand narrative of the origins, possibilities and outlook for humankind. Every grand story locates the present context as part of a wider and structured temporal whole, thus pre-organising our anticipations of possible short-term futures as well. (2011: 347)

However, I don't agree that there is a structured temporal whole. In the three ways that time can be structured in relation to history—neutrality, plurality, and constructedness—it is precisely the notion of wholeness that is being constructed.

The Dalit movement inspired by Dr Ambedkar's leadership, has its origins in India but has, since the early twentieth century, become a transnational phenomenon (Zelliott 1996; 2004). As the FEDO website describes, this non-governmental organization in Nepal, founded in 1994 by Dalit women, aims 'to promote Dalit rights, eliminate caste and gender-based discrimination and to promote justice and equality in Nepalese society' (FEDO 2012b). The preamble in the mission statement of the Feminist Dalit Solidarity Organization, the Nepali Dalit Women's Charter for New Nepal Building Process 2007 states:

> Since only non-Dalit women have access to the facilities and opportunities that are made available by the government for women, Dalit women have been further isolated from the state structure. Nepal is in one of the poorest countries in the world because of the state's discriminatory policies towards Dalits from time immemorial. (FEDO 2012c)

It is worth noting, in the extract above, how Dalit identity is formulated in terms of gender, class, and caste (Rao 2009; 2008; 2003; Rege 2004; 2006) but also only in juxtaposition with its hegemonic other—this adjacent status illuminates the presence or absence of rights. This latter deficit is experienced particularly in relation to the history of untouchability (Gheeta 2009; Gorringe 2004; Mendelsohn and Vicziany 1998; Zene 2000). The preamble also places these particularized identities in the context of structure and position. Most significantly, the text is infused with the notion of history as overlapping with, but also distinct from, 'time immemorial'. The last sentence of the preamble indicates that statehood commandeers history and annexes (to use Foucault's word) the longue durée of time in which Dalit identity has existed, prior to and during the Nepali state.

The larger network of the umbrella organization – the International Dalit Solidarity Network (ISDN) – gives FEDO a wide base of identity-formation, one in which competing narratives of time and history play out both trans-regionally and on the global scene (see AIPTN 2009; BDERM 2009; BDHR 2006; Charsley and Karnath 1998; Hardtmann 2009; Narayan 2006). Gramsci's depiction of subaltern resistance to hegemonic forces has often been interpreted as signifying a binaristic dynamics; on closer investigation, it is through negotiation across hegemonic and counter-hegemonic forces that 'revolution,' or political change takes place. It is significant that FEDO lists among its partners and donors organizations such as the Australian government, the European Union, Womankind Worldwide, the Dan Church Association, the Minority Rights Group, the World Bank and the International Movement Against All Forms of Racial Discrimination. In the transition from modernity to postmodernity, FEDO not only demonstrates the nuanced understanding of power that Gramsci indicates but also practices the mediation between dominant and subjugated knowledges, to intervene in history, which Foucault analyzes in his 'Two Lectures' on power.

The Indigenous Women's Organization was established in Washington (USA) in 1985 'as a grass roots initiative at a gathering of over 200 Indigenous women' (IWN 2012). Similar to FEDO, IWN negotiates the straddling of history and time by interposing their identity, both imposed and self-defined. While marginality is imposed on them by the history of colonialism and present-day hegemonic conditions, they identify as 'strong, committed indigenous women activists who dedicate themselves to generating a global movement that achieves sustainable change for [their] communities.' They describe their training programs and publications as tools that 'each and link Indigenous women around the world in a network of support that includes award winning artists, activists, authors, community leaders, educators, attorneys and traditional healers' (IWN 2012). Just as the Dalit women's organization, the IWN allies with a network larger than can be contained by the monolithic state (for the Dalits, see Shah 2001; 2002). Among the funders are the Ford Foundation, the Unitarian Universalist VEATCH program at Shelter Rock, the Tides Foundation, and the City of Austin. Ishay comments about the discernible shifts in the late twentieth century: 'Post-Fordism after the Second World War has both created new informational sites of economic activity and at the same time decentralized the arenas of social and economic interactions' while it has also weakened the power of the state to 'mediate between capital ...

and workers and the poor' (2004: 191). The role of religious affiliation or sponsorship is prominent in both FEDO and IWN; this discussion does not focus on Gramsci's careful analysis of the place of religion in subaltern identity, but it is certainly worth pursuing as a major element in transnational solidarity movements (for particular reference to Dalits and Christianity, see Clarke 2000; Webster 2007; Zene 2000; 2002).

In both cases, however, globalization from above works to pluralize forms of disempowerment, and create multiple narratives of time and history in order to perpetuate that marginalization. It is also becoming more evident that globalization from below allows for differential knowledges to adjust to newer conditions of disempowerment that call for newer strategies of intervention (Bhagavan and Feldhaus 2008a; 2008b). The abiding dilemma is that the search to arrive into history becomes conducted on hegemonic terms—through programs and training constructed within the frameworks of prevailing powers. Less visible but present and active are the strategic interventions based on 'indigenous values' (IWN 2012) that change the nature of the discourse and, as is the hope, of structures themselves.

References

Ackerly, B.A. and Sapra, S. 2006. On women and citizenship: Silence and speech in transnational women's movements. Paper presented at the annual meeting of the International Studies Association. Town and Country Resort and Convention Center, San Diego, California, USA, http://www.allacademic.com/meta/p100816_index.html, accessed on 25 June 2012.

Adam, B. 1994. Perceptions of time. In *Companion Encyclopedia of Anthropology, Humanity, Culture and Social Life*, edited by T. Ingold. London: Routledge, 503–26.

AITPN 2009. The experience of Bangladesh. Asian Indigenous and Tribal People Network, http://www.aitpn.org/UN/UPR-Bangladesh-2009.pdf, accessed on 14 January 2013.

Aronowitz, S. 2009. Gramsci's concept of political organization. In *Perspectives on Gramsci: Politics, Culture and Social Theory*, edited by J. Francese. New York: Routledge, 7–19.

BDERM, NU and IDSN 2009. The human rights situation of Dalits in Bangladesh, their socio-economic problems, legal and constitutional protections, and the issues of discrimination on the basis of caste and lower status. Bangladesh Dalit and Excluded Rights Movement, Nagorik Uddyog and International Dalit Soldarity Network, http://www.upr-info.org/IMG/pdf/IDSN_BGD_UPR_S4_2009_InternationalDalitSolidarityNetwork_JOINT_upr.pdf, accessed on 14 January 2013.

BDHR (Bangladesh Dalits' Human Rights) and IDSN (International Dalit Solidarity Network) 2006. Consultative meeting on the situation of Dalits in Bangladesh. Dhaka, Bangladesh, 18 October.

Banerjee, P. 2006. *Politics of Time: 'Primitives' and History-writing in a Colonial Society*. New Delhi: Oxford.

Bergman, I. 2006. Indigenous time, colonial history: Sami conceptions of time and ancestry and the role of relics in cultural reproduction. *Norwegian Archaeological Review* 39(2): 151–61.

Bhagavan, M. and Feldhaus, A. 2008a. *Speaking Truth to Power: Religion, Caste, and the Subaltern in India*. New Delhi: Oxford University Press.

—. 2008b. *Claiming Power from Below: Dalits and the Subaltern Question in India*. New Delhi: Oxford University Press.

Bourdieu, P. 1992. Réponses. *Pour une Anthropologie Reflexive* (avec L.J.D. Qacquant). Paris: Seuil.

Boydston, B. 2012. What exactly does the Occupy movement want? *Humanist* 72(1): 20–23.

Braudel, F. 1984. *The Perspective of the World*. London: Collins.

Bunyard, T. 2011. Debord, time and history. *Historical Materialism* 19(1): 3–36.

Campbell, E.R.A. 2011. A critique of the Occupy movement from a black Occupier. *Black Scholar* 41(4): 42–51.

Charsley, S.R. and Karnath, G.K. 1998. *Challenging Untouchability: Dalit Initiative and Experience from Karnataka*. New Delhi: Sage.

Christian, D. 2011. History and time. *Australian Journal of Politics and History* 57(3): 353–65.

Clarke, S. 2000. *Dalits and Christianity: Subaltern Religion and Liberation Theology in India*. New Delhi: Oxford University Press.

Coe, C.D. 2001. Domesticating time: Two contemporary continental critiques of history. *Clio* 30(4): 417–43.

De Certeau, M. 1988. *The Writing of History*, translated by T. Conley. New York: Columbia University Press.

Eberhard, W. 1965. *Conquerors and Rulers: Social Forces in Medieval China*. Leiden: Brill.

Eisenstadt, S.N. 2000. Multiple modernities. Special issue edited by S.N. Eisenstadt. *Daedalus* 29(1).

Ermarth, E.D. 2010. Time is finite: The implications for history. *Rethinking History* 14(3): 321–41.

Fabian, J. 1983. *Time and the Other: How Anthropology Makes its Object*. New York: Columbia University Press.

FEDO. 2012a. Strategy. Feminist Dalit Organisation, http://fedonepal.org/np/index.php/our-work/strategy, accessed on 14 January 2013.

—. 2012b. History. Feminist Dalit Organisation, http://fedonepal.org/np/index.php/about-us/history, accessed on 14 January 2013.

—. 2012c. Dalit women's charter. Feminist Dalit Organisation, http://fedonepal.org/np/index.php/resources/dalit-womens-charter, accessed on 14 January 2013.

Foucault, M. 1980. *Power/Knowledge: Selected Interviews and Other Writings, 1972–77*, edited by C. Gordon, translated by Gordon et al. New York: Pantheon Books.

—. 2007. Security, territory, population. *Lectures at the Collège de France, 1977–1978*. London: Palgrave Macmillan

Fraser, J.T. 1980. Out of Plato's cave: The natural history of time. *Kenyon Review* 2(1): 143–62.

Friese, H. 2010. Times, histories and discourse. *Rethinking History* 14(3): 405–20.

Geertz, C. 1973. Thick description: Toward an interpretative theory of culture. In *The Interpretation of Cultures. Selected Essays*, edited by C. Geertz. New York: Basic Books, 3–30.

Gell, A. 1992. *The Anthropology of Time.* Oxford: Berg.

Gheeta, V. 2009. Bereft of being: The humiliations of untouchability. In *Humiliation: Claims and Context*, edited by G. Guru. New Delhi: Oxford University Press, 95–108.

Giddens, A. 1979. *Central Problems in Social Theory. Action, Structure and Contradiction in Social Analysis*. London: Macmillan.

Gorringe, H. 2004. *Untouchable Citizens: Dalit Movements and Democratization in Tamil Nadu.* New Delhi: Sage.

Gramsci, A. 1911. Oppressors and oppressed, http://socialiststories.net/liberate/Oppressed%20and%20Oppressors%20-%20Antonio%20Gramsci.pdf, accessed in July 2014.

—. 1971. *Selections from the Prison Notebooks*, translated and edited by Q. Hoare and G.N. Smith. London: Lawrence and Wishart.

—. 1978. *Selections from Political Writings 1921–1926*, translated and edited by Q. Hoare. London: Lawrence and Wishart

Green, M. 2002. Gramsci cannot speak: Presentations and interpretations of Gramsci's concept of the subaltern. *Rethinking Marxism* 14(3): 1–24.

Green, M. and Ives, P. 2009. Subalternity and language: Overcoming the fragmentation of common sense. *Historical Materialism* 17(1): 3–30.

Guha, R. 1988. On some aspects of the historiography of colonial India. *Subaltern Studies* I: 37–45.

Gurevich, A.J. 1976. Time as a problem of cultural history. In *Cultures and Time*, edited by Gardet et al. Paris: The UNESCO Press, 229–45.

Haidt, J. 2012. The moral foundations of Occupy Wall Street. *Reason* 43(8): 33–9.

Hall, S. 1988. *The Hard Road to Renewal: Thatcherism and the Crisis of the Left.* London: Verso.

Hardtmann, E.M. 2009. *Dalit Movement in India: Local Practices, Global Connections*. Delhi: Oxford University Press.

IDSN 2012. What are the key issues affecting Dalits today? International Dalit Solidarity Network, idsn.org/caste-discrimination/key-issues/, accessed on 14 January 2013.

Ishay, M. 2004. Promoting human rights in the era of globalization and interventions: The changing spaces of struggle. *Globalizations* 1(2): 181–93.

IWN 2012. History of IWN. Indigenous Women's Network, http://www.indigenouswomen.org, accessed on 14 January 2013.

Kuokkanen, R. 2011. Indigenous economies, theories of subsistence, and women: Exploring the social economy model for indigenous governance. *American Indian Quarterly* 35(2): 215–40.

Louai, E.H. 2012. Retracing the concept of the subaltern from Gramsci to Spivak: Historical developments and new applications. *African Journal of History and Culture* 4(1): 4–8.

Mendelsohn, O. and Vicziany. M. 1998. *The Untouchables: Subordination, Poverty and the State in Modern India*. Cambridge: Cambridge University Press.

Mignolo, W. 2001. *Coloniality of Power and Subalternity, The Latin American Studies Reader*, edited by I. Rodriguez. Durham and London: Duke University Press.

—. 2005. On subalterns and other agencies. *Postcolonial Studies* 8(4): 381–407.

Moore, M. 2012. The purpose of Occupy Wall Street is to occupy Wall Street. *Nation* 294(14): 12.

Morera, E. 2000. Gramsci's critical modernity. *Rethinking Marxism* 12(1): 16–46.

NACLA 2012. Occupy: Resistance to global capitalism in the Americas. *NACLA Report on the Americas* 45(2): 41–5.

Narayan, B. 2006. *Women Heroes and Dalit Assertion in North India: Culture, Identity and Politics*. New Delhi: Sage.

Patomäki, H. 2011. On the complexities of time and temporality: Implications for world history and global futures. *Australian Journal of Politics and History* 57(3): 339–52.

Perrett, R. 1999. History, time, and knowledge in ancient India. *History and Theory* 38(3): 307–21.

Persram, N. 2011. Spatial and temporal dislocations of theory, subjectivity, and post()reason in the geocolonial politics of subaltern studies. *Cultural Studies* 11(1): 9–23.

Pletsch, C.E. 1977. History and Friedrich Nietzsche's philosophy of time. *History and Theory* 16(1): 30–39.

Pollitt, K. 2012. Women: Occupy the Left. *Nation* 294(21): 10.

Prakash, G. 1994. Subaltern studies as postcolonial criticism. *The American Historical Review* 99(5): 1475–90.

Rao, A. 2003. *Gender and Caste*. New Delhi: Kali for Women.

—. 2008. Who is the Dalit? The emergence of a new political subject. In *Claiming Power from Below: Dalits and the Subaltern Question in India*, edited by M. Bhagavan and A. Feldhaus. New Delhi: Oxford University Press, 11–27.

—. 2009. *The Caste Question: Dalits and the Politics of Modern India*. Berkeley and Los Angeles: University of California Press.

Rege, S. 2004. Dalit women talk differently: A critique of 'difference' and towards a Dalit feminist standpoint position. In *Feminism in India*, edited by M. Chaudhuri. London: MacMillan, 211–25.

—. 2006. *Writing Caste/Writing Gender: Narrating Dalit Women's Testimonies*. New Delhi: Zubaan.

Ricoeur, P. 1983. *Temps et* Récit, *Vol. I-III*. Paris: Seuil.

Rosengarten, F. 2009. The contemporary relevance of Gramsci's views on Italy's 'Southern question.' In *Perspectives on Gramsci: Politics, Culture and Social Theory*, edited by J. Francese. New York: Routledge, 134–44.

Schneider, N. 2012. From Occupy Wall Street to occupy everywhere. *Nation* 295(13): 13–17.

Shah, G. (ed.) 2001. *Dalit Identity and Politics*. New Delhi: Sage.

—. 2002. *Dalits and the State*. New Delhi: Centre for Rural Studies.

Shield, R.W. 2009. Identifying and understanding indigenous cultural and spiritual strengths in the higher education experiences of indigenous women. *Wicazo Sa Review* 24(1): 47–63.

Smail, D.L. 2011. History and the telescoping of time: A disciplinary forum (introduction). *French Historical Studies* 34(1): 1–6.

Spivak, G.C. 1988. Can the subaltern speak? In *Marxism and the Interpretation of Culture*, edited by C. Nelson and L. Grossberg. Urbana: University of Illinois Press, 271–313.

—. 2005. Scattered speculations of the subaltern and the popular. *Postcolonial Studies* 8(4): 475–86.

Srivastava, N. and Baidik, B. 2012. *The Postcolonial Gramsci*. New York: Routledge.

Stacul, J. 2005. Natural time, political time: Contested histories in northern Italy. *Journal of the Royal Anthropological Institute* 11(4): 819–36.

Swanson, J. 2009. Gramsci as theorist of politics. *Rethinking Marxism* 21(3): 336–43.

Therborn, G. 2003. Entangled modernities. *European Journal of Social Theory* 3(3): 293–305.

Webster, J.C.B. 2007. *The Dalit Christians: A History*. Delhi: ISPCK.

White, H. 1978. *The Content of the Form: Narrative Discourse and Historical Representation*. Baltimore and London: Johns Hopkins University Press.

Zelliott, E. 1996. *From Untouchable to Dalit: Essays on the Ambedkar Movement*. New Delhi: Manohar.

—. 2004. *Dr. Babasaheb Ambedkar and the Untouchable Movement*. New Delhi: Bloomoon Books.

Zene, C. 2000. 'We too are Humans!' (Amrao je manus!): The Rishis' Struggle for a Religious/Human' Identity. In *SOAS Working Papers in the Study of Religions*. SOAS, 69–98.

—. 2002. *The Rishi of Bangladesh: A History of Christian Dialogues*. London: Routledge Curzon.

—. 2011. Self-consciousness of the Dalits as 'subalterns': Reflections on Gramsci in South Asia. *Rethinking Marxism* 23(1): 83–99.

Chapter 7
The Passive Revolution of Spiritual Politics: Gramsci and Foucault on Modernity, Transition and Religion

Jelle Versieren and Brecht de Smet

The following chapter compares the methodology of Gramsci and Foucault deployed in their investigations into the nature of modernization and transition. Throughout the text, their perspectives on the relation between religion and modernity serve as a main theoretical thread, knotting different historical case studies, such as France, Italy, and Iran together. The text opens with a discussion of Gramsci's concept of modernity, which is understood from a thoroughly immanent, historicist, and humanist philosophical framework. The conception of modernity is supported and complemented by an elaboration of the notion of hegemony. Subsequently, the movement of the French Revolution is considered as the archetypical trajectory of modernity through a 'classic' formation of bourgeois hegemony. However, Gramsci noted that the real historical process forcefully rejected this archetypical development in favour of particular transformations, which could be understood as a 'passive revolution'. In his studies of Italian history Gramsci recognized the roots of the 'passive revolutionary' transition towards modernity, which came to dominate most Western nations.

After the elucidation of Gramsci's conception of modernity, attention is turned towards Foucault's notions of the modern. A first encounter between Gramsci and Foucault is set up via the entwinement of the concepts of passive revolution and hegemony with those of biopower and governmentality. Next, Foucault's concrete reading of the Iranian Revolution of 1979 as a form of 'political spirituality' is examined, and found to be lacking because it could not integrate the cultural hybridity of Khomeini's Shi'ism with Iran's transitory political economy.

Modernity in Gramsci's Notebooks: Methodology, Historicism, Dialectics and Critique of the Present

In order to render Gramsci's worldview intelligible, it is necessary to approach the *Prison Notebooks* not as a fragmentary and topical collection of diverging historical and intellectual commentaries, but as a developing, yet logical whole of thoughts (Thomas 2009). In an epoch of revolution and counter-revolution and swift societal transformations, the Italian Marxist investigated the determinations of change and transition in contemporary societies. Gramsci conceptualized 'modernity' as a concrete historical process: the tendency of the capitalist mode of production to expand, develop, and become universal in its different political, ideological and cultural forms, shaped by particular ensembles of social forces. He concluded that the interplay between existing universals and particular contingent elements brought forth a new set of universals upon the disintegration of ensembles of social relations. The bourgeois revolutions in Europe constituted just one moment within a century-long chain of attempts by the capitalist class to carve out their own economic and political spaces within the feudal order. Before the advent of modernity, the bourgeoisie defended its own direct particular interests vis-à-vis the rulers of absolutist or despotic regimes – what Gramsci called the 'economic-corporate' phase. Time and time again the bourgeois class failed to permanently impose its own agenda on the political and economic policy of budding nation-states until it became the dominant political force. Thus, with the aim of understanding how a subordinated class successfully created itself as a unified social force, i.e. forming a historical bloc in order to take political control, Gramsci presented a grand historiography of intellectual, social, political, cultural, psychological, economic, institutional and religious transformations as 'hegemonic' forces, which led to the domination of the universals of capitalist production.

Gramsci's concept of modernity as a historical process did not entail a linear reconstruction of the present. Thomas's research on Gramsci's historicist methodology raised awareness about the epistemological status of his concepts and the ontological status of history as a dialectical, organic, and open totality. This awareness stems from the fact that the interpretation and deployment are also products of social scientific practices throughout time (Thomas 2009: 8–31). Thomas refutes the Althusserian critique in *Reading Capital* that Gramsci's historicism shared the same scientific error as the positivist logico-historical Marxists, who conflated the dialectical constitution of a determined concept with its historical-genetic becoming. From Althusser's point of view, the validity of a concept is derived solely from its historical concrete substance (Althusser and Balibar 1970: 91–4). Furthermore, he conflated Hegel's historicist interpretations of the formation of philosophical concepts with the formal procedures of thinking about the unity of thought and being – dialectical logic. Althusser assumes the coincidence of an order of existence defined by linear historical time – i.e. the history of philosophy – with a conceptual order defined by logical time – i.e. reflective thinking about realized actuality. However, the conceptual order is driven by absences, repetitive mediations and possibilities, which, when applied to history as an appearing self-mediated positivity in linear historical time, shows us history as an ensemble of multiple temporalities. The Hegelian dialectic does not present history as unified, linear and self-enclosed (Read 2005). It enables conceptual arrangements of a mediated process, which breaks the preconceived set of relations, and, consequently, continuously fills the concepts with meaning.

The dialectic defines the intentions of the interpretation of historical meaning, and meaning continuously expands the truth of those intentions.

Gramsci indicated that the concept of hegemony holds the key to an understanding of the political determinants of the transition to modernity. Marx had already commented that the rise of the bourgeois state eliminated the political character of civil society and abolished the particularist nature of politics. The sphere of civil society was torn from political society, and man as a private individual with particular interests was separated from man as a citizen of the universal community. The political sphere abolished the social distinctions of 'birth, rank, education, and occupation' in principle, but 'far from abolishing these factual distinctions, the state presupposes them in order to exist, it only experiences itself as a political state and asserts its universality in opposition to these elements' (Marx 1992: 219).

Gramsci developed Marx's concept of bourgeois society and defined the contradictory totality of the historically matured differentiation of civil and political society as the 'integral State' (Morton 2007: 89). In the bourgeois age, the equilibrium was no longer maintained between estates, but between the spheres of political and civil society, and between the modes of governance of domination and hegemony. Whereas domination is the concept of 'naked' and 'top-down' class rule, whereby the ruled constitute the passive object of the integral state, hegemony entails the active acceptance of the bourgeoisie's class leadership by subaltern groups, because of its prestige, its directive capacities, its cultural aura, its technocratic ability to 'manage' society, etc. In order to become a hegemonic force, a party had to forge an organic connection between the spontaneous philosophy of its social base and its own worldview. Gramsci distinguished between, on the one hand, popular religion as an integral part of 'spontaneous philosophy' – a whole array of gelatinous and often contradictory concepts of the world he described as, 'the entire system of beliefs, superstitions, opinions, ways of seeing things and of acting' (Gramsci 1971: 323); and, on the other hand, philosophy proper, which was a coherent and logical body of ideas.

History does not logically constitute the concept of hegemony, nor does the concept a priori find the necessary expression in historical processes. In order to develop an understanding of a social formation, its historical resources have to be processed by conceptual devices, which are developed themselves in the process of investigation and interpretation. Gramsci's historicism consists of a reciprocal relation between his historical materialist analysis of the capitalist social formation and his philosophy of praxis, in which he finds himself as 'an element of the contradiction and elevates this element to a principle of knowledge and therefore of action' (Gramsci 1971: 405). Hegemony emerged as a concept within Gramsci's own practico-theoretical activity (praxis) as a communist during the two years of the biennio rosso and its Fascist aftermath. An expansion and deepening of Lenin's understanding of the position of the proletariat vis-à-vis other subaltern forces in a shared political project, 'hegemony' became a key concept in the historical understanding of the rise and degeneration of the bourgeois state and modernity.

Gramsci deployed the concept of hegemony in order to rupture, in a historical and logical sense, the self-referentiality of modernity as the bourgeois epoch (Thomas 2009: 134). In the Ancien Régime, the bourgeoisie emerged as the class most capable of defeating the dominance of the aristocracy, and the need for its own emancipation coincided with that of society at large. The class was able '… to radicalize the elements of crisis that have slowly been strengthened and, finally, to promote the advent of a different social formation, destined to live, for a longer or shorter period, an historically significant and operative life, bearer of real transformations' (Gramsci in Thomas 2009: 153). Hegemony was the capacity of the bourgeoisie to consolidate its position as a progressive and directive political force, and to represent its own particular interests as the general or common good.

Gramsci and France: A Historical Formation of Bourgeois Hegemony

In Gramsci's notebooks the Renaissance is depicted as a regressive, reactionary moment, whereas the Reformation presented itself as a new ethico-moral formation challenging the dominant feudal order. The Renaissance was a result of the failure of the political viability of the republican communes in the Italian city states. The humanists, as a secularized social stratum within an expanding urban environment, refused to act as the organic intellectuals of the merchants and rich master craftsmen. Instead they became the traditional intellectuals of aristocratic rulers from whom they received status and a comfortable income. They promoted a high culture and disconnected themselves from the popular layers of society. In other words, they produced a corpus of high ideals in order to protect parochial prerogatives.

Commune elites failed to absorb the clergy as traditional intellectuals, because the papal state policy positioned itself as a political force above the city states (Gramsci 1996 [1931]: 378–9). Gramsci's analysis of the Catholic religion emphasized the fundamental difference between the Church as an international and local institutional organization, and the clergy as a class-caste or class-order. The international components allowed the Church to play a distinctive role in the power struggle of sovereign powers, but as a local institution it had to integrate itself in the feudal institutional-political order. Nonetheless, the Church provided also the organizational framework for a communal social force in which the principles of faith were transformed into the tools for the moral-intellectual leadership of the clergy who expressed the universalist-papist world view. These organizational traits, represented as a religious society, were at odds with its direct economic interests as a class-caste. In Western Europe during the commercialization of feudal society, the clergy underwent a process of social differentiation: in rich regions the urban middle strata became the preferred recruiting pool, while in rural backward regions the clergy still constituted a part of the upper classes. In early modern times the urban clergy blended in the numerous political and administrative offices (Munck 1990). In absolutist France the clergy was the largest single landowner and expressed itself as a conservative force in defending the feudal system of rents and taxations. In times of crisis, the clergy as a caste risked to be disassociated from its own communal form of organization.

The Reformation started as an organic, mass expression of 'the popular', initiating the idea of political sovereignty and negating the universal claims of the Catholic Church as a caste of priestly intellectuals. Driven by 'innovating and mass-mobilizing activities of the new religious teachers' (Fontana 1993: 39), the Reformation appeared as a national-popular movement (Gramsci 1996 [1930]: 143). It opened up a potential space to negotiate state policy between, on the one hand, the economic-corporate attitude of the well-off of the third estate and, on the other, the political aspirations of the proto-bourgeoisie. Local circumstances and the capacities of the particular assemblages of social forces against the resilience of the feudal order determined the concrete outcome of these struggles.

After two centuries of religious wars and factional struggles between kings and aristocrats, the European nation states came into existence. In absolutist France the crown centralized, although not in a unified manner, the exercise of political power through the mediation of personal networks of the local gentry and the imposition of judicial and financial administration. Despite the weakening of manorial rights in the process, the aristocracy relied on the institutions of the crown to maintain its customary prerogatives in new forms of proprietary political power (Meiksins Wood 1991). The aristocracy secured its surplus extraction from seigniorial taxation, tax farming contracts and different sorts of exclusive property rights on communal means of production (Mooers 1991). Lower nobles, lacking strong financial reserves or important connections, hoped to get elected as officers of the state.

In the provincial cities and the Parisian metropolis the bourgeoisie consisted of many class fractions. A rich layer of master craftsmen subordinated the production system of the guilds under a complex system of subcontracting and patent rights (Littler 1982; Lis and Soly 2008). Other fractions focused on buying land and titles, or the accumulation of venal offices (Lucas 1973; Woloch and Brown 2012). The income strategies of the bourgeoisie depended on the capacity of the absolutist state to expand occupational promotions, urban investment opportunities, tax collection benefits and the supply of land entitlements. Their economic-corporate interests were tightly interwoven with the national state and its local institutions, but at the same time they depended on the financial gains in intermediate bodies, corporate benefits and fragmented jurisdiction (Meiksins Wood 1991). The absolutist state exercised a limited form of political hegemony in the shape of an institutional-economic equilibrium between the aforementioned social class fractions. Absolutist France survived several grave financial difficulties by separating the interests of the nobility and the rich bourgeoisie from those of the lower urban classes and the tax farmers (Mousnier 1970). It could centralize the political forces of the late medieval federation of classes or class fractions in the urban commercial environment without eliminating corporate institutions and structures (Gramsci 1996 [1930]: 24).

Throughout his analysis of the crisis of the French absolutist state Gramsci discerned that the policy of equilibrium and separation came to a halt when it was no longer possible to merge the economic-corporate interests of the aristocracy with those of the bourgeoisie through moderate reforms in an aristocratic parliamentary setting. Any temporary solution stirred up the political debates around the alliances and splits between king, aristocracy and bourgeoisie. These proposed reforms revealed the fundamental incapacity of the absolutist state to maintain the political equilibrium. The collective action of the popular classes propelled the difficulties of institutional reform to a full-scale organic crisis in which economic-corporate interests were transformed into political demands addressing society as a whole (Gramsci 1996: 97).

Hegemony stands at the crossroads of the Gramscian historicity of modernity. It combines a historical investigation into concrete social relations and forces, such as the French revolution, with a symptomatic rereading of the bourgeois conceptual framework of modernity, and with the creation of a gradually expanding systematic toolbox. Hegemony functions as an index of this historicity (Thomas 2009: 134). The western transition to modernity, as exemplified by Gramsci's analysis of French national history, can be seen as the formation of a political and ideological hegemony, in which the bourgeoisie succeeded to institutionalize the social conditions of the capitalist relations of production. The 'myth' of the French Revolution represented modernity's ethico-political moment: '... a creation of concrete phantasy which acts on a dispersed and shattered people to arouse and organize its collective will' (Gramsci 1971: 125–6). However, Neil Davidson (2012) has clearly shown that the immense success of a total political transformation of the French people-nation was an exception in the history of bourgeois revolutions, the accomplished form of a political revolution (Buci-Glucksmann 1980: 54).

In most of France's neighbouring countries the bourgeoisie was unable to develop itself as an integral hegemonic force. Gramsci aimed to explain the nature of an apparent transitional interregnum in which neither a full restoration, nor the revolutionary birth of a new social formation could be achieved (Gramsci 1996 [1930]: 33). In most European countries, the transition to modernity was driven by a 'passive revolution': a series of small-scale economic reforms that initiated molecular transformations, and which were based on the partial hegemony of one or more class fractions over the other ruling and subaltern social layers. 'Passive revolution' is Gramsci's interpretation of

> ... the persistent capacity of initiative of the bourgeoisie which succeeds, even in the historical phase in which it has ceased to be a properly revolutionary class, to produce socio-political transformations, sometimes of significance, conserving securely in its own hands power, initiative and hegemony, and leaving the working classes in their condition of subalternity. (Losurdo in Thomas 2009: 197)

Not the archetype of the French Revolution, but 'passive revolution' in its many forms of appearance became the political cell-form of capitalist modernity. Through his study of the Risorgimento Gramsci elaborated the Italian particularities of the 'passive' transformation process towards modernity.

Unlike its French counterparts, throughout the Middle Ages the Italian bourgeoisie was not able to develop itself as a coherent political force. Socially locked in an economic-corporate state and spatially divided between North and South class fractions, it was unable to rally popular forces behind a modernist project of nation state building and economic transformation. The bourgeoisie chose to emulate the aristocratic competitors: thus its culture and intellectuals became profoundly anti-democratic and reactionary (Gramsci 2007 [1930]: 205). Italian unification was realized by military conquest of Piedmont from above, and not by a mass movement from below. The Italian state became the facilitator of a limited bourgeois hegemony, instead of its organic outcome (Gramsci 1971: 105). From 1848 onwards, Ancien Régime personnel and radical-popular intellectuals were not politically defeated, but gradually absorbed and integrated into the apparatus of the new state (Gramsci 1971: 58–9). Thus the radical Action Party of Garibaldi and Mazzini, which had the potential to lead a popular mass movement, was instead pacified by the right-wing Moderates.

The absence of a political revolution paralleled a lack of cultural-religious transformations that would reorient the dominant feudal worldviews towards bourgeois notions. In Italy, the bourgeoisie had to win the support of the peasants in the south vis-à-vis the landed power of the church (Gramsci 1982 [1930]: 163). However, the Action Party only affirmed its anticlerical philosophy, and did not offer the farmers the ideological means to connect their popular religion to a national-bourgeois worldview. Unlike the universalism of French bourgeois culture, the celebrated 'Italian' cultural expressions remained locked within a caste of urban intellectuals (Gramsci 1971: 63). There was no genuine attempt to forge a national Italian culture as the sediment for a modern state. Neither did the Action Party create the material base for such an ideological connection. Wary of its revolutionary potential, the Action Party refused to implement anti-feudal land reforms in the south, even suppressing spontaneous rural revolts. In contradistinction, the Moderates '… did not distribute ecclesiastical property among the peasants, but they used it to create a new stratum of great and medium landowners tied to the new political situation, and did not hesitate to lay hands on landed property, even if it was only that of the Orders' (Gramsci 1971: 102). This crude transformation of rural relations blocked a complete transition towards capitalist social relations in the Italian countryside, in addition to politically pacifying the peasant masses – thus the particular path of Italy's 'passive revolution'.

Foucault's Crisis of Modernity and the History of the Present

There is little debate about the relationship between Foucault's methodology and Marxist perspectives. Foucault and several authors who align with his genealogical project (for example Poster 1984) did and do not sufficiently grasp the conceptual 'differences in unity' between dialectical thought, historical materialism, and Marx's political economy (Paolucci 2003). Foucault continued a tradition of criticizing the fictitious image of Marxist thought as being logico-historical and Hegelian thought as a hypostatization of history and as a secular theology. Nonetheless, Gramsci's Marxism and Foucault's genealogical perspective share a mutual core element: the historical and conceptual status of modernity as a historicity, in which knowledge has its own relative autonomy qua transformations within its articulation with power strategies. Foucault's historical investigations of Western history and present cannot be fully grasped unless the historical a priori enters the arena (Major Poetzl 1983; O'Farrell 1989; Mahon 1992; May 1995; Visker 1995; De Oliveira 2012). History analysed through the prism of knowledge-power exists through the contingent, unstable, and fragile production of an ontological real, but nominalist social reality. At the same time, the practices of knowledge and strategies of power regulate the established identities of subjects, not nothings, and set limits to the reality-reference in a certain historical age (Foucault 1991 [1975]: 23).

Foucault's analysis of the status of modernity was from its inception a philosophical and historical enterprise. For Foucault, Kant's critique remained the prime example of a humanist delusion. Kant functions as a transitional thinker towards modernity in which the Cartesian knowing subject has been transformed into both a subject and object of knowledge (Major-Poetzl 1983: 161). The Cartesian subject and its knowledge were grounded in an order of representation, natural or divine, while Kant's subject constitutes itself as the centre, origin and limit of knowledge. Kant's transcendental subject possesses fixed, limited, and transhistorical faculties of reason, in which it permits to know itself as an empirical object. The subject as a noumenon can only empirically know itself by the a priori knowledge of the transcendental finite conditions. This transcendental-empirical double interprets a subject within its own normativity and circularity (Racevskis 1983: 60). This subject represents itself as 'Man' as the origin of knowledge, the transcendental limit, which Foucault calls the modern 'invention of man'. The anthropological status of the modern subject as 'Man', the 'originary', fictitiously grounds the transcendental and is grounded by the same transcendental. Therefore the anthropology of 'Man' creates a transcendental transposition of the noumenon as itself in order to overcome the empirical limit (Han 1998: 17–37). The knowledge of modern human sciences, the acts of representation of the same representations (although representation and analysis are separated) is unscientific because it naturalizes the historical a priori: 'The human sciences … become that knowledge of that in Man which escapes him' (Cousins and Hussain 1984: 54).

Contrary to the classical episteme, Kant studied the act of representation besides its actual deployment, but did not ground these acts in a historical setting, therefore lacking an articulated view on the anthropology of man and the analysis of modern empiricities (Gutting 1989). Nonetheless, it was Kant who erased the role of spirituality in subjectivation in favour of reason (O'Farrell 1989: 73).

This humanistic form of rationality suspended the question of self-understanding because knowledge of man and ethics cannot be distinguished (Angus 2000: 187). Pace Kant's critique, Foucault's genealogical method is the conceptual turn of transforming historical ideas about social reality and the subject into power/knowledge relations without a repetition of the anthropological categories. Knowledge as a set of practices and the strategies of power do not spring from a preconfigured and preconstituted knowing subject who interprets history as the historical acts and thoughts of an essential human nature. 'Anti-humanist' resistance is possible when the anthropological concepts have been transformed into a complete new set of historical categories and power practices, and when the genealogical point of view can offer 'spaces' of resistance within the processes of analysis of modern regimes of truth (Visker 1995).

The relation between Kant, anthropology, and the human sciences allowed Foucault to break with the philosophical metaphysics of modernity, revealing the human sciences as discursive practices of ordering knowledge and exclusion, or the production of knowledge with strategies of power as regimes of truth. The transcendental subject supposes a continuous progression of reason in the history of ideas, while Foucault focuses on the relations of knowledge within discursive formations and regimes of truth (Cousins and Hussain 1984: 94). This is the explicit connection between the critique of philosophy and the research into the historical a priori in history.

Foucault did not pay much attention to the role of religion as a complex of dispositifs or technologies until his (unfinished) project on power, subjectivity, and sexuality, and in several auto-critiques in his later lectures at Collège de France. He identified church institutions as crucial sites of technologies of behaviour. Nonetheless, he never wrote a concrete historiography of the Church as a network of religious organizations, but studied its effects in other regimes of power (Carrette 2000: 31). Foucault asserted that a new form of power had been born between the confined walls of early medieval monasteries. Besides the fact that monasteries functioned as a hierarchy of power relations, it could not obtain a degree of domination over the clerical inhabitants without fixed rituals of salvation, obedience and penance, and the practice of confession as a technique of power. This technique did not just consist of a one-sided subjection of a body, but invested in the transformation of pleasure into desire to confess. In a similar way, Christian institutions did not only impose moral codes on society, but successfully inserted ethical guidelines in the techniques of the self, which can be defined as the self-imposed process of both individualized normalization and a disclosure of the self through the idea of self-knowledge (Racevskis 1983; O'Farrell 1989; Strozier 2002). Both the ethical problematic of the self-relation and the technique of power were driven by binary situations: body/flesh and desire, piety and sin, etc. This kind of pastoral power, expressed the ability of Christianity to form communal local sites of power in which knowledge was connected to the notions of the common good and corporatist stratification of the social. From this constellation the deployment of alliance crystallized in which blood and family ties grounded the first discourses on sexuality.

Gramsci and Foucault: Commensurable and Complementary Concepts

Foucault's interpretation of early modernity and absolutism in *Discipline and Punish* (1991 [1975]) and the first volume of *The History of Sexuality* (1978 [1976]) expresses a more elaborate conjunction between power-knowledge of several dispositifs and the Marxist class analysis (Lemert and Gillan 1982: 8–10). Visker (1995) already showed the conceptual ambiguities of knowledge and power, whereas Carrette (2000) emphasized the fact that Foucault encountered great difficulties to see the interconnected relations between Christianity as a belief system and its existing social practices. A social formation as an aggregate of class relations does not directly determine the locality of the dispositifs, but does shape a general field of possibilities of mechanisms of power (Strozier 2002: 69). Marxists, according to Foucault, do not see this differentiation and reciprocity and reduce modern forms of power to the politico-discursive form of law and reduce political philosophy to the relation between law and property relations. Both Gramsci and Foucault emphasized the incomplete, fractured, and particularized – i.e. capillary – political potential of social control of absolutism. The exercise of sovereign absolutist power focused on the preservation of law and rule of a certain geographical domain, what Arrighi (1994) called the territorial logic. Although Foucault located the 'birth' of modernity at different points of the timeline – because each locality of power relations in a dispositif has its own specific temporality – a specific articulation of forces and power can be discerned.

While Gramsci directed his attention to changing class relations, political mediation, and the nation state's lack of a proper political hegemony, Foucault succeeded in analysing the limits of sovereign power as a force which only could be exercised when directed to a social specific. The Gramscian modern bourgeois state expanded its hegemonic forces because the techniques and practices of the body politic proliferated throughout the political anatomy of society. Certain procedures were established to control the bodies of society (Lemert and Gillan 1982: 75). Disciplinary power, rooted in the dispositif of the prison or the military, disseminated across regulatory forces. Sovereign power had been displaced and articulated via the juridico-discursive construct of law (Smart 1983: 85). But the moment of passive revolution was impossible without the ability of political forces to establish a set of procedures to control the population as the aggregated political economy of bodies. The explicitly ethico-political hegemony of the bourgeoisie in the salient style of the French Revolution was increasingly complemented or replaced with the growing capillary and technocratic capacities of ruling classes to govern, manage, and regulate the social existence of the subaltern classes. This passive revolution driven by biopower and discipline signalled a new economy of judicial power, standardization of legal codes, and the definite unification of judicial space (Foucault 1991 [1975]: 77–90). The creation of the national-popular – a precondition of hegemony – also entailed the regulation of political souls and the moral integration of subjects as civil individuals into the political. In the Gramscian integral state, governmental power within the biopolitical field subjected the national-popular to obedient political bodies. In this moment of post-passive revolution, civil society reveals itself as the central processing unit of decentralized centres of state power, from which the most efficient economies of intensification of disciplinary and governmental power emerge (Nealon 2008: 29–48). In these transitions, the Church as a dispositif played an important role to articulate the different kinds of power, a 'Christianization-in-depth', which Foucault detected in the locality of sexual discourses, its role in centuries of religious wars and colonization, and the supportive role of the deployment of alliance (Bernauer 2004: 78–9).

In modern times, the Church and the secular state were brotherly competitors to recruit elements from the popular classes to serve as traditional intellectuals in civil society. The Church lost the moral-intellectual claims on universality in which natural theology and divine revelation became sterile doctrines of the past. The civil institutions of the Church served as the ideological means to obtain concrete power in the political society to overcome its own degradation as merely a subaltern ideological element (Gramsci 1995 [1930]: 12–13, 34; Gramsci 1996 [1931]: 199). The priestly caste politicized itself and effectively participated in the secular procedures of the regulatory mechanisms of domination. This politicization forced the Church to combine two perspectives: on the one hand, the propagation of the long-gone values of the Ancien Régime with an emphasis on the neo-Thomist concept of the common good; and, on the other, a defence of its direct corporate interests in modern society. Eventually, the Church was able to develop the theological notion of the common good into a transitional concept that is situated at the boundary of the direct economic-corporate and the modern political.

Foucault and the Iranian Revolution

With the aim of completing his critique of modernity, Foucault was looking for alternative and non-Western discourses that did not reproduce the modernist reproduction of power (Leezenberg 1999: 67). In his genealogical writings of the first period he stressed the fact that power contingently produced certain forms of knowledge and the objects of knowledge, although a crystallization of dominant discourses takes place (Racevskis 1983: 83). Local power relations and apparatuses are being temporarily integrated in power strategies, but these strategies are instable and do not possess an inherent quality to necessary determine the future chain of successions. Thus, from a genealogical point of view, any political strategy can be immediately countered in order to create a completely new one.

Between 1978 and 1979 Foucault became fascinated with the unfolding process of the Iranian Revolution. He observed the awkward yet somehow organic class alliance between, on the one hand 'traditional' bazaar merchants and the clergy, and, on the other, 'modern' students and industrial workers, and concluded that the revolution did not fit the traditional Marxist scheme (Leezenberg 1999: 68). He was especially interested in the role of religion within the anti-Shah movement –

a radical version of Shi'ism developed and popularized by intellectuals such as Ali Shariati and clerics such as Khomeini. He conceived of the Iranians' mobilization of religion as an 'authentic' way to overcome the modernist technologies of power upon which the dictatorship of the Shah was founded. Furthermore, this interpretation resembled his later fascination for early Christian Gnosticism and mysticism as being radically different from classical philosophy or medieval Christianity in its attempt to design other modes of self-interrogation and self-subjectivation, which he called Parrhesia (Bernauer 2004: 90–92). In Iran, according to Foucault, there is no organic historicity of modern power strategies. The genealogical notion of the 'non-place' as the battlefield between forces has already been occupied by an authentic 'political spirituality' that embodied the Iranians' will, which expressed itself in the determination of the mass mobilizations in the face of deadly police violence. The return to 'original' and 'traditional' Shi'ism was a non-alienated, non-political and authentic way of the Iranian people to reject Western modernity (Leezenberg 1999: 78; Afary and Anderson 2006: 50–51).

Although Foucault conceived of the Iranian revolution as an open site of subjectivation processes that put aside the former power relations of the Shah's regime, he did not turn to a genealogical methodology to understand the relation between the productivity of power and its internal resistance. This production has an auto-negative quality because subjectification is driven by an internal differentiation within unstable identities (Bech Dyrberg 1997: 133). For Foucault, the Iranian subjectivity was solely an act of liberation based on self-constitution and experience of forms of subjectivity by the self through self-recognition. Nowhere does he place self-recognition within a regime of practice. Thus, this act of liberation as self-recognition only faces forms of modern subjectivity as an externality in which the techniques of the self always had a non-modern spirituality: 'The Iranian masses demonstrated the possibility of resistance without participating in or perpetuating a preconceived schema of power' (Ghamari-Tabrizi 2010: 282). The modernization of Iran, the formation of power relations which would create modern subjects, in the end was not characterized by a stalled transition but by a struggle between 'alien' modern dispositifs and 'authentic' traditional techniques of the self giving birth to the experience of revolution. This traditional subjectivity finds its force to proliferate new relations of power in a political form in religion as the active field of knowledge.

Foucault returned to the notion of the authentic, which stands in opposition to his critique of modernity. The Iranian body, the original materiality which is in process of self-recognition as a non-modern subject, played a key role. Foucault's revisions in the genealogical methodology were driven by, on the one hand, the continuous contradiction between the critique of origin as an anthropological sin of modernity and the normativity of modern human sciences; and, on the other, by the recurrent genealogical doubling of the representations of modernity in which resistance seems impossible or only possible within the anthropological mode of being (Visker 1995; Strozier 2002). Foucault tried to circumvent this problematic in his analysis of Iran – which served as an empirical case of the subject turn within the genealogical methodology – by opposing western subjectivity to an original Iranian version.

However, Foucault's enthusiastic embrace of Shi'ite political spirituality was quickly shattered by the development of the Iranian Revolution. Iranians found themselves terrorized by the technologies of repression of the – quite modernist – dictatorship of the Shi'ite clergy. Arguably, Foucault's intellectual faux pas was caused by an orientalist blindness towards the fact that both the Iranian Revolution and the radical Shi'ite discourse were deeply modernist phenomena (Afary and Anderson 2005). Foucault did not grasp the fundamentally transitory character of the Iranian social formation at the time of the Revolution. The French philosopher cast the mobilization of non-Western religious signifiers into the a priori mould of a non-modernist discursive practice. He heralded the spiritual politics of Islam as forms of subjectivity which escaped, rather than articulated modernization.

Shi'ism and Modernity

Because of the relative political and economic independence of the Shi'ite clerical caste from the Persian state, the masses increasingly perceived the clergy as a mediating group between their popular interests and those of the isolated rulers. The Iranian clergy became the bearers of a national-popular project centred on the interpenetration of the 'spontaneous' Islamic religion and popular culture on the one hand, and Twelver theology on the other. However, because the clergy was embedded within the pre-capitalist structure of the 'bazaar economy', there was a contradiction between their modernist political project of forging a national cultural sphere, and their aversion to transform the social relations of production. The bazaar was not a class in itself, but a socio-spatial nexus of production and distribution, where different class fractions such as artisans, merchants, shop owners, etc. were united in corporatist ways. Through bath and tea houses, mosques, community centres, etc., the bazaar fused economic structures with social and cultural forms. Acting as brokers and middlemen of the bazaar, and often tied to its actors through bonds of marriage, the interests of the clergy were entwined with those of the bazaris (Keddie 1981: 244–6; Moaddel 2005: 99–108).

The contradiction between the political and economic poles of the transformation towards modernity was compounded by the penetration of Western capital and the decrease in political sovereignty during the nineteenth century. Imperialism weakened the rise of an Iranian bourgeoisie that could have led the transition to modernity. Instead, the ulama, the bazaar, and even secular intellectuals found each other in a political alliance against foreign intervention and its domestic collaborators, first in the anti-tobacco movement of 1891, then in the Constitutional Revolution of 1905. Military intervention by Russia and Britain put an end to the revolutionary uprising. After World War I the Iranian regime was faced with an organic crisis as its political and economic sources of power had completely collapsed, but the popular mass movement that could have challenged the weakened state had been defeated. In 1921 Minister of War Reza Khan organized a coup, paving the way for Iran's passive revolution. Reza Khan neutralized clerical opposition against the secular-republican Turkish road to modernity, by crowning himself as Reza Shah Pahlavi and promising to defend the interests of the ulama, landlords, and bazaris (Keddie 1981: 90–105).

In order to create a strong national state, Reza Shah had to revolutionize Iran's economy. As pre-modern economic structures, the bazaar, the clergy, and the landlords constituted objective obstacles on the road to modernity. Yet, because the clergy was the conscious and powerful bearer of the national-popular project, the Shah could not easily liquidate or absorb these layers into his own project. This contradiction remained at the heart of the Iranian social formation until the revolution of 1979.

After the defeat and repression of the anti-imperialist National Front movement in the 1950s, the position of the Shah was strengthened. The passive revolution turned to its offensive moment, as Iran's civil society was increasingly subsumed under the political dictatorship. From 1963 onwards, the forceful social and economic transformation process was dubbed the 'White Revolution', entailing land reforms, privatizations, the formation of a new cadre of teachers for the countryside, nationalization of the forests, and profit shares for industrial workers (Keddie 1981: 150–56). These reforms gradually transformed the Iranian social formation, increasing the number of modern middle class and industrial wage workers in the total labour force. However, only a tiny fraction of the population enjoyed the improvements in healthcare and education, and the influx of Western commodities. Not the modernization process in itself, but the authoritarian and exclusivist method of transition would prompt the Iranians to revolt in the 1970s (Abrahamian 1980: 22–3).

The religious opposition had been part of the National Front up until 1953. Yet, at this point the general 'progressive' character of the clergy was already falling apart. Faced with the call by the popular masses and trade unions for social and economic reform, the ulama often allied themselves with the landlords and imperialist forces against the reform movement. The clergy itself was split between conservatives, who did not care much for a political role for the ulama; 'liberals', who advocated a constitutional monarchy; and radicals such as Ayatollah Khomeini, who demanded a direct political role for the clergy (Keddie 1981: 208–10).

In the second half of the 1970s, the ulama increasingly turned against the Shah. Not only did Muhammad Reza Pahlavi encourage the distribution of Western cultural ideas and practices, he also attacked the material base of the clergy's power: their income, lands, and endowments (Keddie 1981: 239–43). The clergy mobilized its traditional corporatist layers: the bazaar and the sub-proletariat. Even though the Shah's transformations had created a modern industrial proletariat and middle classes, the bazaar had continued to exist more or less unchanged. Its number had remained stable because of rural migration to the cities. In 1975 their existence was threatened by the Shah who outlawed their traditional guild structures, reorganizing their members in new, state corporatist unions (Abrahamian 1980: 25–6). Those Iranians from the countryside who could not find work in the bazaar joined the urban lumpen-proletariat, where they became clients of Islamic welfare organizations. Together with the Islamic students, these groups constituted the mass reserves of the clergy.

Because of his radicalism, Khomeini became the vocal leader of most clerical opposition to the Shah. The Shah imagined that he could forge a new state project ex nihilo, as he tried to conjure up the pre-Islamic Persian past in prestigious monuments and festivities. However, this pompous Persian ultra-nationalism was not in any organic way connected to the spontaneous religious-cultural framework of the masses. Conversely, Khomeini's apparent liberation theology did resonate among the Iranian people. On the one hand, just as Foucault emphasized, it expressed the political tasks at hand in an 'authentic' language, using shared cultural categories and signifiers. On the other hand, its anti-imperialist tone and defence of the Iranian 'common good' brought into memory the modern historical alliances and projects of the Constitutional Revolution and the National Front. It was the hybridity of Khomeini's discourse that allowed him to become the national figurehead of the mass movement against the Shah. He was supported by religious and secular opposition forces because he was seen as the individual who expressed both the particular nature of the Iranian Revolution and the general struggle against imperialism.

It is exactly this hybridity – which expresses the transitory character of the Iranian social formation, and which permeates every epiphenomenon of the revolution – that Foucault failed to see.

Gramsci, Foucault, and Transition

Putting together the insights of Gramsci and Foucault on modernity, religion, and transition, one could situate the praxis of spiritual politics in the fluid zone of transition towards modernity. Political spirituality constitutes an unarticulated appeal to an ethics of justice which is rooted in the intersection between the modern and the pre-modern. It is a hybrid construct that mobilizes a hybrid combination of pre-modern and modern notions of corporatism and the common good – a sublation of class society by infusing the capitalist significants of the present-as-becoming with the pre-capitalist signifiers of the present-as-fading-away. Being a particularist political force, a class or class fraction with corporate interests can only obtain forms of political power when it is able to legitimize its project in the discursive form of the 'common good'. In itself, this does not (yet) establish a hegemonic transformation, but enables the respective class to render other subaltern formations as a temporary passive force. This was a political technique of the bourgeoisie in all transitional phases in the European feudal social formations.

For Gramsci, however, the effects of hegemony are highly contradictory. The more authentically hegemonic a class really is, the more it leaves opposing classes the possibility of organizing and forming themselves into an autonomous political force. France is not only the 'classic' country of bourgeois domination and rule, but it is also the 'classic' country of class struggle and revolt. Conversely, the passive revolution, by separating the leadership of allied and opposing classes from their organic base, deprives these social groups of their own political instrument and creates an obstacle to their constitution as autonomous classes (Buci-Glucksmann: 57). Such was the fate of the Italian Action Party, as its cadres were absorbed by the Moderates.

In Iran the budding Pahlavi state was able, to a degree, to bind the intellectuals of the modern capitalist classes to its project in clientilist and coercive ways. Its passive revolution entailed a weak and limited hegemony, and its national project lacked cultural and directive power and prestige. In each situation of crisis the modern petty bourgeois and worker classes turned against the Pahlavi state, as happened with the National Front.

The clergy, for its part, remained largely outside the transformism of the Pahlavi state. As a semi-independent force it sometimes joined the Pahlavi project, as long as its corporate interests were served by such an alliance, and sometimes it participated in – or even led – a counter-hegemonic bloc when the state encroached on its class privileges. The clergy's project was political modernist, in the sense that it aimed to transform its traditional national-corporate religion into the politico-legal framework of a sovereign nation state. At the same moment it was socially and economically pre-modern, as the ulama desired to keep the status-quo of the bazaar economy in the face of capitalist and imperialist encroachment. The assertion of clerical power always expressed its hybrid nature of both a politically progressive and a socio-economically regressive force, vis-à-vis its equally hybrid antipode of authoritarian Pahlavi modernization.

The offensive of the White Revolution pushed the clergy into opposition against the state, whereby the radical wing of Khomeini constituted the directive force. Khomeini sublated the internal and combined contradictions of the clergy's hybridity and the Shah's passive revolution through a Caesarist intervention. What Foucault understood as political spirituality was the dialectic of 'revolution/restoration' taken a step further than its continuous interplay between the Pahlavi state and its counterbloc. The Iranian Revolution was clearly an ethico-political assertion of the popular, and as such the negation of the passive revolution of the Shah. However, through the leadership of Khomeini it was the clergy who acted as Iran's radical Jacobins, initiating a transformation of the democratic modernist project of the Constitutional Revolution and the National Front into the hybrid national-popular demand of an 'Islamic Republic' versus the 'monarchy' in the infamous referendum of 1979.

However, the 'spirituality of politics' was quickly replaced with the 'politics of spirituality' during the struggle for power after the fall of the monarchy, between radical and moderate Islamists, between Islamists and secularists, and between leftists and rightists. Islamist hegemony could only be extended through explicitly political means, such as the 'anti-imperialist' occupation of the US embassy, and, in the end, by waging a 'national' war against Iraq. The swift exhaustion of the ethico-political or spiritual dimension of the Islamist project signalled a return to the cynical politics of passive revolution and top-down modernization. Ideological mobilization was replaced with the vertical hierarchy of bureaucratic clientilism, which became the worldly, material base of the Islamic Republic. In Iran, the halted transition to modernity was continued by the Caesarist clergy, who dissolved the bazaar economy by establishing a novel and hybrid corporatism. Iran became another historical case of transition wherein both the pre-modern, religious-corporatist notion of the common good and the modernist, secular promise of universal political representation was replaced with the repressive mechanisms of an integral state, which mediated rather than sublated the growing antagonistic relations between transitory classes and social forms.

References

Abrahamian, E. 1980. Structural causes of the Iranian Revolution. *MERIP Reports (Iran's Revolution: The Rural Dimension)* 87: 21–6.

Afary, J. and Anderson, K.B. 2005. *Foucault and the Iranian Revolution. Gender and the Seductions of Islamism*. Chicago: The University of Chicago Press.

Althusser, L. and Balibar, E. 1970. *Reading Capital*. London: New Left Books.

Angus, I. 2000. *(Dis)figurations. Discourse/Critique/Ethics*. London: Verso.

Arrighi, G. 1994. *The Long Twentieth Century*. London: Verso.

Bech Dyrberg, T. 1997. *The Circular Structure of Power*. London: Verso.

Bernauer, J. 2004. Foucault's philosophy of religion. In *Michel Foucault and Theology*, edited by J. Bernauer and J. Carrette. Aldershot: Ashgate.

Brown, S.B. and Woloch, I. 2012. *Eighteenth-Century Europe*. New York: W.W. Norton & Company.

Buci-Glucksmann, C. 1980. *Gramsci and the State*. London: Lawrence & Wishart.

Carrette, J.R. 2000. *Foucault and Religion*. London: Routledge.

Cousins, M. and Hussain, A. 1984. *Michel Foucault*. New York: St. Martin's Press.

Davidson, N. 2012. *How Revolutionary Were the Bourgeois Revolutions?* Chicago: Haymarket Books.

De Oliveira, N.F. 2012. *On the Genealogy of Modernity: Foucault's Social Philosophy*. New York: Nova Science Publishers.

Fontana, B. 1993. *Hegemony and Power. On the Relation between Gramsci and Machiavelli.* Minneapolis: University of Minnesota Press.

Foucault, M. 1991 [1975]. *Discipline and Punish. The Birth of the Prison*. New York: Vintage Books.

—. 1978 [1976]. *The History of Sexuality. Volume I: An Introduction*. New York: Pantheon Books.

—. 2009 [1977–1978]. Security, territory, population. *Lectures at the Collège de France 1977–1978*. New York: Picador Books.

Ghamari-Tabrizi, B. 2010. When life will no longer barter itself. In defense of Foucault on the Iranian revolution. In *A Foucault for the 21st Century*, edited by S. Binkley and J. Capetillo-Ponce. Newcastle upon Tyne: Cambridge Scholars Publishing, 270–90.

Gramsci, A. 1971. *Selections from the Prison Notebooks*. New York: International Publishers.

—. 1982. *Prison Notebooks Volume I*. New York: Columbia University Press.

—. 1995. *Further Selections from the Prison Notebooks*. London: Lawrence & Wishart.

—. 1996. *Prison Notebooks Volume II*. New York: Columbia University Press.

—. 2007. *Prison Notebooks Volume III*. New York: Columbia University Press.

Gutting, G. 1989. *Michel Foucault's Archaeology of Scientific Reason*. Cambridge: Cambridge University Press.

Gillan, G. and Lemert, C.C. 1982. *Michel Foucault. Social Theory and Transgression*. New York: Columbia University Press.

Han, B. 2002. *Foucault's Critical Project*. Stanford: Stanford University Press.

Keddie, N.R. 1981. *Roots of Revolution. An Interpretive History of Modern Iran*. Binghamton: Yale University Press.

Leezenberg, M. 1999. Michel Foucault on the Islamic Revolution in Iran. In *Cultural History after Foucault*, edited by J. Neubauer. New York: Transaction Publishers, 63–82.

Lis, C. and Soly, H. 2008. Subcontracting in guild-based export trades: Thirteenth–eighteenth centuries. In *Guilds, Innovation and the European Economy, 1400–1800*, edited by S. Epstein and M. Prak. Cambridge: Cambridge University Press.

Littler, C.R. 1982. *The Development of the Labour Process in Capitalist Societies*. London: Heinemann.

Lucas, C. 1973. Nobles, bourgeois and the origins of the French Revolution. *Past & Present* 60(1): 84–126.

Mahon, M. 1992. *Foucault's Nietzschean Genealogy*. Albany: State University of New York Press.

Major-Poetzl, P. 1983. *Michel Foucault's Archaeology of Western Culture*. Chapel Hill: The University of North Carolina Press.

Marx, K. 1992. *Early Writings*. London: Penguin Group.

May, T. 1993. Between genealogy and epistemology. Psychology, politics and knowledge. *The Thought of Michel Foucault*. Pennsylvania: The Pennsylvania State University Press.

Meiksins Wood, E. 1991. *The Pristine Culture of Capitalism*. London: Verso.

Moaddel, M. 2005. *Islamic Modernism, Nationalism, and Fundamentalism*. Chicago: The University of Chicago Press.

Mooers, C. 1991. *The Making of Bourgeois Europe*. London: Verso.

Morton, A.D. 2007. *Unravelling Gramsci. Hegemony and Passive Revolution in the Global Economy*. London: Pluto Press.

Mousnier, R. 1970. The Fronde. In *Preconditions of Revolution in Early Modern Europe*, edited by R. Forster and J.P. Greene. Baltimore: The Johns Hopkins Press, 131–60.

Munck, T. 1990. *Seventeenth-Century Europe*. London: Macmillan.

Nealon, J.T. 2008. *Foucault Beyond Foucault*. Stanford: Stanford University Press.

O'Farrell, C. 1989. *Foucault. Historian or Philosopher?* London: Macmillan.

Paolucci, P. 2003. Foucault's encounter with Marxism. In *Current Perspectives in Social Theory 22. Critical Theory: Diverse Objects, Diverse Subjects*, edited by J. Lehmann. Oxford: JAI, 3–60.

Posadas, J.D. 2010. 'Political spirituality', 'revolution' and the limits of politics: What was Foucault talking about in Iran? In *A Foucault for the 21st Century*, edited by S. Binkley and J. Capetillo-Ponce. Newcastle upon Tyne: Cambridge Scholars Publishing, 291–307.

Poster, M. 1984. *Foucault, Marxism and History*. London: Polity Press.

Racevskis, K. 1983. *Michel Foucault and the Subversion of Intellect*. Ithaca: Cornell University Press.

Read, J. 2005. The Althusser effect: Philosophy, history, and temporality. *Borderlands* 4(2): s.p.

Smart, B. 1983. *Foucault, Marxism and Critique*. London: Routledge.

Strozier, R.M. 2002. *Foucault, Subjectivity and Identity*. Detroit: Wayne State University Press.

Thomas, P.D. 2009. *The Gramscian Moment*. Leiden: Brill.

Visker, R. 1995. *Michel Foucault. Genealogy as Critique*. London: Verso.

Chapter 8
Post-Neoliberal Regional Integration in Latin America: Alianza Bolivariana para los Pueblos de Nuestra América (ALBA)

Efe Can Gürcan and Onur Bakıner

One of the most exciting phenomena in global politics since the mid-1990s has been the rebirth of the Left in Latin America. Socialist, social democratic, and centre-left parties assumed political power in the majority of Latin American countries, while numerous social movements have transformed the political landscape in the areas of economic distribution, rights of women, the indigenous, and landless peasants, the use of natural resources, and so on. Accompanying the rise of left-wing political parties and social movements, efforts to forge close economic, political and cultural cooperation across countries in the service of progressive causes have gained momentum. This chapter offers a theoretically informed perspective on a pioneering post-neoliberal regional integration effort: Alianza Bolivariana para los Pueblos de Nuestra América (ALBA).

Our fundamental premise is that the theory and practice of regional integration have become key fields of struggle in the aftermath of failed neoliberal restructuring in much of the world, and especially in Latin America. While the early theory and practice of regionalization focused exclusively on efficiency-driven market integration and the consequences of integration on national sovereignty (the neoliberal paradigm), in the twenty-first century the emerging consensus is that regional integration should address socioeconomic, political and cultural inequality through top-down and bottom-up decision-making to pose a counter-hegemonic challenge to neoliberalism. By counter-hegemonic, what is meant is the alignment of progressive forces that seek to overcome domination embedded in structures of material production, political decision-making, and the production of knowledge and social values in late capitalism.

We argue that post-neoliberal regional integration has emerged as a political, economic, and cultural alternative to neoliberal hegemony, whose processes of economic production and reproduction, political decision-making, and knowledge/norm creation have dominated capitalist globalization. Pointing out the differences and points of contact in the works of Antonio Gramsci (1891–1937) and Michel Foucault (1926–1984) with regards to the nature of social control, knowledge production, and political institutions in modern societies, we assert that resistance to material and symbolic domination should take place at the confluence of economic, political, and cultural counter-hegemonic struggles. Furthermore, we aim to reintroduce the significance of political agency in the form of revolutionary leadership into debates on emancipatory politics.

Supranational political alliances can be a genuine revolutionary alternative, a reformulation of Gramsci's Machiavelli-inspired *Modern Prince*, (Gramsci 2007: 122–205) to the shortcomings of today's nationally based hegemonic and counter-hegemonic politics. We provide empirical evidence for various achievements of regional initiatives within the institutional framework of the Alianza Bolivariana para los Pueblos de Nuestra América [Bolivarian Alliance for the Peoples of Our America; ALBA in Spanish acronym]. Yet, we conclude on two cautionary notes. First, it is too soon to celebrate post-neoliberal regional integration in Latin America as an irreversible achievement of socialist politics. Second, regionalism can play the transformative counter-hegemonic role ascribed to it by progressive scholars, politicians and activists only if initiatives like ALBA can inspire a sense of supranational identity and political legitimacy. Regional entities in Latin America still resemble venues for inter-state (if not inter-presidential) dialogue and cooperation, which poses the danger of linking the future of post-neoliberal regionalism too closely with personalities, like Hugo Chávez, Evo Morales and Rafael Correa, and nationally based political projects.

The chapter is organized as follows: the first section offers a reappraisal of the works of Gramsci and Foucault in the context of capitalist globalization and its aftermath. Then we discuss the implications of regional integration for contemporary struggles for economic, political and cultural power. The next section offers an account of neoliberalism and the resurgence of the Left in Latin America, followed by an exploration of regional integration efforts in Latin America, with specific emphasis on post-neoliberal forms of regional cooperation and the case of ALBA. The last section provides an evaluation and critique of post-neoliberal regional integration.

Domination, Resistance and Agency in the Works of Gramsci and Foucault

Despite their divergent epistemologies, reading Gramsci and Foucault in dialogue offers significant points of contact, which not only serves the intellectual curiosity to compare and contrast two contending views on modern societies, but also promises to take thought and action in new directions. We focus our attention on three theoretical problematics where such a reading can provide new perspectives on global governance in general, and regional integration more specifically: (i) the constitutive role of knowledge production and discursive practices in creating, maintaining, legitimizing and transforming power relations; (ii) the epistemological status and practical challenges of resistance in the face of near-total domination; and (iii) the role of human agency, especially that of revolutionary leadership, in reconstructing emancipatory politics.

Power and Knowledge

First, and most obviously, both thinkers have taken a keen interest in the production of knowledge and values in civil society. For Gramsci, 'consent' is the key to understanding how capitalism has managed to survive economic and political crises. The realization that economic and political hegemony in a mass capitalist society inevitably relies on the production of consent within civil society leads Gramsci to explore the interaction between the top-down processes of government and bottom-up processes of norm production among societal actors. The coherence of a system of domination relies on the production of values and knowledge that create a shared 'common sense', which also serves to eliminate the emancipatory potential of historical actors or alternative claims to truth. Put simply, Gramsci's understanding of hegemony consists of a 'cultural, moral and ideological leadership over subordinate groups' by which is ensured the 'active and practical involvement of the hegemonized groups' (Gramsci, 1999: 423–4). In pessimistic terms, history does not necessarily move toward progress, truth or freedom. Nonetheless, the Gramscian notion of 'hegemony' is not a totalizing dystopia that paralyzes social transformation; to the contrary, contradiction is built into the production of a historically embedded common sense, which turns processes of cultural production (i.e., the creation of knowledge and social values at relative autonomy from the production of state power) into domains of struggle.

Normalization of thought and behaviour is a concern guiding much of Foucault's writing, as well. However, his approach is decidedly different from Gramsci's. Foucault likewise starts from the premise that the domain of knowledge and norm production is relatively autonomous from the state or the economy. Yet, Foucault de-centres further these processes, going beyond Gramsci's distinction between civil society and the expanded state. Foucault and Foucauldian scholars reveal the ways in which 'normal' behaviour is produced through the capillary operations of medical, sexual, racial, and economic discourses, often involving 'a whole army of technicians' who take the lead in the production of knowledge through discursive practices (Foucault 2005: 18). The concatenation of these discourses leads to a distinctive power regime, called 'disciplinary' power. What gives coherence to modern domination is not merely the perpetuation of capitalist hegemony in the final analysis, but the existence of a shared epistemic core that seeks to normalize and discipline members of society at each domain of social interaction. The central question for Foucauldian political theory has always been how the micro-dynamics of disciplinary power and the logic of social control through technologies of rule, rationalities, and institutions in mass societies – what he calls 'governmentality' (Foucault 1991) – reinforce each other.

The renewal of interest in Gramsci and Foucault owes greatly to their respective analyses of the relationship between ideas and power in the age of capitalist globalization. Agents of global capitalism have not only attacked the numerous achievements of working-class movements and the safety nets established under developmentalist, welfarist or socialist governments throughout much of the twentieth century; neoliberal restructuring has also taken the form of an ideological attack, which ironically hails the end of ideology while defending an ambitious and ideologically motivated social engineering project across the globe. In part the ideological offensive is carried out by identifiable agents, like neoclassical economists, international financial institutions, major media outlets, and a broad spectrum of right-wing, centrist, and even self-designated 'leftist' political actors. Yet, the hegemony of neoliberalism has relied as much on the ideational power of the economic and political elites as on the justification and increasing normalization of modes of thinking and acting that perpetuate an unreflective obedience to market efficiency, competitiveness, individualism and consumerism. Critics of mass culture have amply documented the extent to which obedience is produced and reproduced through such unwitting normalization mechanisms as TV ads or lifestyle magazines. In Gramscian terms, neoliberalism has become a totalizing common sense, a halfway between everyday wisdom and various claims to scientific expertise, to the extent that alternative social imaginations appear nonsensical, irresponsible, and even dangerous.

Resistance

Both Gramsci and Foucault have targeted economistic and state-centric forms of reductionism in their writings. Even though Gramsci follows the Marxist conception of history as characterized by class conflict, he regards class domination as a multi-faceted phenomenon that cannot be reduced to the relations of production, or the actions of a coercive state. Social hierarchies are produced and reproduced through the mutually reinforcing functioning of the capitalist economy and the socio-political system, which itself is the site of a dialectical tension between the coercive power of the state and the domain of civil society (Demirovic 2003: 222). These multiple sites of power tend to reinforce capitalist hegemony while at the same time laying bare its contradictions.

Foucault's understanding of history rejects a unifying underlying framework, such as class conflict. Yet, Foucault realizes that while history is not structured rationally, it is not entirely chaotic, either. In other words, the multiple effects of power (whether they reflect relations of class, social status, gender, or hierarchies imposed by legal and medical norms) tend to converge upon a set of epistemic assumptions, concrete policies and social norms at a given point in history (Foucault 1994). The question for Foucault, as well as for Gramsci, is: how do such disparate domains of power, with their own logics of operation and different conclusions about ordering society, converge on a relatively stable set of principles that give a sense of coherence and continuity across production and consumption practices, the functioning of the state, and social norms? Accompanying this fundamental question is a related one: is resistance to domination possible when all areas of life seem to be governed by mutually reinforcing power relations?

The production of social norms invites the question of resistance and social transformation. Gramsci appears markedly more optimistic than Foucault, who is quite suspicious of attempts to ground resistance in the laws of historical dialectics or a metaphysics of emancipation. Gramsci suggests going beyond the framework of resistance, and pays particular attention to the possible ways in which 'transformative resistance' can be achieved. It is worth noting that Gramsci, whose work has come in response to the historical defeat of working-class movements, is no naïve optimist. Nonetheless he finds the seeds of transformation in the dialectical unravelling of existing relations of class domination, quite unlike Foucault. However, the revolutionary potential immanent in existing relations of domination merely opens the door for political action; the dialectic does not have a definite, predetermined direction.

Gramsci sees in the founding of new institutions the seeds of social transformation and emancipation. Constitutional arrangements undertaken under the leadership of capitalist classes are strategic hegemonic tools for the subordination of working masses:

> Any law in this respect which emanates from bourgeois power has just one significance and just one value: it means that in reality, and not just in words, the terrain or the class struggle has changed. And insofar as the bourgeoisie is compelled to make concessions and create new juridical institutions on the new terrain, it has the real value of demonstrating an organic weakness of the ruling class. (Gramsci 1978: 10)

By contrast, counter-hegemony depends on the 'organic power' of the working class, which necessitates not only the prevalence of a critical consciousness and what Gramsci calls 'national-popular collective will', but also the possession of the capacity of self-government, the capacity to supersede the economic achievements under capitalism, and the development of collective initiative and creativity along with a capable leadership (Gramsci 1978: 93, 417). The acquisition of such 'organic power' rests on the establishment of an institutionalized structure (which was supposed to be the 'factory councils' in Gramsci's Italy). He expects that a transformed institutional environment would provide the necessary ground for the emergence of a collective and organic working-class leadership, as the working class turns from a 'class-in-itself' to a 'class-for-itself' by also being able to represent the broader interests of working masses.

For Foucault, there is no standpoint outside of the existing discursive relations that would provide social actors with the leverage to act and think toward human emancipation. Gramsci's defense of revolutionary institutionalization finds no echoes in Foucault, despite (or perhaps because of) his careful documentation of the disciplinary character of a variety of modern institutions, like the mental hospital and the prison. Yet, he famously states: 'Where there is power, there is resistance, and yet, or rather consequently, this resistance is never in a position of exteriority in relation to power' (Foucault 1978: 95). As is well known, his later writings shifted toward a search for liberation, as demonstrated in his interest in 'care of the self', and he took an activist stance concerning many of the political issues of his day. Yet, Foucault always refused to formulate a systematic politics of emancipation, either in the form of concrete, programmatic proposals, or as normative theory. His key contribution to the theory and practice of emancipatory politics is an attitude of skepticism: self-labelled progressive movements might end up reproducing the epistemic prejudices and oppressive practices that they claim to overcome.

Leadership

How should human agency be conceptualized in today's emancipatory politics? The discussion above strongly suggests that no individual or collective actor is entitled to the role of trans-historical emancipatory agency. Yet, political leadership cannot be ignored in any form of political practice. On this subject, Gramsci offers a close reading of Machiavelli, whose theory of political action helps Gramsci step outside deterministic readings of Marx. According to Machiavelli, political action cannot be reduced to, or comprehended in terms of, any prior moral doctrine or conception of history (Gramsci 2005: 134; also see Honig 1993). In the end, any politics (including emancipatory politics) has no grounds for success but its own capacity to assess and act upon existing political forces. Like Foucault, Gramsci would concede that resistance is not about fulfilling a metaphysical principle of emancipation. Yet, transformative political agency can bridge the gap between the sheer contingency of human affairs and the striving for a just society – hence Gramsci's *Modern Prince*:

> The modern prince, the myth-prince, cannot be a real person, a concrete individual. It can only be an organism, a complex element of society in which a collective will, which has already been recognised and has to some extent asserted itself in action, begins to take concrete form. History has already provided this organism, and it is the political party – the first cell in which there come together germs of a collective will tending to become universal and total. (Gramsci 2005: 129)

Gramsci concedes that politics has always relied on the separation of the rulers and the ruled: 'The first element is that there really do exist rulers and ruled, leaders and led' (Gramsci 2005: 144). However, this does not mean that leadership is an ontological fact, or the natural consequence of an immutable human nature: 'In the formation of leaders, one premise is fundamental: is it the intention that there should always be rulers and ruled, or is the objective to create the conditions in which this division is no longer necessary?' (Gramsci 2005: 144).

He notes that the party consists of three fundamental elements: the mass element, the leadership enjoying 'cohesive, centralizing and disciplinary powers', and an 'intermediate element, which articulates the first element with the second and maintains contact between them, not only physically but also morally and intellectually' (152–3). Thus, Gramsci seeks to provide a solution to the problem of leadership by highlighting the importance of balanced representation, or what he calls the 'theorem of fixed proportions' (190–92). In other words, the relationship of representation between the leadership and the masses has preoccupied Gramsci, but his writings do not provide a clear account of how this separation can be overcome; instead, he provides a workable solution.

Foucault is credited with 'cutting off the king's head' in studies of power. Rather than focusing on political leadership, he has devoted his explorations to the ways in which the discourses of a particular historical-epistemic era circulate through subjects, regardless of their position as rulers or the ruled. Not surprisingly he has been criticized for ignoring the transformative aspects of human agency, such as the human capacity to think and act outside the limits of a given situation. Furthermore, it is not clear from his account whether certain principles and procedures of social communication and political decision-making can enhance human freedom.

Paulo Freire's work on pedagogy provides interesting insights into the role of leadership in emancipatory struggles. The *Pedagogy of the Oppressed* (Freire 1970) is, not unlike Marxism and postcolonial theory, a powerful critique of hierarchy and oppression. However, Freire's project offers liberation for not only the oppressed, but also the oppressor, through a dialogical process of mutual understanding and solidarity (Freire 1970: 34). Oppression is a 'limiting situation', and not the total closure of communicative possibilities – which is often interpreted as Freire's response to Frantz Fanon's pessimism in the face of colonial injustice (Shaull in Freire 1970: 9–15). The elimination of the oppressive relationship depends critically on the realization, on the part of the revolutionary leadership, that revolution can only be with the oppressed, not for them: 'The only effective instrument is a humanizing pedagogy in which the revolutionary leadership establishes a permanent relationship of dialogue with the oppressed' (Freire 1970: 55). The relationship between the leadership and the masses is not one of delegative representation, instrumentalization, and unidirectional consciousness-raising (which he calls 'propaganda'); the solution of the 'teacher-student contradiction' (Freire 1970: 59) points to a radically participatory, egalitarian and dialogical emancipatory politics that aims to transform not only adult education, but all societal processes through which collective opinion and will are shaped.

Freire's pedagogy offers valuable insights into the possibility of emancipatory politics in late capitalist societies. First, the reflection of the oppressed in assessing (revolutionary) praxis should enjoy epistemological primacy in any transformative process. Post-neoliberal regional integration (or any other project with political-institutional, socioeconomic and cultural implications) should avoid the pitfalls of leader-driven institutionalization and the consequent 'democratic deficit' often associated with previous regional integration efforts, such as the European Union. Second, new institutions should be oriented toward forging genuine and comprehensive dialogue about the means and ends of regional integration. The danger of over-bureaucratization and the resultant ossification of power relations between the ruler and the ruled should be avoided. Third, a healthy dose of skepticism (à la Foucault) is necessary in evaluating the transformative potential of such grandiose (and self-designated) titles as 'Bolivarian', 'counter-hegemonic', as the power to regulate subjects and structure social relations is inherent in every discursive formation. Nonetheless, discursive change need not merely mean the replacement of one form of rigid epistemic assumptions for another. The aspiration for human emancipation cannot be separated from an egalitarian and participatory political project that seeks to achieve collective self-reflection by overcoming the divide between the teacher and student, rulers and the ruled, and theory and praxis.

Building on the discussion above, we understand emancipatory politics as emerging out of transformative resistance to the socioeconomic, political, and cultural manifestations of power that seek to simultaneously discipline and normalize its objects. Political change is an agency-based endeavour for which personal and collective leadership is necessary; yet, no agent has a priori privileged access to the role of emancipatory leadership. Counter-hegemonic alternatives should seek to build novel institutional and cultural structures ('organic power') to provide alternatives to existing institutional arrangements, discursive formations and knowledge-production procedures. We show in the following sections that post-neoliberal regional integration has emerged as a clear demonstration of how new institutional arrangements capable of generating critical consciousness and a new articulation of national-popular collective carry the hope of developing new economic imaginaries and encouraging popular initiatives.

Regional Integration as a Site of Domination and Resistance

Regional entities have emerged as key players in global political economy. While some accounts tend to consider regional integration as an inevitable consequence of economic, political and cultural globalization, others point out that the new economic and political reality is in any case less 'global' than 'regional' (Zysman 1996), which refers to the high degree of cooperation within, and protectionism across, geographically and politically defined regional blocs (Gamble 2001).

A key question is whether regionalism perpetuates hierarchies between social classes, countries, and regions. Realist international relations scholars stress that great powers opt for international institutions in order to 'lock in' their dominant position in the international state system, as they anticipate a decline in their relative power (Keohane 1984). Taking his cue from the 'hegemonic decline' thesis, Kavous Ardalan (2010) claims that today's regional integration schemes mark a shift away from the regionalism of the Cold War era, when the bipolar international order and limited economic liberalism among capitalist nations were shaping cross-national cooperation efforts. Instead, contemporary neoliberal regional integration has emerged at a time of US supremacy, although various cooperation schemes also reflect the recent reality of hegemonic decline.

Regional integration no doubt reflects the complex dynamics of the interaction between the fast-changing state system and capitalist globalization. Nonetheless, it would be wrong to reduce regionalism to the self-interested decisions of political elites. Regional cooperation opens up new venues of political struggle for a number of actors. Some of the struggles take place over the divisions within the ruling class. Take this example from Europe: 'During the early 1980s, most firms that were the national and European "champions" generally tended to perceive globalisation as a threat rather than an opportunity and pressed for a relaunch of the European project on very different terms from the neoliberals' (Gill 1998a: 11). The same supranational project has inspired different hopes among those who see in the European Union 'a possible way out of the crisis of national social democracy' (Strange 2006: 197).

Regional cooperation in other geographies has likewise taken the form of a hegemonic struggle (in the Gramscian formulation) within and between social classes and political agendas, rather than a unidirectional project. To this day, the dominant conception of regional integration privileges trade liberalization within and across regions, security cooperation (often in line with the security interests of hegemonic powers inside and outside of the region) and a limited degree of political integration (Gürcan 2010). In the post-World War II era, when the global economic system relied on a compromise between the free trade regime dictated by international financial institutions and national economic policies based on Keynesian, welfarist, and developmentalist ideas, regional integration was a means to promote trade among countries with relatively similar economic structures. The erosion of this compromise in the 1970s and 80s provoked a new hegemonic struggle, whereby a crucial sector of the nationally based and transnational capitalist class, along with politicians and policy experts, began to lobby aggressively for a new conception of regionalism that would complement, rather than offer limited protection from, the forces of global capital. Either new regional entities were created (e.g. MERCOSUR in Latin America) or the existing ones took a sharp neoliberal turn (e.g. the EU following the Single Market Initiative of 1986).

It did not take long before resistance to neoliberal regional integration asserted itself. In part, the early resistance was 'a defensive reaction mounted by those left out of the mosaic globalization, particularly in zones outside the macro-regions' (Mittelman 1996: 208). Social democrats in various European countries argued for the reproduction of the national welfarist model at the supranational level, as quoted earlier. In southern Africa, and Southeast and East Asia, some regional schemes (like SADC in the early 1990s) fought to maintain the developmentalist, redistributive state in the face of economic liberalism (Mittelman 1996: 195). It is safe to argue that the boldest national and supranational reactions to neoliberalism have come from Latin America in the 2000s (Gürcan 2010). The next section deals with the aftermath of neoliberalism in Latin America.

Neoliberalism and Post-Neoliberalism in Latin America

Arguably, neoliberal restructuring has produced more impact on Latin America than anywhere else in the developing world in the 1980s and 1990s. Neoliberalism has signaled political authoritarianism in much of the region. This is not surprising because the elimination of fundamental political and socioeconomic rights, and the hard-won achievements of workers', peasants', and women's struggles, could not be achieved easily under political regimes with even the slightest democratic openness. Chile is a case in point: neoliberal restructuring by the (in)famous 'Chicago Boys' took place with the support of Augusto Pinochet's military regime, which overthrew the democratically elected socialist government of Salvador Allende in 1973, banned all political parties and social organizations, suspended the constitution, and unleashed a bloody campaign of terror against all progressive sectors. In Argentina and Peru, Presidents Carlos Menem and Alberto Fujimori (respectively), who campaigned on clearly non-neoliberal political platforms, reneged on their campaign promises once elected. Fujimori soon orchestrated a 'self-coup': he closed down the Congress and suspended basic civil liberties with the aid of the military in 1992, and ruled Peru dictatorially for eight more years. Even in countries where democratic elections and basic liberties were not formally suspended, opponents of neoliberalism met widespread repression, as exemplified in the 1989 massacre of protestors in Caracas, Venezuela (an incident known as Caracazo) and ongoing police violence elsewhere in the region.

Neoliberalism failed to deliver on its economic promises to the masses: 'Latin America under neoliberal rule has lagged far behind its economic performance of the period of 1960–80, under the now largely discredited model of import substitution industrialization' (Macdonald and Ruckert 2009: 4). Early on, stories of the Chilean 'miracle' and Argentine recovery served as ideological justification for advocates of neoliberalism across the globe, but these success stories proved illusory. The fragile Argentine model ended with one of the worst economic crises the country has witnessed in its history, which led to the virtual collapse of the middle class overnight; and when Pinochet left office in 1990, the poverty rate in Chile was at a staggering 40 per cent! It seems that the miracles of neoliberalism worked for a minority that constituted the economic and political elites, while the rest was left to deal with unemployment, poverty, social marginalization, and accompanying social problems in the absence of social safety nets. It took Latin American and Caribbean countries 25 years to reduce poverty back to the 1980 levels (quoted in Macdonald and Ruckert 2009: 4).

As argued earlier, neoliberalism cannot be understood as a merely top-down political or economic transformation. Competitiveness, market efficiency and individualism have become increasingly more entrenched in sociological imagination, as the mainstream media and a number of intellectuals promoted neoliberalism as the unique path to development (Dello Buono 2010: 11). Latin America's populist-developmentalist and socialist projects of the past have been portrayed as naïve utopias at best; and totalitarian dystopias at worst.

The normalization of neoliberalism as the only viable alternative has pervaded scholarship to such an extent that even leftist movements are exhorted to accept the overbearing presence of market forces and make decisions accordingly (Castañeda 2006). Political responsibility is reduced to unquestioning reverence for the dominance of the national and global market.

It was in this context of neoliberal hegemony, which manifested itself at the level of governmental decision-making as well as society-wide norm production and diffusion, that New Leftist politics took shape in Latin America. Considered by many to be historically defeated in the 1980s and '90s, the Latin American Left has since managed to capture government in the majority of countries, but as importantly, progressive social movements have transformed the basic terms of political debates on economic policy, social security, human rights, indigenous politics, environmental degradation, reproductive rights, and the treatment of ethnic, 'racial', cultural and gender minorities.

Not all left-leaning political movements are anti-neoliberal. As the examples of Chile's Socialist Party and Brazil's Workers' Party suggest, some political movements have acknowledged the fundamental premises of neoliberalism, such as limiting or even eliminating the state's role in economic production, monetary policy, and trade policy. The success of the neoliberal 'Left' depends on its capacity to provide a minimal safety net for the poorest citizens, while leaving the basic economic structure and social hierarchies intact. For example, the coalition of Christian Democrats and Socialists in Chile has managed to reduce the poverty rate from 40 to 16 per cent between 1990 and 2006, while it has been very careful not to challenge economic inequality, which had increased enormously under Pinochet's dictatorship, making Chile one of the most unequal nations even by the standards of Latin America. Similarly, Brazil's Lula governments continued the economic agenda of predecessors by providing poverty relief without alienating the powerful business class.

Other governments have moved beyond this model, which remedies only the most egregious consequence of neoliberalism, i.e. extreme poverty, while still tolerating, and even promoting, gross inequalities in areas like educational opportunities and healthcare, and upholding legal and political structures that normalize and perpetuate these inequalities. Governments in Venezuela, Bolivia, Ecuador, and to some extent Argentina, have undertaken redistributive policies and massive nationalization campaigns, and in some cases, ratified new constitutions to recognize basic education, healthcare, and cultural survival as inalienable rights. In Ecuador, the new constitution safeguards the rights of pacha mama [Mother Earth], in great part thanks to pressures from indigenous and environmentalist groups.

Detractors note that these measures amount to little more than a new form of populism fuelled by windfall revenues on natural resources and tailored to serve the interests of ambitious strongmen [caudillos] who are trying to remain in power by giving hand-outs to the impoverished masses and abolishing constitutional term limits. While it cannot be ignored that the personalization of politics (especially in the case of Venezuela) may endanger the long-term accomplishments of socialist constitutions and policies, anti-neoliberal governments have already scored two key victories: (i) they have crystallized some of the hard-won gains of social and political movements in the form of fundamental rights; and (ii) they have shifted the Latin American (and global) debate away from whether post-neoliberal politics is at all possible to what kind of post-neoliberalism is feasible and desirable.

Post-Neoliberal Regional Integration in Latin America: The Case of ALBA

Aware of the need to create a new, counter-hegemonic 'common sense', the promoters of post-neoliberal regional integration have reconfigured concepts and symbols in innovative ways. The Spanish acronym for the Bolivarian Alliance for Our America, ALBA, means 'dawn'. The name makes a reference to Simon Bolívar, the Venezuela-born liberator whose (frustrated) dream of uniting the entire Spanish-speaking Americas inspired generations of Latin American intellectuals and politicians. The choice of 'Our America' [Nuestra América] is also quite intentional, referring to the title of the famous essay written by José Martí, the intellectual forefather of Cuban independence, who promoted the cultural solidarity of Latin America in the face of emerging American imperialism in the late nineteenth century. Needless to say, out of the multiplicity of the interpretations associated with the legacies of Bolívar and Martí in Latin America (Dawson 2010), the leaders of these pioneering regional integration efforts select a specific historical lesson – one that advocates anti-imperialist pan-American solidarity.

Economic cooperation treaties signed under the ALBA system are called People's Trade Agreements (Tratados de Comercio de los Pueblos, TCPs) rather than conventional Free Trade Agreements. The semiotic shift aims to unsettle the identification of trade with profit maximization. Instead, the promoters of TCPs argue, the goal of trade should be to enhance the fair distribution of prosperity for all members of the participating societies. Likewise, multinational companies created under the ALBA system are called grannacionales [an approximate translation would be great-nationals], rather than multi-national corporations. Accordingly, some observers associate ALBA's approach with the principle of 'cooperative advantage' as the basis of mutual economic relations, rather than the comparative (and by corollary, competitive) advantage model advocated by standard economic theories (Artaraz 2012: 31). Thus, the ALBA leadership seeks to build novel discursive configurations that serve to forge a new (inter)national-popular collective will.

The origins of ALBA go back to 2001, when various Latin American states, trade unions and social movements explicitly reacted against the crisis of the 'actually existing' integration model and rejected the US vision of hegemonic regionalism (Gürcan 2010). Efforts to abolish the Free Trade Area of the Americas [Área de Libre Comercio de las Américas; ALCA in Spanish acronym] resulted in the official formation of ALBA in 2004 under the leadership of Cuba and Venezuela. The ALBA initiative now embraces various other Latin American states, such as Bolivia, Nicaragua, Ecuador, Dominica, Antigua and Barbuda, and Saint Vincent and the Grenadines, as well as Grenada, Haiti and Uruguay as observer states. ALBA's main goals include the eradication of illiteracy through literacy programs that have reached more than 3,000,000 people; community development through social missions; disability programs that have reached more than 900,000 people; health sovereignty through the Latin American School of Medicine, which has thus far funded more than 1,730 students from 70 countries; cultural and communication sovereignty (ALBA Culture Fund-Houses of ALBA, ALBA-TV, Radio of the South and TeleSur); fair trade through TCPs and the Unified System for Regional Compensation [Sistema Único de Compensación Regional, SUCRE]; and food sovereignty (ALBA-TCP N.D.-a: 3).

Advocating an alternative model of all-round development, ALBA opposes the capitalist model of 'transnational' or 'multinational' corporations. Instead it promotes grannacionales, which are active in a myriad areas including food, environment, science and technology, fair trade, culture, education, energy, industry and mining, health, telecommunications, transportation and tourism (ALBA-TCP N.D.-a: 1, ALBA-TCP N.D.-b). All decisions are made with the consensus of the member states in grannacionales. In turn, the Bank of ALBA provides grannacionales and other development projects with financial support, as a counter-model to what the World Bank (WB) and the International Monetary Fund (IMF) represent. The goals of the Bank of ALBA are described as follows: 'to contribute to economic and social development, reduce poverty and asymmetries, strengthen integration, and promote a fair, dynamic, harmonious and equitable economic exchange among the ALBA members, inspired by the principles of solidarity, complementarity, cooperation and respect for the sovereignty of peoples' (Banco-del-ALBA N.D.: 2). In 2010, the Bank of ALBA's capital reached more than $85 million (Correo-del-Orinoco 2010). According to César Giral, its president, the Bank is a mechanism by which the peoples of ALBA are liberated from the domination of such hegemonic institutions as the IMF and WB (Correo-del-Orinoco 2010). Giral sees SUCRE, ALBA's common monetary currency, as crucial for promoting regional development (Correo-del-Orinoco 2010). By September 2012, 419,000 SUCRE transfers were realized within the ALBA region (Correo-del-Orinoco 2012). Estimates indicate that the amount of SUCRE operations will reach more than $900 million by the end of 2012. Furthermore, it is estimated that the commercial transactions between Venezuela and Ecuador using SUCRE account for at least 50 per cent of the two countries' commercial exchange (SUCRE-ALBA 2012).

The media power that ALBA has developed serves as a major catalyst in the (inter) national-popular integration of the entire region as well as in extending the reach of the counter-hegemonic symbolic articulations of Latin American solidarity. One has to take into account the current structure of the Latin American media, marked by high levels of concentration of ownership and content importation, to understand the significance of ALBA's media initiative. According to Salö (2007: 12), in 1996, only 6 per cent of the total audiovisual imports to Latin America originated from within the region, while 86 per cent of the imports came from the US. In 1998, the percentage of TV programs coming from the region amounted to 30 per cent. Launched in 2005 in reaction to the 'media hegemony' of CNN, NBC, UNIVISION and Fox News, which together control 85 per cent of the news sector in Latin America (Faivre d'Arcier-Flores 2007; Arcila Calderón 2005), TeleSur is jointly owned by Venezuela (51 per cent), Argentina (20 per cent), Cuba (19 per cent), and Uruguay (10 per cent) (Guerra 2012; New-Internationalist 2006). The channel thus emerged with the slogan of 'Our North is the South' along with an advisory board that includes Nobel Peace Prize winner Adolfo Pérez Esquivel, writer Tariq Ali, Free Software Foundation creator Richard Stallman and actor Danny Glover (Latin Trade 2005; New-Internationalist 2006).

The programming of TeleSur also reflects the channel's concern to create an (inter)national-popular collective will and promote a counter-hegemonic process of cultural integration. The TV program called Maestra Vida aims to generate an atmosphere of discussion on the values, ethics and ideals of an imagined shared Latin American identity (Faivre d'Arcier-Flores 2007). Latitud América intends to 'socialize intellectual production' in Latin America by hosting various artists from the region. Esfera Cultural sheds light on everyday life in different places in Latin America, while América Tierra Nuestra displays the local traditions, customs and cultural production of Ibero-American people. CineSur, Clásicos, Documentales TeleSur and Memorias del Fuego aim to contribute to the collective memory of Latin American peoples through full-length and short films and documentaries (Faivre d'Arcier-Flores 2007).

In sharp contrast to previous experiences of regionalism that mostly rely on security- and economy-driven top-down policies, the ALBA experience sets forth bottom-up strategies of alter-globalism, the major component of which is the active inclusion of critical social movements in the integration process (Gürcan 2010). Therefore, the core structure of ALBA includes the Council of Social Movements (CSM), which assists the work of the Council of Presidents and Council of Ministers in deepening the integration process. Claiming the revolutionary heritage of important figures, the CSM of ALBA proclaims its adherence to the principles of inclusiveness, openness and diversity by embracing a wide range of social movements and associations representing the indigenous, Afro-descendants, peasants, workers, the youth and teachers (ALBA-TCP 2009b: 180, 182–3). The council is responsible for presenting its proposals and projects to the Council of Presidents and evaluating the work of the latter as well as assisting to the work of grannacionales (ALBA-TCP 2012).

In many respects, the CSM of ALBA has emerged as the catalyst for a regional norm creation effort (horizontalism, inclusion, complementarity, cooperation, solidarity, coexistence, direct and participatory democracy, social justice and equity) that aims to eradicate the exclusionary legacy of neoliberalism in the continent. The CSM affirms that its main task is to contribute to the development of common agendas for the benefit of the peoples, in addition to the implementation of a new development paradigm relying upon the principles of participation and assistance through social movements (ALBA-TCP 2009b: 183–4).

Another bottom-up initiative parallel to the CSM of ALBA has been the Articulación de Movimientos Sociales hacia el ALBA (AMSA) [Coordination of Social Movements towards ALBA], which involves more than 30 critical social movements, including the Movimento dos Trabalhadores Rurais Sem Terra [Landless Rural Workers' Movement, or MST], Frente Popular Darío Santillán [Darío Santillán Popular Front], Organization in Solidarity with the People of Africa, Asia, and Latin America (OSPAAL), La Vía Campesina, Coordinador Nacional Agrario de Colombia [National Agrarian Coordinator], Movimiento de Liberación Nacional [National Liberation Movement of Mexico, or MLC], Movimiento de Campesinos de Santiago del Estero [Santiago del Estero Peasant Movement], Central de los Trabajadores de Argentina [Workers' Centre of Argentina], and Movimiento Campesino Paraguayo [Paraguayan Peasant Movement] (Juventud-Rebelde 2010; AMSA 2012b: 4). AMSA defines itself as a regional initiative made up of critical social movements that are driven by such values as anti-imperialism, anti-neoliberalism, anti-patriarchialism, equality, freedom and emancipation (AMSA 2012b: 2). It formulates its concrete tasks as follows: the struggle against militarization, military bases, the criminalization of social protest and the aggressions of the empire; the battle against multinational companies, privatization and denationalization; confronting the climate crisis and protecting the rights of Mother Earth, the rights of indigenous peoples of Our America and the struggle for living well; and international solidarity between brother peoples (AMSA 2012b: 6). AMSA appears to be a highly active agent of counter-hegemonic regional integration from below, as it takes part in regional activism and mobilization on a wide range of issues including the struggle against the Canadian mining industry, solidarity with the Paraguayan people after the impeachment of President Fernando Lugo, advocacy of women's rights (such as the legalization of abortion, respect for the women's body and gender equality), and the struggle against the commodification of life (AMSA 2012a).

For ALBA, education constitutes an area of primary importance for the counter-hegemonic transformation of the region, as clearly reflected in the 2009 Declaration of Managua for the Educative Union of the ALBA. The declaration considers education to be a crucial means for consciousness-raising and mobilization against capitalism, and for the revolutionary transformation of the region. The declaration highlights two major tasks to promote the counter-hegemonic production of knowledge: the eradication of illiteracy and promotion of post-literacy processes by internationalist brigades; and the establishment of a regional structure of undergraduate and graduate education that prioritizes such areas as geopolitics, sciences of education, food sovereignty and hydrocarbons, based on common curriculum projects and new information technologies (Lorán 2009; ALBA-TCP 2009a; Radio-Nacional-de-Venezuela 2009). The Third Meeting of the Council of Ministers of Social Areas held in the city of Cochabamba on March 19, 2011 approved a new financing of $25 million for the eradication of illiteracy and promotion of post-literacy processes in the region (Banco-del-ALBA 2011). One should note that projects addressing educational problems are not only developed by the presidents of member countries, but are also shaped through public discussions involving numerous scholars, teachers and students. The University 2010 International Conference that took place in Havana on 12 February 2010 is an example in point: it brought together grassroots actors with 15 ministers, 12 deputy ministers and 213 university directors (Jiménez and Barrios 2010). Similarly, the Third Workshop on Education for ALBA, held 14–15 April 2010 in Caracas, laid emphasis on the need to counter the capitalist-elitist paradigm of higher education that fails to comprehend the real needs of the people (ABN 2010).

Concrete steps have been taken toward the creation of a common curriculum in the ALBA area. According to Arturo Collado, the Secretary of the Consejo Nacional de Universidades de Nicaragua (National Council of Universities of Nicaragua, CNU), the initiative of the Red de Universidades de los Pueblos del Alba (The Network of Universities of the Peoples of the ALBA, or UNIALBA) has led to a cooperation in more than 33 areas including food security, health care, scientific development and environmental protection (Patria-Grande 2011). In the context of UNIALBA, Cuba designed master's programs in informatics for Venezuela, Bolivia, Ecuador and Nicaragua (Cuba-Standard 2010). By 2012, Nicaraguan universities gained accreditation both in Ecuador and Venezuela (Tuleando 2012). Telémaco Talavera, the president of the NCUN, drew attention to the importance of the struggle against 'feudal', 'mercantilist' or 'individualistic' logics that undermine the principle of solidarity under the UNIALBA initiative (Chávez 2012).

Assessing ALBA: Supranationality, Leadership and Counter-Hegemony

Perhaps no other question has been as central to socialist, communist and anarchist politics as that of agency: who (i.e. which individuals, social classes or political organizations, if any) will occupy the leading position in the revolutionary process, and in whose name? It is not the task of this chapter to recapitulate the historical debates, but socialists and communists across the globe have been divided between a nationalist camp that advocates the capture and revolutionary transformation of the existing nation-states, and an internationalist camp that promotes the global solidarity and coordination of the working class as the only feasible way to challenge globalized capitalism. As the Soviet Union adopted the 'socialism in one country' approach under Stalin, and as postcolonial societies opted for independent nation-states in the wake of World War II, the nationalist camp took the upper hand. Throughout the rest of the twentieth century, socialist and communist political parties and insurgencies have devoted their resources first and foremost to taking over state power and enacting national-level policies to transform societies.

The nation-state remains the basic unit of decision-making today, both in the eyes of the ruling elites and their opponents. However, the primacy of the nation-state as the only framework relevant for politics has been challenged by pressures for economic, technological and cultural globalization, supranational decision-making, and subnational movements that strive for social and political change in relative autonomy from the inadequacies and biases of national-level decision-making. Needless to say, there is nothing inherently emancipatory about the increasing presence of non-state actors in world politics, or the delegation of sovereignty to supranational, international, regional or subnational decision-makers. Capitalist globalization and accompanying processes of internationalization and regionalization have often eliminated, rather than advanced, the political and economic gains made under welfarist and developmentalist national governments. Although the nongovernmental sector emerged with progressive agendas such as the protection of human rights or elimination of world poverty, some of the major NGOs (but by no means all) ended up reproducing and legitimizing existing hierarchies – in a way, strengthening global 'hegemony' in the Gramscian sense (Demirovic 1998). Despite the risk of co-optation, however, various social and political movements have managed to conceive of post-nationalism as a moment with emancipatory potential. Counter-hegemonic regional integration in contemporary Latin America is without doubt the expression of such optimism.

Latin America has its own peculiar history of the clash between regionalism and national sovereignty. Since the independence wars that ended Spanish and Portuguese colonial empires on much of the hemisphere (1810–1824), the idea of pan-Americanism has inspired intellectuals, politicians, military leaders, and millions of citizens. Simon Bolívar's frustrated attempt to unite Spanish-speaking America under a republican government has remained an enduring dream – not incidentally, the cooperation scheme that brings together leftist Latin American governments is called the Bolivarian Alternative. Yet, it was Bolívar himself who once likened Latin American unity to 'sowing seeds into the sea', as he witnessed the division of liberated Spanish-speaking territories into independent republics. To this day, independent nation-states in the Western Hemisphere have guarded their territorial sovereignty jealously, and challenges to sovereignty have often taken the form of imperialist meddling (almost always by the US) rather than some form of Bolivarian pan-Americanism or socialist internationalism.

Even when the option of political union was discarded, a sense of Latin American identity based on shared cultural characteristics or similar political experiences has remained strong. Ever since the end of the nineteenth-century, a peculiar form of Latin American nationalism that defines itself in contradistinction to European and North American cultural and political expansionism has inspired liberal-minded elites, and occasionally, conservatives, too. Its twentieth-century variant has enhanced the popular appeal of nationalist leaders like Mexico's Lázaro Cárdenas and Argentina's Juan Domingo Perón, as well as generations of socialist and communist politicians and guerrilla leaders, who described their struggle as a regional (and global) struggle against American imperialism and its domestic collaborators. Yet, despite the attractions of this supranational imagination, progressive politics in Latin America, just like its reactionary counterpart, has for the most part remained national, with only limited and issue-specific inter-state cooperation.

We argue that today's post-neoliberal regional integration brings the tension between two approaches to leftist politics to the forefront: the supranational imagination rooted in socialist internationalism and Bolivarian pan-Americanism (in the specific case of Latin America), and the political reality of the nation-state system in which revolutionary politics is tied to governments' capacity and willingness to enact policy change within their sovereign limits. On the one hand, we observe the embryonic formation of alternative regional projects and initiatives, like ALBA and the TCPs, and counter-hegemonic struggles over the policies and identity of existing regional schemes, like MERCOSUR and UNASUR. ALBA's founding documents make constant reference to the promotion of supranational exchanges across civil society actors, thereby promising to move beyond the state-centric vision of regional politics. On the other hand, all these institutions constitute no more than inter-state agreements, if not outright inter-presidential dialogue. At least until now, none of the supranational institutions (the Parliaments of MERCOSUR or UNASUR, or any of the councils within ALBA) have transformed themselves into bodies that make decisions independently of the constituent states, or offer a sense of identity and democratic legitimacy beyond those bestowed upon them by the member states. The fate of counter-hegemonic regional integration depends less on the cooperative networks between state and non-state actors or the growth of supranational institutions capable of resisting and transforming capitalist globalization than the political fortunes of Hugo Chávez's successor, Evo Morales and Rafael Correa – and those of their friends and foes across the region.

Gramsci registers the paradigmatic shift in terms of political agency in mass societies when he states that the modern Prince will be a political party representing a social class, rather than an individual. Echoing his words, we argue that revolutionary political agency cannot be a nationally based social class or government (let alone individual) in the age of capitalist globalization and hegemonic regional integration. If the claim that regionalism has emerged as a site of counter-hegemonic struggles has any value, then it should be acknowledged that agency requires a network of governmental and nongovernmental actors who can build horizontal mutual relationships regardless of the political clout of their national governments and who are willing to delegate some degree of policy-making power to supranational institutions. Latin American societies have the potential to pioneer non-elitist forms of regional integration, quite unlike the hegemonic European Union model, which has suffered from elitism and lack of democratic control at every level of supranational expansion and deepening. Yet, the success of such integration depends critically on transforming what today appears to be inter-presidential dialogue toward forms of genuine supranational cooperation, hence the importance of insisting that the development institutions consolidate cooperation- and solidarity-driven values and norms, as well as the establishment of stronger social protection mechanisms.

Conclusion

The ALBA initiative has already made inroads into strengthening counter-hegemonic regional integration at the level of political institutions, economic practices, and symbolic/discursive relations. It has been striving to develop a critical consciousness and an (inter)national-popular collective will by bringing to the forefront hegemonic knowledge creation through such educational and cultural initiatives as UNIALBA, TeleSur, Radio del Sur, AMSA, ALBA TV, ALBA Culture Fund-Houses of ALBA; it has reconfigured regional integration within the context of non-market and cooperation/solidarity-driven values and norms; it has sought to build a more inclusive and socially responsible economic and political environment through the adoption of post-neoliberal policies and creation of political structures via numerous treaties and agreements (TPCs, Council of Presidents, Council of Ministers, Council of Social Movements); and finally it has established social and financial protection mechanisms, such as ALBA's own bank, in order to contain systemic financial dislocations.

Yet, it is too soon to conclude that ALBA has transformed regional integration in an irreversibly progressive fashion in Latin America. The Alliance looks to be an inter-state (and even more problematically, inter-presidential) cooperation scheme that may not outlive its founders. As of this writing, the political turmoil in Venezuela following Hugo Chávez's health threatens the survival of the national and international structures put in place under his rule. Nonetheless, there are reasons to be optimistic about the possibility of a participatory and democratic founding of supranational institutions capable of posing a viable counter-hegemonic alternative to neoliberal regionalism and globalism. International civil society networks that have changed the terms of basic political debates in Latin America for the past two decades may take up the cause of progressive politics regardless of national-level policy shifts. ALBA does not have a constitution or permanent, time-tested supranational institutions, but the set of core values shared by constituent governments (and an important portion of the public) may shed light on the future of the project. Perhaps it is best to anticipate future developments with Gramsci's peculiar mixture of 'pessimism of the mind' and 'optimism of the will' (Gramsci 1994: 299).

References

ABN 2010. Educación: Mecanismo que erradicará analfabetismo de países del bloque [Education: Mechanism that will eradicate illiteracy in the countries of

the bloc], http://www.alianzabolivariana.org/modules.php?name=News&file=article&sid=6241, accessed on 28 September 2012.
ALBA-TCP. 2008. Declaración política del consejo de movimientos sociales del ALBA-TCP [Political declaration of the Council of Social Movements of ALBA-TCP], http://www.iadb.org/intal/intalcdi/PE/2008/02145.pdf, accessed on 28 September 2012.
—. 2009a. Declaration of Managua. For the educative union of the ALBA, http://www.mppeu.gob.ve/web/uploads/documentos/documentosVarios/pdf18–12–2009_10:07:07.pdf, accessed on 28 September 2012.
—. 2009b. Manifiesto general de la Primera Cumbre de Consejos de Movimientos Sociales del ALBA-TCP [General manifesto of the first summit of the Council of Social Movements of ALBA-TCP], http://biblioteca.clacso.edu.ar/ar/libros/osal/osal27/26PCCMS.pdf, accessed on 28 September 2012.
—. 2012. Consejo de movimientos sociales del ALBA-TCP [Council of Social Movements of ALBA-TCP], http://www.alba-tcp.org/contenido/consejo-de-movimientos-sociales-0, accessed on 28 September 2012.
—. N.D.-a. Bolivarian Alliance for the Peoples of Our America/Alba-TCP, http://www.alba-tcp.org/public/documents/pdf/Ingles/ALBA_Pamphlet.pdf, accessed on 28 September 2012.
—. N.D.-b. Grannacional en el marco del ALBA-TCP [Grannacional under ALBA-TCP], http://www.alba-tcp.org/public/documents/pdf/Grannacional.pdf, accessed on 28 September 2012.
AMSA 2012a. Movilización [Mobilization], http://www.albamovimientos.org/category/movilizacion/, accessed on 28 September 2012.
AMSA 2012b. Periódico del ALBA de los Movimientos Sociales hacia la Cumbre de los Pueblos [Periodical of AMSA], http://www.albamovimientos.org/2012/06/periodico-del-alba-de-los-movimientos-sociales-hacia-la-cumbre-de-los-pueblos/, accessed on 28 September 2012.
Arcila Calderón, C. 2005. Qué es telesur? Revista Latinoamericana de Comunicación. *Chasqui* 92: 44–51.
Ardalan, K. 2010. Globalization and regionalization: Four paradigmatic views. *Journal of International Business Research* 9: 71–101.
Artaraz, K. 2012. Cuba's internationalism revisited: Exporting literacy, ALBA, and a new paradigm for South–South collaboration. *Bulletin of Latin American Research* 31: 22–37.
Banco-del-ALBA 2011. Acta de la tercera reunión del Consejo Ministerial del área social del ALBA-TCP [Act of the third meeting of the Council of Ministers of Social Areas of ALBA-TCP], http://www.bancodelalba.org/acta-de-la-tercera-reunión-del-consejo-ministerial-del-área-social-del-alba-tcp.html, accessed on 28 September 2012.
—. N.D. Proyectos en ejecución-Banco del Alba [Current projects – Banco del Alba], http://www.bancodelalba.org/descargas/info-alba2.pdf, accessed on 28 September 2012.
Castañeda, J. 2006. Latin America's left turn. *Foreign Affairs* 85: 28–43.

Chávez, K. 2012. Se constituirá la Universidad del ALBA (UNIALBA) [The University of ALBA will be established], http://www.elpueblopresidente.com/realidades/8316.html, accessed on 28 September 2012.

Correo-del-Orinoco 2010. Banco del Alba cuenta con más de 85 millones para impulsar el desarrollo de los países miembros [ALBA Bank has more than 85 million to promote the development of member countries], http://www.correodelorinoco.gob.ve/economia/banco-alba-cuenta-mas-85-millones-para-impulsar-desarrollo-paises-miembros/, accessed on 28 September 2012.

—. 2012. Países del ALBA potencian uso del Sucre en transacciones [ALBA countries enhance the use of Sucre in transactions], http://www.correodelorinoco.gob.ve/avances/paises-alba-potencian-uso-sucre-transacciones/, accessed on 28 September 2012.

Cuba-Standard 2010. Havana hosts ALBA meeting, http://www.cubastandard.com/2010/02/03/havana-hosts-alba-meeting/, accessed on 28 September 2012.

Dawson, A. 2010. *Latin America since Independence: A History with Primary Sources*. New York: Routledge.

Dello Buono, R.A. 2010. Latin America and the collapsing ideological supports of neoliberalism. *Critical Sociology* 37: 9–25.

Demirovic, A. 1998. NGOs and social movements: A study in contrasts. *Capitalism Nature Socialism* 9: 83–92.

—. 2003. NGOs, the state, and civil society: The transformation of hegemony. *Rethinking Marxism: A Journal of Economics, Culture and Society* 15: 213–35.

Faivre a'Arcier-Flores, H. 2007. Telesur: Une nouvelle forme de communication? [Telesur: A new form of communication?]. *Autrepart* 1: 227–38.

Foucualt, M. 1978. *History of Sexuality: An Introduction (Vol. I)*. New York: Vintage.

—. 1991. Governmentality. In *The Foucault Effect: Studies in Governmentality*, edited by Burchell, G., Gordon, C. and Miller, P. Chicago: University of Chicago Press, 87–104.

—. 1994. *The Order of Things: An Archaeology of the Human Sciences*. New York: Vintage Books.

—. 2005. *Discipline and Punish*. New York: Vintage Books.

Freire, P. 1970. *Pedagogy of the Oppressed*, translated by Myra Bergman Ramos. New York: Herder and Herder.

Gamble, A. 2001. Regional blocs, world order and the new medievalism. In *European Union and the New Regionalism*, edited by Telo, M. Aldershot: Ashgate.

Gill, S. 1998a. European governance and new constitutionalism: Economic and Monetary Union and alternatives to disciplinary neoliberalism in Europe. *New Political Economy* 3: 5–26.

—. 1998b. New constitutionalism and the reconstitution of capital. Paper to PEWS – Political Economy of the World-System Section of the American Sociological Association Conference: The Shifting Geopolitics of the Modern World-System, Northwestern University, 22–23 March 1998, http://www.meijigakuin.ac.jp/~iism/pdf/nenpo_002/Gill.pdf, accessed on 28 September 2012.

—. 1998c. New constitutionalism, democratisation and global political economy. *Pacifica Review* 10: 23–38.

—. 2003. *Power and Resistance in the New World Order.* New York: Palgrave Macmillan.

Gramsci, A. 1978. *Selections from Political Writings (1921–1926)*. London: Lawrence and Wishart.

—. 1994. *Letters from Prison, Volume I*, edited by Frank Rosengarten, translated by Raymond Rosenthal. Columbia University Press.

—. 1999. *The Gramsci Reader: Selected Writings 1916–1935*. London: Lawrence and Wishart.

—. 2005 [1971]. *Selections from the Prison Notebooks of Antonio Gramsci*, edited and translated by Q. Hoare and G.N. Smith. New York: International Publishers.

Guerra, A.T. 2012. La integración cultural: Una propuesta para América Latina [Cultural integration: A proposal for Latin America]. *Nueva Politica* 1: 11–25.

Gürcan, E.C. 2010. New regionalisms and radical identity formation in Latin America: Towards an 'alter-global' paradigm. *Journal of Social Research and Policy* 1: 19–33.

Honig, B. 1993. *Political Theory and the Displacement of Politics*. Ithaca: Cornell University Press.

Jiménez, M.M. and Barrios, M. 2010. UNIALBA university network: Another step towards integration, http://www.juventudrebelde.co.cu/cuba/2010–02–16/unialba-university-network-another-step-towards-integration, accessed on 28 September 2012.

Juventud-Rebelde 2010. Pronunciamiento de los Movimientos Sociales hacia la ALBA [Statement of the Coordination of Social Movements towards ALBA], http://juventudrebelde.org.ar/content/pronunciamiento-de-los-movimientos-sociales-hacia-la-alba, accessed on 28 September 2012.

Keohane, R.O. 1984. *After Hegemony: Cooperation and Discord in the World Political Economy.* Princeton, NJ: Princeton University Press.

'Media is Reality' 2005. *Latin Trade (English)* 13(11): 15. Business Source Premier, EBSCO*host*, viewed on 11 November 2013.

Lorán, J.M. 2009. Educación: Una bandera de luz [Education: A flag of light], http://www.granma.cu/espanol/2009/diciembre/juev10/educacion.html, accessed on 28 September 2012.

Macdonald, L. and Ruckert, A. 2009. Post-neoliberalism in the Americas: An introduction. In *Post-Neoliberalism in the Americas*, edited by L. Macdonald. New York: Palgrave Macmillan.

Mittelman, J.H. 1996. Rethinking the 'new regionalism' in the context of globalization. *Global Governance* 2: 189–213.

New-Internatioanlist 2006. Interview with Aram Aharonian, Director General of TeleSUR, http://www.newint.org/columns/makingwaves/2006/01/01/aram-aharonian/, accessed on 28 September 2012.

Patria-Grande 2011. Países del ALBA estrechan vínculos en educación universitaria [ALBA countries tighten their ties in university education], http://www.patriagrande.com.ve/temas/internacionales/paises-alba-estrechan-vinculos-educacion-universitaria/, accessed on 28 September 2012.

Radio-Nacional-de-Venezuela 2009. Impulsan constitución de Red de Universidades de los Pueblos del Alba [Formation of the Network of Universities of the Peoples of the ALBA]: http://www.rnv.gov.ve/noticias/?act=ST&f=20&t=114288, accessed on 28 September 2012.

Rajagopal, B. 2003. *International Law from Below: Development, Social Movements and Third World Resistance*. New York: Cambridge University Press.

Salö, F. 2007. Telesur: 'Tele-Chavez' or the public service of Latin America? A case study. C-level thesis, The Södertörn University College.

Strange, G. 2006. The Left against Europe? A critical engagement with new constitutionalism and structural dependence theory. *Government and Opposition* 41: 197–229.

SUCRE-ALBA 2012. Ecuador consolida el sucre en operaciones comerciales [Ecuador strengthens the sucre in its commercial operations], http://www.sucrealba.org/index.php/noticias/102-noticia070820121, accessed on 28 September 2012.

Tuleando 2012. Ecuador y Venezuela reconocerán títulos universitarios [Ecuador and Venezuela will recognize university degrees], http://www.tuleando.com/2012/07/13/ecuador-y-venezuela-reconoceran-titulos-universitarios/, accessed on 28 September 2012.

Zysman, J. 1996. The myth of a 'global' economy: Enduring national foundations and emerging regional realities. *New Political Economy* 1: 157–84.

Chapter 9
The Hegemony of Psychology: The Practice and Teaching of Paediatrics in Post-Invasion Iraq

Heather Brunskell-Evans

Introduction

In this chapter I take one small piece of research as a case study to assess the connections and dissonances between Gramscian and Foucauldian analyses of the micro-politics of government in post-invasion Iraq. The research is called 'Psycho-social Paediatric Training in Iraq: Perspectives of Trainers and Students' by Al-Obaidi et al. (2013). It was conceived and carried out from 2009 onwards when the violence and murder in Iraq had somewhat abated, its infrastructure had been partially restored and the transition to Iraqi self-governance was taking place. The proposition of the research is that Iraqi paediatric care should clinically address the 'psycho-social' needs of children, and that child psychology should be incorporated into paediatric training in teaching hospitals. One of the key claims is that revised paediatric practice would not only contribute to the healing of the generation of children and adolescents whose well-being had been substantially eroded by the environment of armed conflict but it would also help in some measure with the healing of Iraqi society.

Neither Gramsci nor Foucault wrote in the context of the 2003 largely US-led invasion and occupation of Iraq, however there is a body of Gramscian and Foucauldian scholarship which analyses this as an example of US imperialism and neocolonialism. My intention here is not to become too embroiled in the broad aspects of this literature, nevertheless I hope my focus on one small area 'on the ground' can contribute to comparative Gramscian and Foucauldian critical approaches to the kinds of micro-political relations that have emerged out of the US attempt at regime change. I explore the following question: After the initial violence and coercion deployed in the invasion and occupation between 2003–2007 how would Gramscian and Foucauldian approaches conceptualize the role of the Iraqi doctors and their truth-telling in demanding and freely mobilizing psychological discourses imported from the Western scientific canon and thus from the culture of the occupying forces? My theoretical point of entry is a comparison between the respective methodologies of Gramsci and Foucault with regard to the issue of humanism.

The Council for Assisting Refugee Academics (CARA)

My interest in the politics of the US invasion and the subsequent government of Iraq was intensified by my work for the Council for Assisting Refugee Academics (CARA), a long-standing charity with which I have been involved since 2009, in particular with its most recent programme, the Iraqi Research Fellowship Programme (IRFP). The IRFP is concerned with the restoration of intellectual capital in Iraq through the academic and financial support of Iraqi scholars who, in fleeing from the murder of academics in the post-invasion period, became exiled or otherwise displaced, thus depleting and diminishing the intellectual resources of the Iraqi Academy. The killing of academics was part of a wave of attacks on Iraq's professional middle classes that included doctors, journalists, judges and lawyers, as well as religious and political leaders (Adriaensens and Fuller 2009). The majority of murders took place in the universities of Baghdad, Basra and Mosul, perhaps reflecting the leading position of these universities as well as the potential role of the cities where they were located as capitals of areas in an Iraq divided along the major ethno-sectarian lines (Adriaensens and Fuller 2009).

In my role as a facilitator on the IRFP I supported capacity-building and networking through quarterly workshops at the Columbia University Middle East Research Centre, at Amman in Jordan (see Brunskell-Evans and Moore 2012; Moore and Brunskell-Evans 2013). The overall purpose of the workshops was to foster the capacities of scholars so they could produce research outputs of relevance to the building of social and academic capital within Iraq, to nurture lasting international research collaborations between Iraqi and Western scholars, and to re-engage selected Iraqi academics in exile. I facilitated the particular team whose project is described in this chapter. It comprised two Iraqi trainee paediatric doctors in situ at the Child Central Teaching Hospital in Baghdad, an Iraqi psychiatrist in exile in the US, and a Western psychologist who acted as the principal investigator.

What is intriguing about this research is the paediatricians' initial hypothesis that children were routinely brought by their parents to the accident and emergency ward on the basis of some or other alleged injury. In the absence of any injury the doctors began to believe that the child was somatizing psychological trauma, a phenomenon to which the parents could not admit because of the cultural stigma in Iraqi society associated with mental health. Moreover, the paediatricians were mindful that they themselves had received no training in child psychology. It was the hypothesis and their acute awareness of their own lack of expertise that led the paediatricians to seek funding from CARA to research into paediatric care in Iraq.

Psychosocial Paediatric Training in Iraq

Al-Obaidi et al. (2013) administered a questionnaire to 56 paediatricians at the Child Central Teaching Hospital in Baghdad. The aim of the study was to evaluate the knowledge and perspectives of these professionals regarding psycho-social approaches to child and adolescent health. Firstly the results outline the absence of current training in psychology, an issue about which the authors were already painfully aware. They delineate factors potentially contributing to this phenomenon. Iraqi Higher Education had been substantively degraded before the US invasion as a result of 13 years of economic embargos; the invasion and the bombing of Iraq's infrastructure resulted in internal fighting, the attrition of academics, and the lack of access to current Western scholarship and up to date resources and teaching materials. Secondly the results clearly demonstrate the concept of the psycho-social was unfamiliar to the respondents who had only hazy ideas as to what it meant. Although they shared some awareness approximately 30 per cent of respondents said they did not fully understand the term and even after explanation nearly 40 per cent were yet to be convinced of its relevance. Moreover they expressed low incentive for including this knowledge into the paediatric curriculum and cited the daily pressure of dealing with urgent physical health needs and high caseloads as taking precedence. The authors speculate that there are deeper, unconscious reasons for the respondents' reluctance to embrace psycho-social perspectives, and propose that since it would situate the aetiology of presenting complaints in the realm of mental health this approach is confronting to the medical practitioners who have deeply held contrasting values stemming from their own culture.

In contradistinction to the opinions of the respondents, some of whom were their teachers to whom traditionally they would show academic deference, Al-Obaidi et al. conclude that clinical care of children informed by psycho-social perspectives should inform preventive and primary care services. As such they recommend paediatricians be trained in identifying and managing mental health problems in children and in communicating these to parents. By incorporating psycho-social approaches into paediatric care this will not only potentially reduce the work stress of practitioners who currently attempt to alleviate symptoms without knowing their cause, the prospective benefit in deploying psychology will foster more positive approaches within Iraqi communities to mental health issues and thus help steer Iraq to a more rational approach to re-building society.

Critical Analysis

My function in this particular project was to facilitate not critique it, however during workshop discussions I was privately quite clear that the proposed quantitative (and thus in the Iraqi academic view, objective) research was highly theoretically determined in ways Al-Obaidi et al. were un-reflexive about. I was troubled that in being silent about this issue I was complicit in power relations that normally I would take as the object of my critical concern. Firstly as a social theorist I analyse psychology for its possible role in producing identities rather than objectively revealing them. Secondly I had been politically opposed to the war in 2003, seeing it as the illegitimate invasion of a sovereign state by the US, one of whose purposes was the Westernization of Iraq. My concern therefore was that I and other academics, indeed CARA as a UK charity, in our genuine attempt to mitigate the effects of the invasion and the occupation on Higher Education, were unwittingly valorizing Western perspectives, approaches and knowledges. Thirdly I withheld from the research team the fact that I participate in debates in the Western academy about the epistemological status of psychology and other human sciences. This was out of an anxiety that I might impede their research.

In taking this case study as a platform from which to re-assess Gramscian and Foucauldian theoretical perspectives my intention is not to de-legitimate the utterly humanitarian endeavour of Al-Obaidi et al. to help relieve the suffering and trauma of children in war-torn Iraq, nor is it to foster cynicism in the face of their desire to contribute in some measure to healing Iraqi society. On the contrary, I join with them in trying to re-imagine research for reclaiming the academy in Iraq and in thinking about how Iraq, in its process of self-transformation after regime change in 2003, can progressively re-arrange practices on the ground. Thus it is the explanatory power of Gramscian and Foucauldian conceptual frameworks that is my focus rather than 'failings' of the research project.

In the first two sections below I compare and contrast Gramsci's method, the philosophy of praxis, with Foucault's methods, archaeology and genealogy. Each theorist has chosen to analyse modern capitalist liberal democracies by deploying a method whose first principle is to critique the idea that human beings have a 'nature'. It is through the respective lenses of this approach that Gramsci and Foucault reflect upon power, the human sciences, freedom and ethics as these pertain to modern Western government. In the final section I apply the issues raised by this comparison to an analysis of the case study.

Gramsci: Modern Capitalist Liberal Democratic Governance

The Philosophy of Praxis: 'Man', Knowledge and Power

Gramsci posits the principal question that different Western philosophies have historically asked is 'what is Man'? (1971: 351). In modernity the problem of man usually begins with 'the so-called problem of "human nature" or the so-called "man in general"' (1971: 355). The idea of 'man in general' is 'an attempt to create a science of man … which starts from an initial unitary concept, from an abstraction in which everything that is "human" can be contained' (1971: 355). The philosophy of praxis innovated by Marx involves the idea that 'man "becomes", he changes continuously with the changing social relations' (1971: 355). Gramsci argues the philosophy of praxis demonstrates that 'there is no abstract "human nature" fixed and immutable … but that human nature is the totality of historically determined social relations, hence an historical fact' (1971: 133). The human being is not the starting point of history, but its point of arrival: 'the nature of the human species is not given by the "biological" nature of man'; 'human nature' is the 'complex of social relations' (1971: 355). He insists on the value of this methodological approach with regard to 'the science of politics and history' (1971: 133).

If it is true that man cannot be conceived of outside of a particular complex of social conditions, Gramsci insists the question needs to be asked as to whether even sociology can 'study these conditions and the laws which regulate their development' (1971: 244). Since the will and initiative of human beings, in transforming the social conditions of their existence, cannot be left out of the account, he reflects that sociology cannot be an objective science and thus the issue of human 'science' itself has to be posed (1971: 244). He is not proposing knowledge pertaining to the human being should be abandoned, nor that truth, because it is produced in particular social and political contexts, is relative, but rather it is necessary to distinguish whether the truth created is 'arbitrary' or whether it is 'rational – i.e. "useful" to men in that it enlarges their concept of life, and raises to a higher level (develops) life itself' (1971: 245). The Enlightenment philosophies which affirmed man's humanity as residing in the faculty of reason, and the more current concept of 'human nature' as founded in biology or psychology are '"scientific utopias" which have taken the place of the previous religious utopia in which humans were thought of as the sons of God' (1971: 356).

By describing psychology as a utopian knowledge Gramsci is not denigrating it for its lack of rigour rather he is questioning whose utility is best served by it. In his view society is broadly divided into two fundamental classes with regard to the economic means of production, and he places psychology within the context of its usefulness to the dominant class. Rather than an immutable essence to 'nature' social and class relations are responsible for the conditions in which human beings experience themselves. In one sense the formulation of psychology was rational in that it released the human being from a previous oppressive interpretive framework. The religious and scientific utopian knowledges are expressions of complex revolutionary movements – the transformations from the medieval world to the classical world, and from the classical world to capitalist liberal democracy – which have laid the most powerful links in the chain of 'man's' historical development. Gramsci links these transformations as stages to the eventual achievement of freedom, as we shall see shortly.

The State and Civil Society

Gramsci posits that in a capitalist liberal democracy bourgeois control of the state's economic (and coercive) resources is insufficient to explain why subaltern groups consent to class domination. In exploring this phenomenon he develops the concepts of hegemony and ideology. Hegemony is a tacit form of leadership rooted in a dominant set of ideas and concepts that determines the social and cultural practices that constitute every-day life. Although hegemony incorporates the ideological it is also distinct in that hegemony includes the dialectical relation of economic class forces. The current political system is the first in history whereby the dominant class assimilates the entire society into its own social, cultural, political and economic interests. This phenomenon first emerged in the nineteenth century when the bourgeoisie presented its own particular interests as universal such that bourgeois ideology became the 'common sense' of all classes which was also taken as 'good sense' (1971: 323). Ideology was not a trick imposed on the workers to eternally deceive them, rather it functions not by obscuring truth as in tying together divergent ideas into singular interpretive framework or consciousness.

In modernity the bourgeoisie occupy the position of a hegemon, legitimating and leading a political system that promotes its own interests through achieving a generalized consensus superseding class. This involves the bourgeoisie in taking account of the interests of the groups over which they exercise hegemony so that equilibrium is formed. The sacrifice made to their own interests by the ruling classes cannot 'touch the essential: for though hegemony is ethico-political it must also be economic, must necessarily be based on the decisive function exercised by the leading group in the decisive nucleus of economic activity' (1971: 161).

Gramsci's emphasis on consent and on persuasion leads him to construct a theory of intellectuals and their role of leadership in hegemony. The notion of the intellectual as a distinct category of person independent of social class is a myth; although intellectuals have a certain class-less aura, ultimately their status derives from the various dominant class formations to which they belong. 'Traditional' intellectuals such as doctors, academics, lawyers, and teachers disseminate knowledge (such as psychology) appropriate for bourgeois hegemony and thus act as agents of reciprocal communication between civil society and the state. In liberal modes of government the state and civil society cannot exist separately from each other and both levels correspond to the function of hegemony. Moreover, whilst the liberal state is limited and circumscribed, responsive and subordinate to civil society, it will resort to direct domination or coercion in moments of crisis when 'spontaneous consent' has failed (1971: 12).

Freedom and Ethics

The measure of freedom enters into the life of the human being since it is possible for the objective conditions to exist in which he or she is not subjugated to the physical and external conditions of existence. That the objective conditions exist is insufficient, it is necessary to know them and to know how to use them. Although all human beings reflect and interpret the world, there are limits to this thoughtful activity, as we have seen with the concepts of hegemony and ideology, since it takes place 'unconsciously, its outcome determined by society' (1971: 323). Conceptions of the world are 'mechanically imposed by the external environment', for example through the language we speak and through received wisdom, through our 'common' sense and shared morality that emerges from the entire collective system of beliefs and opinions (1971: 323).

In contrast to traditional intellectuals, organic intellectuals can replace bourgeois ideology with an alternative interpretive horizon suitable to the needs of the working classes. Organic intellectuals are defined on the one hand by their role in production and in the organization of work, and on the other hand they are distinguished by their function in directing the ideas and aspirations of the dominated social class to which they organically belong. Hegemony is key to both bourgeois and to proletariat power: it is insufficient to get control of material coercive resources or economic assets since power is equally located in non-material resources so that even if the proletariat were to seize the means of production through revolution they would be unable initiate real social change if they did not also instantiate new hegemonic practices. Theory which is grounded in the standpoint of the oppressed is necessary because the non-theoretical finds it difficult to go beyond appearances and therefore cannot, except in vague terms, identify the enemy to freedom. In order for the proletariat to be freed from oppression organic intellectuals need to construct new more appropriate knowledges that support human freedom. Political agency and contingently formed consent form the integral basis for a counter hegemony. The concepts of hegemony, ideology and political power are thus inextricably entwined and mutually constitutive.

Gramsci argues the possibility of freedom and liberty can be sought in the activity of organic intellectuals universalizing the interests of the working classes so other classes will consent to the creation of a new order. Man in this sense is 'concrete will' and creates himself through: (i) giving a specific and concrete direction to will; (ii) identifying the means which will make this will specific and concrete; and (iii) 'contributing to modify the ensemble of the concrete conditions for realising this will to the extent of one's own limits and capacities and in the most fruitful form' (1971: 360). Ethical improvement is the collective activity directed outward to modify external relations both with nature and between men, in local contexts of social groupings up to society as a whole. It is for this reason Gramsci argues 'man is essentially "political" since it is through the activity of consciously directing other men that man realises his "humanity", his "human nature"' (1971: 360).

Conclusion

The philosophy of praxis allows Gramsci to argue that human nature is not fixed but is continually swept up and transformed in the heat of human history. There is an equation between philosophy and politics, thought and action, in that thought transforms human beings and makes them different from what they were previously. This founding methodological manoeuvre transforms the dichotomies found in liberal political thought that are made possible by and adhere to the idea that the human being has a universal immutable human nature: individual/society, objectivity/irrationality, public/private, and state/civil society.

Although Gramsci has refuted the psychological ontology of 'man' he too delineates a minimal ontology to the human being. There are three fundamental human characteristics – the creative domination of the material world through labour, the intellect and the will – capacities that are both constituted by power relations and have a pivotal role in their transformation. As well as being constitutive of the human being he also posits that power relations are at some level extrinsic to the human being. Although he does not give power a conscious intention, he poses the question of power in terms of its possession by the bourgeoisie and as that class's ultimate aim i.e. their economic advantage. In this sense power is sovereign and is exercised from the top down – the individual is that upon which it lands to subdue and oppress. Since power is thus both constitutive of the human being and yet extrinsic to the individual, I conclude that the philosophy of praxis is ultimately humanistic. A teleological element to Gramsci's thought suggests that the human being is progressing through history to reach a place free of the power of class domination, a transformation and self-realization ultimately staged with regard to the means and mode of production.

Foucault: Modern Capitalist Liberal Democratic Governance

Archaeology and Genealogy: Man, Knowledge and Power

Foucault's archaeological and genealogical approach in exploring the philosophical and political question of 'man' is more radical with regard to 'his' plasticity than the philosophy of praxis. Archaeology also refutes that psychology is a science and demonstrates that by developing forms of truth regulated by codes of scientific reason, psychology constructs 'man' and his human 'nature'. Psychology has not finally brought into rational consciousness that which had hitherto been obfuscated by ancient beliefs, philosophies, folk lore or prejudice. Before the end of the eighteenth century, Foucault contends, 'man did not exist' (1970: 308). Nor is psychology, as in Gramscian thought, a scientific utopia commensurate with the needs of capitalist liberal democracy and bourgeois hegemony. Genealogy is a later methodological strategy than archaeology and one that sustains its anti-humanist approach. It analyses the role of psychology and medicine in making up our current identities (e.g. as beings with an essential biological and psychological nature) within the diverse relations established between human scientific reason and liberal political reason from the nineteenth century to the present. In the genealogical view 'man' is immanent within power/ knowledge relations and not that upon whom they act.

Foucault (1977; 1979) describes how in the seventeenth and eighteenth centuries challenges to the excessive powers of the monarchy and the church, the growth of capitalism, and industrialization and urbanization, signified a shift in the axis of governmental control from sovereign power over subjects to the normalization of the population. Normalizing power evolved out of two basic but interlinked forms that focussed on the body: firstly, in the classical age it centred on the individual body and the control and optimization of its forces, and the parallel increase in its docility; secondly, somewhat later in the eighteenth century it focused on the species body and its biological processes for example the level of health and life expectancy, birth rates, patterns of disease and so on, as these were brought into regimes of governmental scrutiny and calculation. Although in the nineteenth century biopolitics were indispensable to the development of capitalism which depended on the controlled insertion of bodies into the machinery of production and on the adjustment of phenomena pertaining to population to economic processes, the maintenance of capitalism was not power's overarching objective. The combined effect of the anatomo-politics and biopolitics had as its objective not the protection of sovereign interests of the state, capitalism or the bourgeoisie, but the social control of population through technologies of normalization achieving social stability, welfare and security.

Normalization was achieved with the help of the human sciences, in particular psychology and medicine, which provided an axis of normalcy/abnormalcy for correct human functioning. Foucault argues that with the breakdown of the pre-modern theological soul and of religious conscience, psychology and medicine were integral in mobilizing a new form of institutional supervision around the concept of the psyche or the 'secular soul' whose welfare is to be ministered to not by the priest but by the doctor (1977: 30). Medicine became the first positive knowledge to take the form of expertise according to the surveillance of normalcy whereby the individual and the population were not only to be 'known' but to be the subject of calculated regimes of reform in relation to secular objectives (Foucault 1973). The newly constituted social arrangement of the private nuclear family of the nineteenth century was a privileged site for the medical surveillance of population, in particular the regulation of mothers and children (Foucault 1979). It was the middle-class family which first became the object of psychoanalytic and psychological scrutiny, and it was in this family that modern childhood was conceived, born and subsequently continuously monitored across all social strata. Fostering children as future citizens is no longer assigned to the responsible parent exercising moral rectitude and guidance, rather it is assigned to the responsible parent's self-surveillance according to the norms set for meeting children's psychological 'needs'. The well-being of the child and of the family is thus inescapably and constitutively social.

The State and Civil Society

In a lecture entitled 'Governmentality' Foucault (1991) ties together threads from his previous work and elaborates the relationship between biopolitics, the modern Western state, government and society. The neologism governmentality refers to governmental rationality, namely a form of activity that aims to shape, guide, or affect the conduct of individuals and of groups of individuals within the population where the norms for this guidance are laid out in particular by medicine and psychology. This form of rationality emerged as a solution to problems posed to government in the eighteenth and nineteenth centuries by phenomena characteristic of a set of living beings forming a population, the political and economic issues raised by the challenge to sovereign power, and the growth of capitalism. The historical outcome has been the growing importance assumed by normalizing power at the expense of sovereign power and the juridical system of the law.

Sovereignty has not ceased to play a role in liberal government but on the contrary, governmental rationality in the nineteenth century involved an attempt to fathom what foundation in law could be given to the sovereignty that characterizes a state when the state itself was being governmentalized. It is not that the law has disappeared in the regulation and correction of people, but that judicial institutions in the West have been increasingly incorporated into a continuum of medical and administrative apparatuses whose functions are for the most part regulatory. Instead of relying on juridical or sovereign power of the monarch or of the Church to regulate human behaviour, in capitalist liberal democracies normalizing power is linked to the secularization of ethical regimes and operates by the surveillance of individuals and our self-surveillance according to whether or not our conduct is normal as opposed to pathological.

Foucault (2008) reflects further on the relationship between governmentalization and liberalism as a political philosophy. He argues the emergence of biopolitics was inseparable from the growth of liberal political rationality with which they appeared and took on their intensity. Liberal thought does not start with the existence of the state, finding in government the means for achieving its ends, rather it starts instead from society which exists in a complex relation of interiority and exteriority with regard to the state. The question for liberalism is 'how can the phenomena of "population", with their specific effects and problems, be taken into account in a system concerned about respect for legal subjects and individual free enterprise?' (2008: 317).

Freedom and Ethics

Since the human sciences were made possible by contingent epistemic shifts in representation that occurred at the end of the eighteenth century, Foucault proposes that if those epistemic arrangements were to 'disappear as they appeared … then one can certainly wager that man would be erased, like a face drawn in sand at the edge of the sea' (1970: 387). He makes clear that he does not regard the erasure of man as a loss to humanitarian progress and freedom. There are other ways of perceiving and understanding ourselves, of which this model is just one, and in some senses a constricting one. What might the benefits to freedom and to ethics be of questioning such epistemic and political arrangements?

Foucault (1982) says we need to interrogate the costs and benefits to us as individuals of being turned into subjects through normalization. He characterizes this interrogation as philosophy, for 'what is philosophy if it is not a way of reflecting, not so much on what is true and what is false, as on our relationship to truth?' (1994c: 327). What is philosophy if it is not 'the movement by which … one detaches oneself from what is accepted as true and seeks other rules … the displacement and transformation of frameworks of thinking, the changing of received values, and all the work that is done to think otherwise?' (1994c: 327).

'The critical ontology of ourselves must be conceived as an ethos [...] which is at one and the same time the historical analysis of the limits imposed on us and an experiment with going beyond them' (1994b: 319). As such, 'the relationship between philosophy and politics is permanent and fundamental' (1994a: 293).

Conclusion

Archaeology and genealogy, like the philosophy of praxis, seek to grasp subjection in terms of the material constitution of subjects. However, unlike the philosophy of praxis these methods strategically do not start analysis with universals such as 'man', bourgeois power, capitalism and the economic mode of production. Instead of deducing concrete phenomena from universals genealogy starts with concrete practices and passes these universals through the grid of their intelligibility. This anti-humanist methodological manoeuvre has allowed Foucault to analyse liberalism as a method for the rationalization of the exercise of government, one that has been imbued with the principle that one can govern too much and one which regulates itself by reflection on the security and welfare of population.

Power is not a possession of the bourgeoisie exercised as 'power over', nor does it reside in an ideology ultimately tied to bourgeois hegemony, and thus to the economic means of production and reproduction, extending right down to language and common sense. Although relations of power remain profoundly enmeshed in economic relations genealogy demonstrates that its essential purpose is not to serve the economy, nor is economic production and reproduction the universal base upon which all other social and cultural phenomena arise. Genealogy describes how normalizing power (its procedures and techniques) became economically advantageous and politically useful so that more global powers or economic interests were able to engage with it. Power, although it can be consolidated and exercised by sovereign groups, cannot be modelled upon the commodity i.e. as something which one possesses, cedes through force, alienates or recovers. Rather power is constitutive of the individual who is its prime effect and an element in its circulation.

Foucault, as does Gramsci, contests liberal political reason whose language is dominated by dichotomies such as the individual/society and state/civil society but he does so for different reasons. Human 'nature' has been immanent within the power-knowledge relations of Western liberal political theory since the nineteenth century, and is thus bound up with the very idea of society and the practices which promote social welfare. For example it is in the name of public and private welfare that the family has been configured as the locus for fostering physical and mental health. It is here that the child with psychological needs has been produced and then regulated by a complex apparatus of health and welfare services according to the norms set for it by the 'science' of psychology.

Since the human subject is the product of power there is no place of freedom outside of power to which we can escape, rather freedom is achieved through bringing critical enquiry to bear on the concrete practices of liberal government, assessing the costs and benefits of normalization.

Conclusion: The (Dis)Connection between Foucault and Gramsci on the Basis of the Iraqi Case Study

How would Gramscian and Foucauldian approaches analyse the case study and the proposition of Al-Obaidi et al. that psychology should be incorporated into paediatric training in teaching hospitals in Iraq and that in doing so revised practice will not only contribute to the healing of Iraqi children and adolescents whose well-being has been substantially eroded by the environment of armed conflict but will also help with the healing of Iraqi society. In order to answer this question I briefly explore literature which describes the causes and consequence of the US invasion and occupation in distinctively Gramscian or Foucauldian frameworks.

The Case Study

A small body of neo-Gramscian literature uses the key concepts of coercion and hegemony to analyse the US invasion and occupation of Iraq (Dodge 2006; Haugaard 2006; Cerny 2006). The US invaded Iraq for the theft of its material resources and to westernize it with regard to the perceived threat from the Middle East. The invasion and occupation were made possible because the US functions as an international hegemon, linking methods of coercion with leadership and ideological supremacy that is both intellectual and moral in character. However, the occupation reveals a failure in US hegemonic power: not only had the Baathist regime defied the international community for 35 years before the invasion by not turning itself into a liberal democracy, it had also resisted the application of 13 years of US coercive diplomacy. The inability of the US to govern Iraq after the invasion, the murderous sectarian chaos that ensued, and the inability by 2006 to facilitate Iraqi self-government according to advanced liberal principles demonstrates the failure of both US coercive and hegemonic power. In a traditional society such as Iraq where authority is based upon the sanctity of tradition and filial obligations, and the power to command those relations, democracy is outside the conditions of possibility, a lesson the US is slowly learning. Even when the US intention was to explicitly undermine elites and inculcate American style liberalization and democratization the result has been a necessary compromise with religious authorities and paramilitary hierarchies to provide 'order' thus resulting in a loss of legitimacy of hegemony itself.

There is a dearth of Foucauldian analysis of the US invasion and occupation of Iraq although Kelly (2010) is a noticeable exception. He deploys biopolitics as a key concept to analyse the invasion and occupation. The US is a parasitic imperialist state, which, although it may be concerned with imposing Western capitalist democracy, had as its founding and more urgent purpose in invading Iraq the preservation of its own population against the perceived external danger, namely the Middle East Other. He reminds us that Foucault argues unlike pre-modern politics, power is no longer waged in the West on behalf of a sovereign who must be defended but on behalf of the existence and defence of population. The US achieved the almost complete destruction of the Iraqi bio-polity during the invasion and occupation, but this was not gratuitous, rather a general subsuming of any concern for the Iraqi population under the US strategic imperialist and domestic goals. It is an open question whether the US administration sincerely believed that a pro-Western Iraq would result from the invasion. The optimal end result for the US would be that Iraq turned itself into a helpful, functional, bio-political client state, however, the worst case scenario, a failed state, is still better than the pre-2003 intransigent, functional enemy state.

In contradistinction to prognoses of failure described above, the case study seems to exemplify the success of US hegemony. Al-Obaidi et al. view the years leading up to war – years of economic embargos and poverty – followed by the invasion in 2003 as a regrettable interruption to access to Western scientific knowledge whose previous influence on Iraqi Higher Education they applaud. In Gramscian terms they can be seen as traditional intellectuals that facilitate US hegemony in Iraq by helping link civil society with the westernization of the state. They formulate a psychological model of the child and attempt to facilitate not only new medical practices on the basis of this model but also to persuade initially sceptical parents of its efficacy. In doing so, they unconsciously disseminate the cultural, political and economic interests of the invading culture and help consolidate US power in a strategic country in the Middle East. Moreover, the response of the Iraqi parents, in seeking to help their children through medical assistance rather than some other cultural means, can also be seen, despite the anxiety of Al-Obaidi et al., as an example of the success of Western hegemony.

In Foucauldian terms, the ethics of Al-Obaidi et al. emerge from the hegemonic influence of advanced liberal welfare government. The term hegemony here does not include economic class forces, rather it refers to the dominant and valorized paradigm of Western social organization whereby society has been accorded an organic form in medical terms: as a body society is liable to sickness or can be restored to health; individuals describe themselves in the language of health and illness, question themselves and others in terms of normalcy/abnormalcy and take their physical and psycho-social welfare as the legitimate and ethical object of government. The psychological model of the child and the medical practices they advocate emerge in one sense from Western ideology but what has happened involves both much more and much less than ideology. As members of the medical profession the doctors task themselves with monitoring the normalcy of the mental health of children and to induce parents into surveillance of themselves as proper parents. In doing so they are not unconsciously promulgating bourgeois ideology, rather they are involved in ethical self-constitution of identity as experts administering paediatric care to promote psychological and social well-being. The children Al-Obaidi et al. want to liberate from custom will not thereby be liberated from power since they are elements in its bio-political circulation, their needs not mutely awaiting recognition but discursively produced by psychology.

Conclusion

The case study, as we have seen, can be analysed by both Gramscian and Foucauldian approaches as an example of the success of US hegemony. If one accepts that the psychology valorized by Al-Obaidi et al. is bound up in strategies of governing by Western capitalist liberal democracies and that as medical researchers they are unaware of this, how is one to judge whether the humanism of the philosophy of praxis or the anti-humanism of genealogy is the most effective in explicating this phenomenon? Since there is no arbiter or Archimedean point to help us judge, the ability of the concepts to provide tools for resistance can be, in my view, the only measure of the efficacy of each method.

The history of Iraq is not that of a capitalist, liberal democracy, and I am not sure modes of resistance proposed by Gramsci or Foucault can be easily mapped on to the Iraqi context. Nevertheless let us for the moment imagine the Iraqi doctors became conscious in either Gramscian or Foucauldian terms of the power and knowledge relations involved in the government of capitalist Western democracies, how could they, in order to improve their paediatric care, take strategies to contest both the received wisdom of their own culture and that of US hegemony?

A philosophy of praxis takes explicit accounts of the creative and intellectual activity of organic intellectuals, and it places this activity as the central, practical aspect to building a citizen democracy which would be based on and express the will of the people. This primary emphasis on intellectual and creative potentiality is not only a necessary basis for the overthrow of an oppressive system but a requirement for the founding of a new and more open social order. If the aspiration of the progressive Iraqi intellectual is the building of a citizen democracy, in contrast to the oppression of the previous Baathist political regime and the religious and political groups which still currently adhere to it, this would also necessitate resistance to transforming their culture according to Western values and ideals arising from capitalism. Carrying out revised paediatric practice would challenge Iraqi stigmatization of mental health issues but would also necessitate problematizing Western 'science' which favours individualistic explanations and solutions for human conduct. In the Gramscian view counter-hegemony would involve providing an alternative interpretive framework or consciousness that would tie together the factional groups in Iraqi society as one universal block in agreement that the capitalist economic interests of liberal democracies and the human sciences liberal government promulgates fails to achieve a free society and reproduces class divisions. Only after this massive counter-hegemonic achievement could freedom be glimpsed by the Iraqi population. It seems to me that as a strategy for resistance this is too unwieldy and indeed paralysing.

The genealogical route to freedom would be more modest and more achievable. Genealogy does not analyse liberalism as an ideology, nor does it locate political power in hegemony that ultimately protects capitalist interests. Medicine was bound up with the very mutation of political thought into its modern liberal democratic form. Since freedom cannot be sought by creating counter ideologies, what we need to examine are the disciplinary costs as well as the benefits of medicalized subjectification. Critical intellectuals would need to reflect upon a societal ethics configured around both the medicalization of children's welfare and of medical personnel as monitors of it, as opposed for example to other ways of constituting social welfare and well-being that are available in Iraqi culture.

I have no means of knowing which traditional social and emotional structures exist for the care of children within families and communities in Iraq and therefore I can make no judgment as to whether a medicalization of children's distress is a more efficient, rational approach to relieving the trauma of living in a war-torn environment than other available approaches. Perhaps, however, it is possible to accept the somatization of trauma without resorting to psychology to either explain or soothe it, and in doing so resist the hegemonic Western narrative that ethics adhere in evaluative judgments about the normalcy/abnormalcy of human conduct.

References

Adriaensens, D. and Fuller, M. 2009. Wiping the slate clean. In *Cultural Cleansing in Iraq: Why Museums Were Looted, Libraries Burned, and Academics Murdered*, edited by R. Baker, S. Ismael, and T. Ismael. Australia: Pluto Press.

Al-Obaidi, A.K., Corcoran, T., Hussein, M. and Ghazi, A. 2013. Psycho-social paediatric training in Iraq: Perspectives of trainers and students. *Medicine, Conflict and Survival*, Special Issue guest edited by Moore, M. and Brunskell-Evans, H. 29(1).

Brunskell-Evans, H. and Moore, M. (eds) 2012. *Reimagining Research for Reclaiming the Academy in Iraq: Identities and Participation in Post-Conflict Enquiry*. London: Sense Publishers, Inclusive Education Series.

Cerny, P.G. 2006. Dilemmas in operationalising hegemony. In *Hegemony and Power: Consensus and Coercion in Contemporary Politics*, edited by M. Haugaard and H.H. Lentner. Oxford: Lexington Books.

Dodge, T. 2006. The Sardinian, the Texan and the Tikriti: Gramsci, the comparative autonomy of the Middle Eastern state and regime change in Iraq. *International Politics* 43(September): 453–73.

Foucault, M. 1970. *The Order of Things: An Archaeology of the Human Sciences*. London: Routledge.

—. 1973. *The Birth of the Clinic: An Archaeology of Medical Perception*. London: Tavistock Publications.

—. 1977. *Discipline and Punish: The Birth of the Prison*. Middlesex: Penguin Books.

—. 1979. *The History of Sexuality: An Introduction.* Middlesex: Penguin Books.
—. 1991. Governmentality. In *The Foucault Effect: Studies in Governmentality*, edited by G. Burchell, C. Gordon, and P. Miller. London: Harvester Wheatsheaf.
—. 1994a. The ethics of the concern for self as a practice of freedom. In *Michel Foucault: Ethics, The Essential Works 1954–1984*, edited by P. Rabinow. London: Penguin.
—. 1994b. What is enlightenment? In *Michel Foucault: Ethics, The Essential Works 1954–1984*, edited by P. Rabinow. London: Penguin.
—. 1994c. The masked philosopher. In *Michel Foucault: Ethics, The Essential Works 1954–1984*, edited by P. Rabinow. London: Penguin.
—. 2008. *The Birth of Bio-Politics: Lectures at the College de France 1978–79.* London: Penguin.
Gramsci, A. 1971. *Selections from Prison Notebooks*, edited by Q. Hoare and G.N. Smith. London: Lawrence and Wishart.
Haugaard, M. 2006. Power and hegemony in social theory. In *Hegemony and Power: Consensus and Coercion in Contemporary Politics*, edited by M. Haugaard and H.H. Lentner. Oxford: Lexington Books.
Kelly, M. 2010. International bio-politics: Foucault, globalisation and imperialism. *Theoria* 57(123): 1–26.
Moore, M. and Brunskell-Evans, H. 2013. Reclaiming research for the survival of post-conflict Iraq. *Medicine, Conflict and Survival*, Special Issue guest edited by Moore, M. and Brunskell-Evans, H. 29(1).
Rabinow, P. (ed.) 1994. *Michel Foucault: Ethics, The Essential Works 1954–1984, Volume 1.* London: Penguin.

Chapter 10
The Complexity of Social Systems: Could Hegemony Emerge from the Micro-Politics of the Individual?

David Kreps

Introduction

Critical philosophies of social systems have often borrowed from scientific insights into non-social systems (though admittedly with mixed results – see Mirowski 2002; Curtis 2011). General Systems Theory, after somewhat Parsonian (1951) beginnings, has, in recent decades, taken a revealing turn, led by environmental biology, capturing the imagination of a growing number of sociologists with the notion of Complex Adaptive Systems – or put simply, a notion of complexity that is distinct from that which is merely complicated. To use Paul Cilliers's marvellous example: 'I have heard it said (by someone from France, of course) that a jumbo jet is complicated, but that a mayonnaise is complex' (Cilliers 1998: 3). This poses interesting questions for the focus of this volume.

What if there were a suitably Gramscian totalizing – and scientific– approach to understanding social systems, which nonetheless escaped all the reductionist, scientistic pitfalls a deconstructive and poststructuralist Foucauldian would be wont to point out? What if there was a science that could speak coherently about the macro-level of social structures without denying the radical uncertainty at the micro-level of the individual, a theory which supported the tension between radical contingency and free choice at the level of the individual yet was able simultaneously to discern and predict robust and reliable patterns at the level of the collective? What if, in a non-mystical sense, the whole really is greater than the sum of its parts – that a complex whole can 'exhibit collective properties, "emergent" features that are lawful in their own right'? (Kaufmann 1995: viii). Would this science of complexity not grant us a context in which the ideas of both Foucault and Gramsci could sit, no longer conflicting because both contextualized by their new situation? Could not Foucault's micro-politics in society indeed add up to and constitute the central figure of a State that exhibited patterns not dissimilar to Gramsci's descriptions of the hegemonic reach of that centre out into the minutiae of social relations?

As an afterword to this volume, then, I wish the reader to indulge me in an attempt to explore this possibility – albeit only tentatively – as an introduction to the substantive work that would need to follow should the premise outlined in this final chapter be deemed worthy of exploration. First, we must briefly explore what this 'complexity' theory is about.

The Complexity Turn

In the 1990s – during the decade following Foucault's death – the work of Stuart Kaufmann (1995; 2001) became known outside his highly specialized field, through his very accessible books, *At Home in the Universe* (1995) and *Investigations* (2001). Building on the insights of Ilya Prigogine (1977; 1984) and paralleling the ideas of Brian Goodwin (1994), Kaufmann's is a view based upon modern biology, and yet reaching out far beyond it, challenging the reductionist neo-Darwinian orthodoxy of the likes of Richard Dawkins (1989), presenting a new understanding of evolutionary theory that places natural selection as a *secondary*, rather than primary force. The primary force behind evolution, for Kaufmann, is self-organization. This is not a new idea in philosophy, but certainly radical for the twentieth-century science of biology. For Kaufmann, 'Life and its evolution have always depended on the mutual embrace of spontaneous order and selection's crafting of that order' (Kaufmann 1995: 9). Yet these insights into how patterns in the branching of evolution reveal a lawful ordering, how the complexity of teeming variety harbours principles of self-organization, he also extends – as perhaps is often the wont with some popular scientists, but in this case extremely plausibly – beyond the self-organization of flora and fauna. 'The natural history of life may harbour a new and unifying intellectual underpinning for our economic, cultural, and social life' he asserts (Kaufmann 1995: 15). He suspects that 'the fate of all complex adapting systems in the biosphere – from single cells to economies – is to evolve to a natural state between order and chaos, a grand compromise between structure and surprise' (1995).

Acknowledging the march of physics towards a final theory of everything, he nonetheless reminds us that though it may end up explaining how the building blocks of the universe operate, it 'almost certainly will not predict in detail' (Kaufmann 1995: 16). This failure to predict is down to two fundamental branches of physics itself: quantum mechanics, 'which assures a fundamental indeterminism at the quantum level' with all its attendant macro-scopic consequences, and chaos theory, neatly captured in the famous so-called 'butterfly effect' that can see the flapping of a butterfly's wings in Australia cause a hurricane in the Atlantic (Kaufmann 1995: 17). But not knowing the details does not preclude us from building theories that 'seek to explain the generic properties' – for example, 'when water freezes, one does not know where every water molecule is, but a lot can be said about your typical lump of ice' (1995). Kaufmann attempts to develop, through his work, 'classes of properties of systems that … are typical or generic and do not depend on the details' (1995). Giving numerous examples, from the origin of life 'as a collective emergent property of complex systems of chemicals' through to 'the behaviour of coevolving species in ecosystems that generates small and large avalanches of extinction and speciation', Kaufmann finds that the 'order that emerges depends on robust and typical properties of the systems, not on the details of structure and function' (Kaufmann 1995: 19). To grasp how seemingly random connections among discrete and previously isolated units can generate staggering order, Kauffman reduces the notion of complexity to a very simple metaphor with buttons and threads.

> Imagine 10,000 bottoms scattered on a hardwood floor. Randomly choose two buttons and connect them with a thread. Now put this pair down and randomly choose two more buttons, pick them up, and connect them with a thread. As you continue to do this, at first you will almost certainly pick up buttons that you have not picked up before. After a while, however, you are more likely to pick at random a pair of buttons and find that you have already chosen one of the pair. So when you tie a thread between the two newly chosen buttons, you will find three buttons tied together. In short, as you continue to choose random pairs of buttons to connect with a thread, after a while the buttons start becoming interconnected into larger clusters.... A phase transition occurs when the ratio of threads to buttons passes 0.5. At that point, a 'giant cluster' suddenly forms ... [as] most of the clusters have become cross-connected into one giant structure. (Kauffman 1995:56)

Phase transitions are key, too, to many biological systems. As Goodwin describes, the single-celled organisms, or amoebas, in cellular slime mould, a very primitive life-form, have two distinct phases to their life cycle. Whilst food in the form of bacteria is available the amoebas exist as independent, single cells, crawling about in their hunt for and consumption of food. As single-celled organisms, their reproduction consists in growth and division, and during this phase they seem to pay little if any heed to one another. This is in sharp distinction to the second phase of their cycle. Once the food runs out, the amoebas start to signal one another, releasing a chemical that constitutes communication from cell to cell. The release of the chemical creates a centre to which cells receiving the signal start to move – at the same time also releasing a burst of the chemical themselves. In laboratory conditions, in a petri dish, these movements quickly form complex and beautiful spatial patterns. This aggregation, moreover, then morphs gradually into a multicellular organism:

> the initially simple aggregate of cells becomes progressively more complex in form, and the cells in different positions differentiate into specific cell types. The final structure consists of a base, a stalk that rises up from the base, and on top a 'fruiting body' made up of a spherical mass of spores that can survive the absence of food and water. When conditions recur that allow growth, the spores are released from the fruiting body and germinate – each one producing an amoeba that feeds, grows, and divides – and the life cycle starts again. (Goodwin 1994:47)

In this way the theory of complexity – and its attendant principles of self-organization – is not tied to simple computational aggregations such as the buttons and thread example, nor merely the world of biology as in the cellular slime mould example above, but capable of evincing patterns in all manner of complex adaptive systems – like the social and political worlds that are the focus of Gramsci and Foucault.

In 1998, Paul Cilliers took the next logical step, with his ground-breaking book, *Complexity and Postmodernism*, in which he lays out the many and varied confluences between – in particular Derridean, deconstructive – poststructuralist thought, and this new science of complexity. By 2005, an entire special issue of *Theory, Culture and Society* – including a new essay from Cilliers – was given over to consideration of the Complexity Turn in which sociological thought was beginning to absorb the impact of these new ideas (Urry 2005).

Cilliers's (1998) intervention on complexity theory concentrates on neural networks and poststructuralist thought. Cilliers lucidly points out a fundamental issue that must be grasped about complexity:

> It is useful to distinguish between the notions of 'complex' and 'complicated'. If a system – despite the fact that it may consist of a huge number of components – can be given a complete description in terms of its individual constituents, such a system is merely *complicated.* Things like jumbo jets or computers are complicated. In a *complex* system on the other hand, the interaction among constituents of the system, and the interactions between the system and its environment, are of such a nature that the system as a whole cannot be fully understood by analysing its components. Moreover, these relationships are not fixed, but shift and change, often as a result of self-organisation. This can result in novel features, usually referred to in terms of *emergent properties.* The brain, natural language and social systems are complex. (Cilliers 1998: viii)

There are important differences in approach that must be undertaken between studying something which is complicated, and something which is complex. The analytical method, whilst useful for complicated systems, is counterproductive when trying to understand complex systems. Complexity focuses on the shifting and evolving 'intricate *relationships*' between components. 'In "cutting up" a system, the analytical method destroys what it seeks to understand' (Cilliers 1998: 2). Furthermore, interactions are not restricted to being *physical* – they can also be described as 'transference of *information*' (Cilliers 1998: 3). These interactions are both *rich* – 'any element in the system influences, and is influenced by, quite a few other ones', and *non-linear* – 'small causes can have large results, and vice versa. It is a precondition for complexity' (Cilliers 1998: 3).

These rich, non-linear information exchanges, moreover, are short-range, resulting in the phenomenon of recurrency. Information being received primarily from each components' immediate neighbours can go through many 'hops', resulting in wide-ranging influence, and there can be 'loops in the interactions' – activities can affect themselves through direct feedback or after a number of intervening stages (Cilliers 1998: 4). Such 'feedback' can be *positive* (enhancing, stimulating) or *negative* (detracting, inhibiting). Both kinds are necessary.

Complex systems 'are usually open systems, i.e. they interact with their environment'. By contrast, 'closed systems are usually merely complicated' (Cilliers 1998: 4). This is of crucial significance in environmental theory, where for much of the twentieth century – at least since Tansley (1935) – a nineteenth-century organicist metaphor of natural equilibrium has been the defining characteristic of the term Tansley coined, 'ecosystem'. Yet, as many ecologists in the last decade or so of the twentieth century found through painstaking study (see Hagen 1992; Botkin 1992), the natural world in fact displays no such equilibrium at all, and the notion of ecosystems has undergone a radical rethink. As Cilliers notes, 'Complex systems operate under conditions far from equilibrium. There has to be a constant flow of energy to maintain the organisation of the system and to ensure its survival. Equilibrium is another word for death' (Cilliers 1998: 4).

This constant flow of energy was first described by Ilya Prigogine (1984: 143), who coined the term 'dissipative structure' to describe systems that are sustained by the persistent dissipation of matter and energy. As Kaufmann asserts, 'in dissipative systems, the flux of matter and energy through the system is a driving force generating order' (Kaufmann 1995: 21). The image of a whirlpool of water at the plug-hole in a bathtub is a useful illustration. If the tap is left running, the whirlpool persists, bringing order to the constant flow of water (Goodwin 1994: 10). It is here, in this inherently unstable nonequilibrium, where, according to Kaufmann, 'life exists at the very edge of chaos' (Kaufmann 1995: 26). Living cells are themselves 'nonequilibrium dissipative structures', and the very nature of evolution – and especially of the coevolution of many systems, such as species in an environment – is to attain the 'edge of chaos, a web of compromises where each species prospers as well as possible but where none can be sure if its best next step will set off a trickle or a landslide' (Kaufmann 1995: 29).

But as Cilliers is at pains to underline, for all this chaos and flux, these remain discernible systems, with pattern and order. As he asserts, 'complex systems have a history. Not only do they evolve through time, but their past is co-responsible for their present behaviour' (Cilliers 1998: 4).

Unlike merely complicated systems, susceptible to analysis, this order does not arise through the control of one part of the system over another.

> Each element of the system is ignorant of the behaviour of the system as a whole, it responds only to information that is available to it locally. This point is vitally important. If each element 'knew' what was happening to the system as a whole, all of the complexity would have to be present in that element. (Cilliers 1998: 4)

The reader will undoubtedly by now be sharing my fascination with the possibilities of applying this notion of complexity to the understandings of both Gramsci and Foucault.

Cilliers takes his readers through a fascinating tour of how this breakthrough in scientific theory not only challenges the reductionist analytical approach of previous scientific endeavour, but that poststructuralist thought 'is sensitive to the complexity of the phenomena under consideration' (Cilliers 1998: 22) in a range of ways he devotes his book to explaining. In particular, he rehearses Derrida's argument against the theory of representation – so crucial to much of analytical thought – stressing that Derrida's 'argument against representation is not anti-scientific at all. It is really an argument against a particular scientific strategy that assumes complexity can be reduced to specific features and then represented in a machine. Instead', Cilliers continues, 'it is an argument for the appreciation of the nature of complexity, something that can perhaps be "repeated" in a machine, should the machine itself be complex enough to cope with the distributed nature of complexity'.

Though, of course, 'Whether our technology can manufacture such a machine remains an open question' (Cilliers 1998: 86). As Kaufmann asserts, the fundamental problem with reductionist thought when applied to complex systems is that to represent a complex system one must, of necessity, reproduce the system in its entirety. The representation, usually something like an algorithm – the 'shortest description' which can capture the essential elements of a system – can only capture the entirety of a complex system, because a complex system is already its own shortest description. In computation this is known as an 'incompressible algorithm' (Kaufmann 1995: 22).

Complexity, Gramsci, and Foucault

So where does the Complexity Turn lead us in our consideration of Gramsci and Foucault? By now it will be clear to the reader that the criticisms of Gramsci levelled by Laclau and Mouffe (Torfing 1999:36), who see a nineteenth-century Marxist essentialism at the core of Gramsci's work, are accepted by this author, whose sympathies lie with the Foucauldians and other poststructuralists, on this issue. Despite Morera's suggestion that Gramsci's Marxism carried the germ of a postmodernism deeply sceptical of the 'possibility of objectivity' (Morera 2000:18) – an anti-scientistic and anti-positivist stance derived from the work of Benedetto Croce – it is apparent that compared to Foucault's epistemic stance on the issue, Gramsci's 'absolute historicism', as it comes across in his critique of Croce in Notebook 10, is a far more realist position (Gramsci 2007:371). But can the insistence of the Gramscians on an objective, scientific basis for political science be satisfied with this newly complex evolutionary biology and its implications for complex systems of all kinds? Although, as Demirović reminds us in this volume, for Foucault, 'The precision of theory, its scientific character, was an entirely secondary question' (Foucault 1980: 137), I believe this is nonetheless a very promising avenue for research. Moreover, the nominalism of Foucault, and his inability to see beyond the individual and conceptualize social structures and institutions as collectivities, can similarly be overcome by complexity theory without reducing the details – the individuals and practices that make up such structures – to mere component parts of a mechanistic system. The individual 'responds only to information that is available to it locally' (Cilliers 1998: 4).

Now, there is a long history of metaphors used for understanding the world of the social, borrowed from scientific endeavour. Such a practice does indeed have its detractors, and in particular authors such as Peter Stewart (2001) single out complexity theories as having 'limited use in the study of society', because 'social processes are too complex and particular to be rigorously modeled in complexity terms' (Stewart 2001: 323). Indeed, this author is keen to distance the ideas represented in this chapter from the approach, say, of Luhmann, whose work is one of the more advanced amongst social complexity theorists, but 'can be seen in part as a development of the functionalist theories of Parsons' (Stewart 2001: 326). Luhmann's embrace of Maturana's closed cybernetic 'autopoiesis' runs counter to the open nature of truly complex systems (Padgett 2012: 33).

But such metaphors are useful, particularly with relevant scholarship, as even Stewart (2001) asserts: 'Social processes and phenomena are far too complex for complexity theory to deal with, or profoundly elucidate, without the aid of the resources of the better of existing social theories and studies' (Stewart 2001: 353). We should be on safe ground with Gramsci and Foucault, then.

So, if in the Middle Ages man and his world were understood in light of the metaphor of the clock, and in the nineteenth century the new mechanics made this clockwork all the more complicated and steam-driven, then in the late twentieth century it came as no surprise that people and societies should begin to be understood by the metaphor of the computer. Yet, as Cilliers stresses, 'our technologies have become more powerful than our theories' (Cilliers 1998: 1), and, as Kaufmann points out, it turns out that in fact the 'theory of computation seems to imply that nonequilibrium systems can be thought of as computers carrying out algorithms. For vast classes of such algorithms, no compact, lawlike description of their behaviour can be obtained' (Kaufmann 1995: 23); there being no shorter description, in other words, than the system itself, and evolution itself being just such an incompressible algorithm.

Thus the disciplinated world Foucault paints for us, in which the micro-politics of power relations codetermines our subjectivities within overlapping epistemes of discursive practices, can, in complexity terms, begin to be envisaged as an incompressible algorithm – the shortest description possible of a highly complex constantly shifting system of interpenetrating open systems. Indeed, the 'global', as John Urry points out (2005), 'is comprised of various systems, operating at various levels or scales' and 'each constitutes the environment for each other. Thus criss-crossing "societies" are many other mobile, material systems in complex interconnection with their environments' (Urry 2005: 11). If this picture is accurate, then with the help of Kaufmann's theories, and those of others working in the field of complexity, it may well be possible to evince generic lawlike behaviours in these systems not dissimilar to those attempted by Gramsci. Such patterns would not – could not – be detailed, as Cilliers points out, in his essay in 2005:

> In describing the macro-behaviour (or emergent behaviour) of the system, not all the micro-features can be taken into account. The description is a reduction of complexity. Nevertheless, macro-behaviour is not the result of anything else but the micro-activities of the system. Yet, to describe the macro-behaviour purely in terms of the micro-features is a difficult task. When we do science, we usually work with descriptions which operate mainly on a macro-level, but these descriptions will, more often than not, be approximations of some kind. (Cilliers 2005: 258)

Armed with such approximations of a newly *complex* Gramscian political science, the project of social change might finally overcome the paralysis poststructuralism can be accused of having brought upon it.

Could this metaphor of complexity be useful for bridging the divide between Gramsci and Foucault? Is this indeed a way in which the 'fundamental classes' (labour and capital) might better be reconceived, escaping the essentialism imputed to them even by Gramsci, and aligning them more closely with the new conception of politics to be derived from Foucault? Could hegemony emerge from the micro-politics of the individual? There is clearly much work to be done before such an assertion can be made, and this chapter seeks merely to suggest it as a possibility for further exploration.

As Byrne (2005) concludes, there are some crucial approaches in the social sciences that must be undertaken for this work to begin. Beyond the merely metaphorical apparatus I have presented above, complexity theory will need to become the 'frame of reference' that 'shapes the actual tools of investigative social science themselves' if this project is to have real impact (Byrne 2005: 96). Byrne also asserts that the comparative method in the social sciences will need greater emphasis, firstly 'since recognition of complex causation has always been a foundation of the comparative approach', secondly since 'serious quantitative investigative tools' are beyond the 'limitations of many social scientists', and thirdly because 'the comparative method employed at the level of neighbourhood and city region has very considerable potential for informing the participatory process in policy formation and implementation – for serving as a basis for what is actually an ongoing process very little noticed by social theorists but one with very considerable implications for the nature of politics in post-democratic societies' (Byrne 2005: 96).

Brian Castellani and Frederic Hafferty have, in 2009, published a book on how Foucault (at least) can be used to build a theory of social complexity, *Sociology and Complexity Science: A New Field of Inquiry* (2009). Here they focus on Foucault's interest in trying to understand how social systems change from one state to another – from one set of self-organizing relations to another – and suggest that Foucault's work could be characterized as a study of phase transitions, or tipping points, such as that between amoebas and cellular slime mould, as mentioned above, or from judicial punishment to disciplinary punishment, from taking care of the self to knowing the self, and so forth. They suggest that this is in fundamental respects what Foucault's entire discourse is about, as well as with the inevitable impact these systems and state changes have upon individuals and the care of the self.

How the ideas of Gramsci might fit into this frame remains to be seen. My task here is to suggest that if there are – as this volume seeks to prove – substantive confluences between the work of Foucault and Gramsci that provide us with a far better picture of society and the relationship between the group and the individual than either does on their own, then, given the new interest in how Foucault's work can be seen through the lens of complexity, discovering how complexity theory and the ideas of Gramsci interrelate may well prove to be very fruitful work.

Gramsci's primary concept, hegemony, as we have seen in my Introduction to this volume, understood as involving the articulation of social identities in the context of social antagonism, provides us with an articulation of identity that 'is taken to be conditioned by the deconstruction of the very notion of structure, which reveals the discursive, and thus the contingent, character of all social identities' (Torfing 1999: 14). This reconceived hegemony, moreover, is situated in a far more nuanced social understanding than the traditional Marxist base-superstructure model. As Torfing relates,

> we should conceive of the state, economy and civil society as articulated within a relational totality which has no pregiven centre, and which thus allows for different and shifting relations of dominance between its constituent parts. According to Laclau, (1981:53) such a conception is precisely what Gramsci aims at with his notion of historical bloc. (Torfing 1999: 28)

The historical bloc is a concept Gramsci defines as a 'complex, contradictory and discordant *ensemble*' of the institutional orders of state, economy and civil society (Gramsci 2007: 366). This is indeed very close to Urry's description, in considering the Complexity Turn, of the global as 'criss-crossing "societies" [that] are many other mobile, material systems in complex interconnection with their environments' (Urry 2005: 11).

Certainly the essentialist remnant in Gramsci's thought, as Torfing describes it, which whilst recognizing the political character of the economy continues to grant it a final say in all matters, has to be jettisoned if this reading of the concept of historical bloc provided by Laclau and supported by Torfing is to be accepted. As Torfing notes, examining the original Marxist definition, 'far from constituting a homogenous social sphere from which all traces of politics have been removed, the economy is heterogeneous terrain for political struggles' (Torfing 1999: 38). Accepting this, as Gramsci did, one must today also accept, in the light of poststructuralist discourse theory, that indeed nothing in society is purely infra- or superstructural, but profoundly interpenetrated, coevolving, and *complex.* Indeed, following this line of thought, one discovers that the fact that discourse is not fixed or inevitable actually provides the possibility for power, and for hegemonic practices within the historical bloc. Hegemonic practices, meanwhile, are situated within, and constitute, discourse. 'Hegemony and discourse are *mutually conditioned* in the sense that hegemonic practice shapes and reshapes discourse, which in turn provides the conditions of possibility for hegemonic articulation' (Torfing 1999: 43).

Now, if language – and discourse – is understood as a self-organizing complex system (Cilliers 1998: 125), the conditions of possibility for hegemonic articulation become likewise susceptible to complexity theory. It seems that there is plenty of work linking complexity theory and poststructuralism – Cilliers as the prime example – and work linking complexity directly with Foucault. There seems, in the extant literature I have been able to find, a dearth of any thinking linking complexity and Gramsci. Bogdanov, however, a founding member of the Bolsheviks, is credited with inspiring Bertalanffy's systems theory and the later complexity theory with his 'tektology' notions, and, Gare claims, Gramsci, too 'was probably influenced at least indirectly by Bogdanov'. There may indeed be fruitful possibilities for linkage here.

A Twenty-First-Century Research Programme

In sum, the principle arenas of confluence and dissonance between the two oeuvres of Gramsci and Foucault for twenty-first-century consideration, and thereby perhaps the importance and timeliness of this new volume offering a reassessment of the relationship between the two writers, may indeed lie within the purview of the sociology of complexity.

Complexity theory may enable political thinkers, critical philosophers and sociologists to heal the late twentieth century rift in radical thought between predominantly Marxist-based political thought, in the one camp, and the poststructuralist cadre almost defined by the distrust of what they viewed as the other's essentialism. This would bring both kinds of radical thinkers together into a new domain neither as scientistic as the worst of the one nor as myopic as the worst of the other. An end to this rift would not only help to remove the stigma associated with the concept of socialism, but also help to lift the paralysis associated with the radical uncertainty and contingency of the postmodern. This new rapprochement, moreover, would bring the technicians of computational social science and the localism of the ethnographic community into meaningful conversation with critical philosophy and political science, enabling the creation of widely consensual and robust recommendations for progressive social policy – recommendations perhaps only the worst demagogues of the Right would be free to ignore.

References

Botkin, D. 1992. *Discordant Harmonies* Oxford: Oxford University Press

Byrne, D. 2005. Complexity, configurations and cases. *Theory, Culture & Society* 22(5): 95–111.

Castellani, B. and Hafferty, F.W. 2009. *Sociology and Complexity Science: A New Field of Inquiry*. London: Springer.
Cilliers, P. 1998. *Complexity and Postmodernism*. London: Routledge.
—. 2005. Complexity, deconstruction and relativism. *Theory, Culture & Society* 22(5): 255–67.
Curtis, A. 2011. *All Watched Over By Machines of Loving Grace*. London: BBC.
—. 29 May 2011. *How the 'Ecosystem' Myth has been Used for Sinister Means*. London: The Observer.
Dawkins, R. 1989. *The Selfish Gene*. Oxford: Oxford Paperbacks.
Foucault, M. 1980 [1991]. *Remarks on Marx: Conversations with Ducio Trombadori*. New York: Semiotext(e).
Goodwin, B. 1994. *How the Leopard Changed his Spots*. Princeton, New Jersey: Princeton University Press.
Gramsci, A. 2007. *Selections from the Prison Notebooks*, edited and translated by Q. Hoare and G.N. Smith. London: Lawrence and Wishart.
Hagen, J.B. 1992. *An Entangled Bank*. New Jersey: Rutgers University Press.
Kaufmann, S. 1995. *At Home in the Universe*. Oxford: Oxford University Press.
—. 2001. *Investigations*. Oxford: Oxford University Press.
Laclau, E. 1981. Teorias marxistas del estado: Debates y perspectivas. In *Estado y Poltíca en América Latina*, edited by N. Lechner, Mexico: Siglo XXI, 25–59.
Mirowski, P. 2002. *Machine Dreams: Economics Becomes a Cyborg Science*. Cambridge: Cambridge University Press.
Morera, E. 2000. Gramsci's critical modernity. Rethinking Marxism 12(1): 16–46.
Padgett, J.F. 2012. "Autocatalysis in Chemistry and the Origin of Life" in John F. Padgett and Walter W. Powell (2012) *The Emergence of Organizations and Markets* Princeton, N.J.: Princeton University Press
Parsons, T. 1951 [2001]. *Toward a General Theory of Action*. London: Transaction Publishers.
Prigogine, I. and Nicolis, G. 1977. *Self-Organization in Non-Equilibrium Systems*. London: Wiley.
Prigogine, I., and Stengers, L. 1984. *Order Out Of Chaos*. London: Flamingo
Stewart, P. 2001. Complexity theories, social theory, and the question of social complexity. *Philosophy of the Social Sciences* 31: 323–60.
Tansley, A. 1935. The use and abuse of vegetational concepts and terms. *Ecology* 16(3): 284–307.
Torfing, J. 1999. *New Theories of Discourse: Laclau, Mouffe and Zizek*. Oxford: Blackwell.
Urry, J. 2005. The Complexity Turn. *Theory, Culture & Society* 22(5): 1–14.

Index